Praise

D1554990

"Any consumer would benefit from the money lessons inside. Better yet, many consumers who've tossed aside more traditional money guides will find its story approach refreshing."

> —Ed Mierzwinski, Consumer Program Director, U.S. Public Interest Research Group (U.S. PIRG)

"*The Money Mentor* uses strategy and metaphor to creatively capture the psychological and soulful issues we face when coming to terms with how we value our money and our time."

> —Joan DiFuria, Money, Meaning & Choices Institute

"*The Money Mentor's* personal approach is highly effective in conveying valuable information on reducing debt and building wealth."

> —Ken McEldowney, Executive Director, Consumer Action

"*The Money Mentor* achieves its goals of being both entertaining and informative. I liked the complexity of Iris and found myself traveling with her on her journey to overcome debt and attain financial stability."

> —Annette Lieberman, coauthor of *The Money Mirror: How Money Reflects Women's Dreams, Fears, and Desires*

"If you're marooned on an island without credit cards, debt, or money, you can skip *The Money Mentor*. But if you live in the real world, you won't find a better or more enchanting guide to being a financial survivor!"

> —Rich Hatch, *Survivor* winner and author of *101 Survival Tips*

THE MONEY MENTOR

A Tale
of
Finding Financial Freedom

TAD CRAWFORD

ALLWORTH
P · R · E · S · S

New York

05   04   03   02   01   5   4   3   2   1

Published by Allworth Press
An imprint of Allworth Communications
10 East 23rd Street, New York, NY 10010

Cover design by Derek Bacchus

Front cover: Digital Imagery © Copyright 2001 PhotoDisc,
Inc.; "Money Flying Away" by Dan Farrall

Page composition/typography by
John Cole GRAPHIC DESIGNER, Santa Fe, NM

ISBN: 1-58115-085-7

Library of Congress Cataloging-in-Publication Data
Crawford, Tad, 1946–
     The money mentor: a tale of finding financial
          freedom/by Tad Crawford.
              p.cm.
     Includes index.
     ISBN 1-58115-085-7
     1. Finance, Personal. I. Title

HG179 .C72 2001
332.024--dc21   00-053122

Printed in Canada

with love,

for Susan,

again,

and Christopher,

for the very first time

Table of Contents

Acknowledgments

I t has been my good fortune to have the support and advice of generous friends and mentors whose contributions have benefited all of my books, including *The Money Mentor*.

I am grateful to the readers who offered criticism and encouragement to help transform each draft of the manuscript: Jonathan Goldberg, Annette Lieberman, John McCarthy, Priscilla Rogers, Fred Lanzetta, Cathy Porter, and Hilda Brown.

I would like to acknowledge my agent of twenty-five years, Jean V. Naggar, for her enduring faith in and enthusiastic efforts on behalf of my writing.

I am thankful to Glenn Heffernan, Harriet Pierce, and the rest of the staff at our distributor, Watson-Guptill Publications, for their wholehearted support of this project and the entire publishing program at Allworth Press.

One pleasure of this project was to experience firsthand the insight, competence, and courtesy of my colleagues at Allworth Press. Having enjoyed the professional treatment that so many authors have praised to me, I would like to recognize and say how appreciative I am to Nicole Potter, Anne Hellman, Jamie Kijowski, Michael Madole, Elizabeth Van Hoose, Birte Pampel, Bob Porter, Cynthia Rivelli, and Gebrina Roberts.

I thank my longtime friend, Bill Beckley, for shooting my photo for this book as he once took the photo for my first book.

I am appreciative to Olga Gardner Galvin for her exceptional copy-editing.

For two of my mentors who are no longer here, Elsie K. Mills and Elsie B. Meyer, I want to voice my gratitude for their devotion to the exemplary and their quotidian presence in my inner life.

I also want to express my unbounded appreciation and love for my parents, whose joy in the arts is only one of their many gifts to me.

I owe a special debt to my niece, Elizabeth Keefe, who asked that I read aloud the earliest beginnings of the manuscript and eagerly demanded more.

Finally, I thank my wife, Susan, who makes the possible worthwhile.

CHAPTER 1

Before My Story

Since I am not a writer, my story would probably never have been told if I hadn't met my mentor, who helped me get out from under the burden of debt and improve my financial life. My mentor was neither wealthy nor a man. She seldom told me what to do, although she did encourage me to write about the twists and turns in my own journey to financial freedom. Rather, she helped me understand my life and my finances by her encouragement, examples, and questions. In the course of dealing with my money cares, I learned to see my life as a spiritual adventure. I discovered and developed aspects of myself that I would not have imagined existed. And I found a lifelong friend in my mentor. I believe my story offers a message of hope. As my teacher's wisdom and generosity helped me meet many challenges in my life and eventually free myself from debt, I hope that this retelling will help others. In some ways, my story appears to me to be the story of America at a certain moment in its history, when wealth and debt raced in a rivalry that mastered my life and the lives of so many people around me. My story is about my decision to end my participation in that race; in fact, to imagine my life in a new way that made the idea of a race beside the point.

This book represents an accurate portrayal of a crucial six months of my life, but even my efforts to fit my life into a story are open to questions, since I felt my life was more like a flood, moving me in ways and places that I would never have expected. This story is an account of some difficult and exciting times in the course of that joyous overflowing.

CHAPTER 2

A Visit to the Dentist

When you look at me, you see a young woman of twenty-three with a silver ring through the left nostril of my nose, my dark hair cropped short with highlights of blonde, and my lipstick a dark maroon. I have sparkling brown eyes, a dancer's figure nearly five foot six, and a blend of features that leaves my origins a mystery. I might come from Bali or Peru, Nepal or Turkey, or almost anywhere in the world where people have darker skins. My adoptive parents, James and Mary Cassidy, had been over fifty when an agency found me for them—I was only a few months old. For whatever reason, they resisted my inquiries about my origins. I only know that I came to the United States from another country where my birth parents, for reasons no one ever explained to me, gave me up for adoption.

Jim and Mary had been childless, and they certainly had love to share with me, but they died in their late sixties and left me alone in the world. While growing up, I had been accustomed to their middle-class lifestyle and earned a college degree, but they never taught me anything about money. Nor did managing money seem to be the subject of any of my high-school or college courses. Of course, I majored in dance and art, not finance or economics. When the lawyer figured out the value of my parents' estate, there was hardly anything left. I suddenly realized that they had lived from paycheck to paycheck, both working, and even the value of our home had been reduced to nearly zero by a home-equity line of credit and a drop in real-estate prices.

After I graduated from college, I moved to the city and started auditioning for dance companies. I quickly realized that I would starve if I didn't find some other work, particularly since I needed a lot more training in dance before I would be able to perform in any of the dance companies. So I worked as a waitress. It was easy work to find and didn't require a lot of commitment. I even imagined that the rushing from table to table was choreography of a sort, and that the exercise would help me in my dance classes. I shared a small apartment with two other dancers my age, a strange experience of not enough closet space and lining up for the bathroom in the mornings. Since I had grown up without siblings, I didn't know what to make of our situation, but I felt that I could endure anything if I could only dance.

I think my downfall must have begun before the accident. It's hard to be certain because I was vague about finances, numbers, budgets—actually, budget was not a word in my vocabulary. So when I put on in-line skates for the first time and started downhill—without any instruction; I thought that with my dancer's footwork and coordination I wouldn't have any problems—I soon found myself speeding out of control. There was a moment of fear and an odd exhilaration when I knew that I had lost control and would crash, yet I was still flying on winged wheels down that slope. When it was over, I was sprawled out on the pavement and lucky to have nothing worse that a broken arm.

That was my first experience of being uninsured. When I added up the medical bills, I couldn't believe the amount. I sat down and started to cry. I had accepted a bunch of credit cards in college so I could use their credit lines for just such an emergency. Unfortunately, I had used them for a lot of other things before the emergency happened, but I had enough left on the credit lines to pay the medical bills. Having a broken arm meant that I couldn't waitress and I had to look for new work. I found a job as a receptionist at a small advertising agency. They had a health plan but no dental coverage, so of course the next misery in my life was an unbearable pain in one of my molars that eventually required an inlay.

I didn't have a dentist in the city, so I asked Rachel and Tina, my roommates, and Tina gave me the name of her dentist. He was old, maybe over forty, and actually taught on the faculty of a dental school as well as having his own practice. Off I went to his office in a pricey part of town. I have to say he looked stern when he first came into the waiting room and introduced himself.

"Hi, I'm Dr. Peter Testa."

"Iris Cassidy," I answered, rising and taking in this tall, skinny man with his bald dome of a head and round, gold-rimmed eyeglasses.

"So you're Tina's roommate?"

"That's me."

"And did you give my receptionist four credit cards that were maxed out?"

"But the fifth wasn't," I tried to keep a cheerful front. If I hadn't had to pay in advance, the embarrassment of having lost track of my drawing on the credit lines of the cards could have been put off until after the treatment at least.

"You've set a record for this office," he said, shaking his head. "Well, come on in."

I followed him into the small room with all the dental equipment and settled myself in the chair, my head on the headrest and the light in my eyes.

"We'll start by taking some X rays. That way I should be able to do something today to relieve your pain."

At this point I was also feeling some additional pain because I felt devalued in his eyes. I took his remark about setting a record as a criticism. I wanted to explain about the cost of the broken arm, but I had also spent money on clothes, albums, dance outfits, and even some meals. I didn't understand how the credit lines had been used up so quickly, but I suddenly felt very bad about it. Once Dr. Testa started working, he managed to make me feel worse and worse. It's awful to endure the pain of dental work, but when a dentist delivers a monologue—and it's about you, and you don't agree but you can't say anything because your mouth is stuffed with cotton, clamps, and tubes—

well, I can think of a lot of places I'd rather be.

After studying the X rays on the light box on his wall, Dr. Testa told me the bad news about the gold inlay and the necessity of one more visit to his office. "And I also think that you should have your wisdom teeth out. You're not using them, and they can cause you trouble in the future. It's best to extract them when you're young and healthy."

I thought of the pain and the discomfort that would follow, living on soup and baby food for a week, and it just seemed like my miseries were multiplying much too fast. Anyway, who had asked him about my wisdom teeth? But the fear of future pain vanished when Dr. Testa began squirting a little liquid out of the long needle of the hypodermic that he intended to inject near the hinge in my jaw. I've always been afraid of needles, I don't know why, and I even look away if a doctor has to draw blood for a test. I wanted to jump out of the chair and run, but I had a picture in my head of Dr. Testa pouncing quick as a cat to make sure I stayed put. His first few tries with the needle must have missed the right spot, because he keep thrusting like a fencer until I was ready to beg him to stop.

"Open wide," he said, and I complied.

Now he began his monologue. My childhood dentist, the one that my mom and dad used, had always liked to talk about politics. It didn't matter what party you belonged to, whether you were a child or an adult, a man or a woman; as soon as you couldn't reply, you got to hear his opinions from beginning to end. Dr. Testa seemed to be that way, only worse, because he was talking about me.

"I'm going to surprise you," he started by saying, "and tell you a little secret. I've never maxed out a credit card, not one card. In fact, I hardly use credit cards. Why should I? I've got good credit—people are happy to accept my checks."

I couldn't speak at all, so of course, I didn't answer.

"I always say that my signature on a check is as good as the Secretary of Treasury's signature on our currency. In the old days, when gold backed our money, that phrase 'In God We Trust' had a lot more meaning than it does today, but that's another story." He chuckled, adding, "You won't be here long enough today to hear all about that."

Thank God, I thought, because even though my jaw felt numb, I could feel the drill whirring deep down toward the bottom of my molar. I also didn't know what in the world he was talking about, and he sounded pompous.

"Now I'm going to make an exception to the rule about not using credit cards," he said. "The way they've set things up, you've pretty much got to use them to make rental car reservations, buy tickets over the phone, order products off the Internet, and so on. But when I do that," here he raised his voice for emphasis, "I immediately pay my bill in full as soon as it arrives. I never carry a balance on any credit card. If I had a choice, in fact, I would use debit cards—those are cards that you can only use if you have money in the bank—but some of the car-rental companies insist on credit cards. Now, you're probably wondering what all this means in the big picture." He stepped back, drill in raised hand, and waited with satisfaction for my reply.

"Ah-uh," I answered, wanting him to be quiet but feeling that the sooner he worked his way through his monologue, the sooner he would finish his dentistry and let me leave.

"Open." He stepped forward, adding, "Wider. I'm going to tell you a secret."

For some reason, I didn't want to know this secret.

"It will change your life. Once you know this secret, you have only yourself to blame if you don't find the path to prosperity. You listening?"

I couldn't close my ears. It simply isn't fair when one person gets to talk all the time, even if they're giving you directions to the Fountain of Youth and El Dorado. I like to talk, too.

Taking my silence as encouragement, he continued, "The ancient world had seven wonders, but the famed banker, Baron de Rothschild, couldn't name any of them when someone asked him to. Instead, he said that he would reveal the eighth wonder—compound interest.

"If you have one thousand dollars in a savings account that pays five percent interest, how much would you earn in a year?"

Fifty dollars seemed like the right answer to me, but I couldn't pronounce it and simply opened my eyes wide as if to shrug.

"Give up? Well, it's a trick question. Whatever you answer, I can say you're wrong and prove it. Open wide. For example, what if you answer "fifty dollars"? Most people probably would. That would be the right answer if interest were paid once a year. On the other hand, if interest were paid quarterly, the interest for the year would be more than fifty dollars, and if interest were computed daily, you'd earn even more than if it were computed quarterly. It's because you're earning interest on interest. That's what compound interest is all about.

"Wider please," his thick finger pressed my lower lip painfully against an incisor. "So what does all this mean?"

I was wondering myself, because a few pennies one way or another didn't seem to make much difference to me.

"Compound interest can work for you or against you. I'd say that, in your case, it's working against you."

I would have liked to interrupt him, because I have some self-esteem issues that didn't appear on his radar screen, but of course, I had to keep as silent as if I had taken a vow.

"How does somebody max out a credit card anyway? On not just one credit card, but four?"

I would have liked to tell him. Maybe if he understood what had happened, he wouldn't be so smug. It had to do with being offered a lot of credit cards in my junior and senior years in college and accepting all of them. After all, I didn't have to have income or get a parent to guarantee that payment would be made. And I honestly believed that the credit card companies had big computers that know whether or not you can handle three, seven, or twelve credit cards. They probably had a pretty good idea how much I would be earning after college—a lot better idea than I had, since I had no idea at all—and if those big companies thought it would be enough to pay them back, on top of my college loans, then what could be wrong with accepting the cards?

"It's really simple," he went on. "Cards get maxed out because people believe that paying the monthly minimum is enough. That's just what the credit card companies want them to believe. But if you pay the monthly minimum, you are paying a whole lot of interest. After the first month, you're paying interest on interest. Open wide."

"Do you know how long it takes to pay back two thousand dollars on a credit card if you pay the minimum each month? Assume 19.6 percent interest, although some cards offer a little less than that."

I'm not terrible at math. In fact, music is kind of mathematical and you need a feeling for music in order to be able to dance. But I couldn't fathom what the minimum payment would be if you owed two thousand dollars. Just guessing, I thought maybe it would take two or three years to pay it all back.

Fortunately, I couldn't say anything.

When I didn't answer, he triumphantly supplied, "Twenty-two years. I bet you never imagined that."

"Uh-uh," I had to agree.

"How much in total would you have to pay back for the two thousand plus interest?"

Twenty-five hundred, maybe even three thousand, occurred to me, but I didn't really know.

"Four thousand nine hundred and nineteen dollars," he proudly answered himself. "That's two thousand nine hundred and nineteen dollars in interest for a two-thousand-dollar loan. And it's not usury, it's perfectly legal. Rinse. Now how can you explain why people are willing to pay so much interest? Why do people pay 15–20 percent on credit cards when they can only get 3–4 percent interest on savings deposits and no one else pays as much interest—not for car loans, mortgages, business loans, or anything else that doesn't involve a loan shark?"

I leaned forward to rinse out my mouth, then answered with the first word that came to mind and certainly seemed to apply in my case.

"Stupidity?"

"As P. T. Barnum said, 'There's a sucker born every minute.' Open wide. In fact, many people who pay interest on their credit cards think they don't. They deny the reality of what's going on. Or maybe they plan to pay it off, so they hope that soon they won't be paying more interest. Or they know they pay some interest, but don't realize how high the rates are. After all, where in our educational system are the most basic aspects of personal finance taught? Nowhere, so rather than saying people are foolish, maybe we should say we have a foolish educational system. If we don't teach about the problems, we certainly can't teach about the solutions to those problems."

I was feeling pretty bad at this point, not just from the pain in my mouth but also from the realization that I was a fool who paid a lot more interest than I ever imagined—especially since I'd never given it a single thought, much less a second thought—and, worst of all, that I saw no way out of it. In fact, I wasn't really sure what I owed. I knew roughly what my minimum payments on all of the cards totaled each month, but I had never thought to add up the principal. Or maybe I *had* thought of it but didn't want to know.

"I'll tell you something else about credit cards," he went on, "People spend a lot more money using credit cards than using cash. It's crazy, because after all, our money is worthless paper. If you take a Federal Reserve Note to be exchanged, they'll give you another Federal Reserve Note—not gold and silver, the way they used to. So it's our trust that gives the money value, our willingness to accept it. But we're more reluctant to part with paper money than we are to run up a tab on a credit card. Maybe the fact you get the credit card back, but not the money, makes some difference. I don't pretend to be a psychologist, but it's another reason why using credit cards can be so risky. Not only are you going into debt, but you're going into debt faster than if you didn't use the credit cards. It makes me wonder what will happen when we're all buying stuff on the Internet, using invisible digital money. I'll bet people spend a lot more that way than they would if they had to hand over real money."

I knew he was right, although I couldn't explain why paying with paper money should seem more solemn and real than paying with a credit card. I was glad that the fifth credit card had something left to draw on its credit line, but suddenly I felt afraid about the future. Maybe I'd get a new credit card with a fresh line of credit, but somehow I didn't think so. The last application I sent in had been turned down. Even if I could get another card, I was suddenly wondering where it would all end.

"Somebody might have to borrow cash from his or her family to pay off credit cards, but it would be a good idea."

He meant me; that was obvious. Only I had no family. It was confusing. Maybe I should have told him off and stormed out of there, but I didn't know any other dentists and I had a serious dental problem to solve. He certainly seemed to be competent. And I actually felt that all his talking showed some concern about me. What did he care about credit cards? As he pointed out, he hardly ever used them. So his lecture was for my benefit. But I left his office deeply in need of some human warmth and comfort. I felt numb from head to toe, partly from his barrage of words, partly from the anaesthetic and the dental work.

Putting one foot in front of another like an automaton, I reached in my pocket and pulled out some crumpled dollar bills. If I went without dinner—and I certainly wasn't feeling very hungry—I could take a chance with this money. I walked down a few blocks to the newsstand where I bought my lottery tickets every day after work. One dollar could bring me thirteen million and a new life. Prudently, I only invested half the crumpled bills, four dollars, in the tickets and felt hopeful for a few moments. If I won, I could turn everything around, pay off my debts, pay to start my dance classes again, even move to an apartment of my own. Only I knew I'd never win. How could there be so many contradictions? I felt hopeful at the same moment I knew I was throwing my money away. I walked slowly into the park and dropped down on one of the green benches next to an African-American woman intently reading her newspaper.

I leaned forward, cradling my aching jaw in my hands, and tried to think through my situation. I must owe a lot of money, but I wasn't certain how much. My arm had healed, so I could go back to working as a waitress. But I'd lose the health insurance if I did that. On the other hand, I didn't want to work as a receptionist for the rest of my life. I couldn't decide what to do, so I couldn't figure out what my income might be. Not knowing my income or how much I owed, I felt like my head was in a confusing cloud that made everything hazy. A few times I let go with an involuntary groan, partly because of the throbbing in my jaw but mostly because my thoughts couldn't shape a problem or a solution. I seemed to be the problem. I hadn't thought about things like health insurance, loan repayments, and compound interest. All of it felt like a giant whirlpool sucking me down into depths of which I had no comprehension. I glimpsed another world, not the kind world that my parents had shown me, but a more terrifying world where my most basic needs for health care, shelter, and food might go unmet. I didn't know if I could do it—whatever "it" might be: make a living, make enough money to be free of debt and live a better life. Once the whirlpool sucked me down, how would I ever find the steps to scramble up those watery walls and look at life with a smile again?

CHAPTER 3

Two Women on a Bench

"Honey, you look like you could use a friend."

I couldn't believe that anyone would be speaking to me. I wanted to keep my face buried in my hands, so I wouldn't have to look up and meet the eyes of this witness to my misery. Nonetheless, the warmth of the voice made me lift my head, and I found myself face to face with the woman who had been reading her newspaper. She had folded it neatly and placed it on the far end of the bench. Now her attention was completely focused on me. She looked nearly forty, taller and fuller in the figure than I am. She wore a dark-blue business suit with a white blouse, but her contours made a pleasing flow of curves that softened the image of the business-woman. Around her neck a single strand of white pearls glistened against her skin. She looked at me with a quizzical smile as if wondering why fate had made me choose her bench as a spot to groan in my despair.

"I sure do," I replied, surprising myself by admitting how miserable I felt.

"What's happening with you?"

There are times when you just make up your mind to dive in. I don't know why I trusted her. Some instantaneous reaction that I wasn't even aware of having. I could have tightened up and said I didn't need a friend or walked off in a huff. But she was right. I needed a friend and she was smiling, warm, interested in me for whatever reason. I just opened up like a rain cloud and let it all pour down. I told her about my visit to the dentist, what happened with the credit cards, how he lectured me, then about breaking my arm, and on and on. Someplace in the middle of it all I got around to introducing myself.

"By the way, I'm Iris," I said, wiping my cheeks with my palms.

"Saidah," she replied.

"That's a pretty name."

"Thanks. It's been passed down in my family. So what do you think about what your dentist had to say?"

I shrugged. Telling her my troubles had lifted my spirits a bit, but it hadn't clarified anything. "I guess he's right."

"What do you love most in all the world?" she asked.

"Dancing." I didn't hesitate before I answered.

"Professional dancing? Like ballet?"

"Any kind of dancing. I've studied ballet, but now I'm more interested in modern or jazz."

"How much are you getting to dance?" she asked.

"Hardly at all. I couldn't take classes when I broke my arm. Now I'm working all day so it's hard to get to auditions. If I don't audition, I'll never get to perform. And, truthfully, I wasn't getting any work before I broke my arm."

"So you want to dance for a living?"

"Sure, that would be great."

Saidah nodded her head slowly as if contemplating this idea from a number of angles. "Are you going to take any of that advice the dentist gave you?"

I hadn't thought of it as advice, more like criticism.

"I wouldn't know where to start," I said with a shrug.

"But you have to get started, right?"

"It seems overwhelming."

"Because it's about money?" she asked.

"Maybe. Sure."

"How much do you earn?"

I shook my head. "I can't tell you that." After all, she was a stranger and my salary was embarrassingly small.

"Why not?"

"People don't talk about money."

"But you'd tell me the price of something you bought."

"Right."

"So why is your salary different?"

"Because it's about me. A blouse has a price and, maybe," here I was making it up as I went along, "my salary is about my price—I mean my value in the world. What will people pay for me? I don't feel very good about it and I don't want to talk about it."

"So money is a taboo subject, because we measure ourselves against others in terms of money?"

"Maybe so."

"But is that right?" she asked.

My jaw hurt, and I had no idea where this conversation was heading. We were talking about money at the same time that we were talking about not talking about it. So I just said whatever came into my mind, things I didn't even know I thought.

"No, I don't think so."

"How else could we value people?"

"By whether they're good or bad," I answered. "Loving or cruel, responsible, honest, talented, friendly. There are all sorts of ways."

"But you think people are going to value you because of what you earn?"

"They do that, too," I said.

"Why should you let what they do bother you?"

"Maybe I wouldn't, in a perfect world."

"But this world isn't perfect?" she smiled.

"That's for sure."

"What would happen in a perfect world?"

"I'd win the lottery," I said.

She nodded. "My, my. So you're going to be rich someday. Will the lottery make you happy?"

"Happier than I am now, that's for certain."

Saidah thought for a moment.

"I know a Mexican folk tale that might amuse you. Want to hear it?"

"Sure."

"In the beginning, the gods created men and women. But men and women loved each other so much, the gods began to worry that our happiness would make us forget to worship them. So the gods created money."

I was waiting for more, but I had to smile when I realized the short tale had reached its end.

"Do you ever think what money is?"

I shook my head.

"How about debt?"

"That's when you owe money to somebody, or maybe a company like a bank."

"St. Paul says, 'Owe no debt to anyone, except the debt to love.' What do you think about that kind of debt?"

She had me going. I hadn't given much thought to any of these questions, and she seemed to have thought about them quite a lot. I found myself confused. Unlike Dr. Testa, who loved declarative sentences, Saidah preferred questions. It made me feel that she might know a whole lot more than I had any inkling of. If that were true, I wondered how she had acquired this knowledge. How could I learn what I imagined she might know? I might be walking in a maze, but this cheerful woman looked like she knew the ways in and out.

"It's like the rock 'n' roll song says," I couldn't think of a more intelligent reply, "'Money can't buy me love.'"

Saidah studied me for a few moments, slowly drumming the fingers of her left hand on the green slats of the bench. The leaves slapped overhead as the April breezes approached first from one direction, then another. I looked at the jewelry on Saidah's left hand. On her ring finger I saw a platinum wedding band and an engagement ring with a sparkling diamond. I wondered about her husband, what kind of man would be the right match for a woman like this? Did she have children? On her little finger was an ellipse of turquoise in an ornate silver setting. And on her middle finger was another silver ring, wider, to portray within its girth the trunk and spreading branches of a tree.

"I want to tell you one thing to keep in mind," she finally said. "I can see you're a good person, trying to do the right thing. Don't ever let anybody put you down, not about money, not about anything. Whatever debt you may have, you walk proud. You keep your head up. If it helps you, say something to yourself like, 'I am a good and loving person.' You remember what I'm telling you. Once you start on the path, there's no turning back. You go through the rough times knowing it will get better. It's right up there, at the end of the rainbow, just over the horizon. You've got to get started and you've got to keep going."

I had no idea what to make of this. Starting on what path? It didn't make any sense, yet I felt that she was trying to help me. But to do what?

"Thanks," I said.

"You must think I'm a crazy woman, huh?" She was smiling. "You're wondering what am I talking about?"

"A little bit," I admitted.

"Just remember what I said. In fact, say it for me."

"I am a good and loving person?" I said it as a question, I couldn't help myself.

"You have to sound like you believe it. If you don't believe, who else will?"

"I am a good and loving person."

"That's more like it," she said approvingly, "Now you have to make a plan."

"For what?"

"To pay off those debts of yours."

"But..." I started to protest, feeling she talked about an impossibility.

"You can't be vague about money. Money is meant to measure, to be easily kept track of. It's a helpful tool if we use it the right way. Can you tell me to the penny how much you earn and how much you spend?"

I shook my head.

"Then you have some finding out to do. You list all your income and you list all your expenses. Add up the numbers. See how you're doing. Then make a list of all your assets, what you own, like a car or house, and all your debts. See how much you're paying for interest and how much you're paying to reduce the debt itself. Do this month by month for twelve months so you can see what a whole year looks like. If you have to make guesses or assumptions, make them. Figure out what would happen if you stayed in the job you have, what would happen if you went back to waitressing, what would happen if you just went to dance auditions."

"I'd starve."

She smiled. "I call this part the money plan, but I don't stop there. Beyond that, make a list of everything you do that's of value to other people, even though you don't get paid money for it. Dancing, for example, gives pleasure to the people who see you, even if you don't get paid. Or helping an older person across the street. Or playing with a child. Making dinner for your roommates. Smiling at someone who smiles back. It's what I call the human economy, where you forget money and see how people give back and forth so much value that isn't monetary. At the beginning, it's crucial for you to remember this, to compute it even if the numbers make little sense. How can you place a financial value on the warmth that joins people together? But I want you to see an economics in which you do have value and are not in debt, in which your goodness shines through and you place a high value on it, high enough to keep your spirits up when money worries seem all around you."

I understood what she was saying, but she had gone way beyond me. I had never added up all my income and expenses, much less my nonexistent assets and very real debts. Now she was proposing something like counting the angels dancing on the head of a pin. I imagined a ballet of angels, their leaps and swirling turns aided by the marvelous lifting of their glistening white wings.

"You with me?"

All I could think about was the misery of sitting down and calculating the unforgiving numbers that I knew I would face. I didn't want to do it.

"It's never easy to start," Saidah might have read my mind, "but you have to know. You can't be guessing, wondering, hoping. You have to know to the penny. You have to be clear. But once you know your dollars and cents, I want you to add up the value of everything else you do. The human value. Don't you forget to do that."

"I won't," I nodded, perplexed that this stranger could talk to me so passionately about money and what I should do. And that I would agree to do what she told me, strange though some of her ideas sounded.

"Now about the Seven Wonders of the Ancient World," she said, referring to the story about Baron de Rothschild that Dr. Testa had told me.

"Yes?" I was curious to hear what she'd say.

"Do you know what they were?"

I tried to remember something from school, but all that came to mind was a big statue. I really didn't know.

"I guess I don't."

"I was going to ask you," she smiled warmly, and I felt that she was kidding me but in a way that might help me, "whether you liked the seven wonders better than the eighth. In fact, I am asking you. Why don't you find out what those seven wonders were? Lord knows we could all use more wonder in our lives."

I realized that she was planning to see me again. I had thought that this would be like so many encounters where two people brush by one another in the bustle of the city. Just a chance meeting, not to be repeated. But if she wanted to talk with me about the seven wonders, she was planning to see me again. I liked her, and I could certainly use a friend like her, someone who seemed to know how the world worked.

"I'll try," I said.

"Try?" She raised an eyebrow and I had to smile.

"OK, I'll find out."

"That's more like it."

"But," I hesitated, "when will we talk about it?"

"At the end of the work day, I like to sit on this bench for a few minutes. Just watch the world go by. Maybe read my newspaper." She looked archly at me. "You have a good chance to find me here if the sun's shining."

"What company do you work for?" I asked.

"I work for myself," she said, reaching into her large pocketbook and pulling out a business card and a pen. Carefully she wrote a telephone number on the back on the card, replaced the pen in her purse, and offered me the card. On the top of the card I read:

> ### Saidah Samuels
> M.B.A., Ph.D.
> Financial Planning from the Heart

I was surprised that she was a financial planner, because I wasn't certain of exactly what financial planning encompassed. I guessed that financial planning from the heart must be unusual, but I didn't know any other financial planners and couldn't make a comparison. Her advanced degrees reinforced my sense that Saidah had mastered a lot of information. I suddenly felt uncomfortable, because I realized that she gave advice for a living. She had been giving me advice. Perhaps I should be paying her.

"I wrote the phone number for a group that could be a good resource for you. It helps people who want to solve their debt problems. You'll know when you're ready to go there."

"Should I be paying you?" I blurted out.

She laughed, tossing back her head so her smile greeted the sky. "If you can afford to pay me, there's something you haven't been telling me. You have bank accounts in Switzerland or the Bahamas? Or maybe your mattress is lumpy with those rolls of hundred-dollar bills you sleep on every night?"

I had to admit that she was right. "What I mean..."

"I know what you mean. You want to do the right thing. I appreciate that. Let's just say I enjoyed talking with you today."

"What if we talk tomorrow?" I asked.

"Will you have to pay?"

I nodded. If she said yes, I was going to feel betrayed. I hadn't asked her for advice; in fact, I hadn't even asked her to talk to me. She started the conversation.

"You mean if it's a sunny day?"

"Yes."

"Because I won't be here if it's raining." She was smiling at me. I had no idea that I could be so amusing, especially without trying.

"I'm trying to say that you have to take one day at a time. What I mean, really, is to take one problem at a time. Right now you need to find out where you stand. How much do you owe, will your earnings let you pay off your debt? Once you know that, you can take another step. Never worry about more than one problem at a time. And even take that one problem and make it into a lot of smaller problems. Then you'll be able to make some progress, one step at a time. If you put your problems in a big pile, you'll only be able to solve them if a rich relative dies and leaves you a fortune. If you break problems down, you'll be learning a process, an approach that will always help you. There's no point in worrying about what may happen tomorrow—whether I'm going to be sitting on the bench and, if I am, whether I'm suddenly going to want to charge you fees you can't pay."

"I see what you mean."

"Good. Then I'll tell you something else. There's no point in worrying. It won't do you any good. Worry is just a form of energy. You can use that energy for better or worse. If I were you, I'd take the worry to dance class and use it to make beautiful movements. Or, instead of worrying, you could pray. Or think of the things that really matter: love, friendship, or..." Here she paused in her recital.

"What?" I encouraged.

"Death," she finished.

I must have frowned. "Why?"

"Because it focuses you—and me, too—on what is of value in life." She glanced at her wristwatch. "If I knew that I would die very soon, I would only be willing to deal with essentials. It's healthy and helpful

21

to think about how to solve a problem. But worrying about it constantly is obsession; that won't help us solve anything."

I nodded. She slipped her newspaper into her handbag and rose gracefully. I stood, too. I wanted to ask her: Why me? Why was she trying to help me? I didn't quite know how to say it.

"Saidah, thanks."

"Don't you go thanking me now. You do what you have to do. Then you'll be thanking yourself. See you." She smiled and waved as she walked away, calling back to me, "I'll be thinking about you dancing. I used to dance a little myself."

I watched the easy flow of her walk until she vanished where the path entered among the thick-trunked trees. While Saidah was talking with me, my jaw had actually felt better. I wondered if I dared to face my checkbook and credit card statements. It might be better to wait a day or two so I could recover from the dentistry. I rubbed my arm near the wrist where it had broken. It still felt tender, but it had definitely healed. I exercised it every morning by squeezing a soft rubber ball. I had been waiting to heal, waiting to dance, waiting to change jobs. I didn't want to wait anymore, not even to get the bad news about money. While Dr. Testa's lecture made me feel like burying my head in the sand, Saidah made me want to find out the truth. So I started for home.

CHAPTER 4

What's Under My Bed

At my apartment that night I didn't really know where to begin. It was a one-bedroom apartment, small enough even before three of us started sharing it. Tina and I slept in twin beds in the bedroom, while Rachel slept on a pullout couch in the living room. There was never enough room to hang up clothes and store everything. I kept my financial papers in a green, plastic trash bag that I could flatten by sitting on it and then shove under my bed. I had been putting papers in there since I graduated from college, but I had never taken any of the papers back out. To me, this had proved that my method of handling my finances had worked fine. Only tonight I was going to face this disorderly mass of papers.

Getting down on my hands and knees, I reached blindly under the bed to where I could feel the plastic bag. I pulled, and it slipped out from its hiding place. One problem with the apartment was that there was no place to sit and work, especially not in private. Also, I felt embarrassed to let my roommates see me puzzling over these papers that I had left so long in the trash bag. The best place to work would be the drop-leaf dining table, but Rachel had been making herself dinner. Tina wasn't home yet, so I just sat cross-legged between the twin beds and started dumping the papers on the rug.

I could feel myself grow heavier looking at them. Credit card statements and receipts, bank statements, checks, deposit slips, bills from my broken arm. If a historian only thought about money, this might be a history of my life for the last three years. It made me think of those time capsules that are sometimes placed in the cornerstone of a new building. Instead of being discovered and marveled at by future generations, my time capsule had to be looked at by me. As more and more of the papers flowed out of the bag, I doubted that I would ever be able to put them back again. These papers were like little demons, each with some unpleasant thought to inflict on me. Once I became aware of what these papers said, would I be able to forget about them and return to the bliss of ignorance?

My depression increased as the papers widened in a white lake. How to begin? I got up, took my wallet from my purse, and sat back on the floor. Carefully I emptied my wallet and counted my credit cards. I had eight cards with credit lines and five cards from department stores. If I could just find the most recent statement for each of these cards, I might be able to ignore a lot of the papers. I only needed to find out about my current situation.

I started shuffling through the pile, trying to deal with the top layer first. But soon I realized that I was going to have to make smaller piles to get everything in order. After an hour or more, I had about twenty piles of paper in front of me. I had glimpsed some of the recent numbers as I worked, and my stomach felt as if a block of ice grew in it. I could smell Rachel's cooking, but I had no appetite. In fact, my jaw was hurting again from the dental work, but the pain seemed like an abstraction compared to the bad news in front of me. To make sense of it all, I found a notepad and wrote "Debt" at the top of it. I entered my student loans—nearly twenty thousand dollars—and then I added each credit card. No credit line had allowed me to borrow more than three thousand dollars, but I owed seventeen thousand. Also, while I had managed to pay most of the department store cards when the bills came at the end of the month, one of the stores was threatening to sue me. That was because I had bought about five hundred dollars worth of clothing just before I broke my arm. My injury and the transition from waitress to receptionist had cost me a few weeks of earnings and I hadn't been able to pay that bill. Now it was three months overdue, and the friendly reminders had gradually become demands to pay that progressed to threats to take me to court. I wasn't sure, but I'd probably pay that bill first after I sorted everything out.

Saidah had said to compare my assets, which I knew to be zero, to my debts, which I now knew to be thirty-seven thousand dollars, an unimaginably large number. Next she had told me to figure out my monthly income and expenses. My income was simple—just my salary after taxes. My expenses I had to list down one side of the notepad. I used the old credit card receipts and statements and my checkbook to figure out most of the expense categories—rent, food, clothing, transportation, medical, dance classes, student loans, and a big number for miscellaneous expenses where I knew I spent the money but didn't know on what. Just the annual fees on my credit cards came to more than two hundred dollars. Then I added the monthly payments on my credit cards—more than three hundred dollars, mostly in interest. Suddenly I could see that I was paying more than three thousand dollars a year in interest at rates of between 15 and 20 percent. Maybe I had some inkling that was true, but looking at the number in my own handwriting shocked me.

The next shock came when I added up the numbers. The income didn't require addition—only one entry there. The expenses exceeded the income by over two thousand dollars, and that was before I included making payments on the credit cards. I knew that my salary as a receptionist was more than modest, but I suddenly understood that if I hadn't been borrowing on my credit cards over the last few years, I wouldn't have been able to afford to live as I had. Even when I had made more money as a waitress because I got good tips, I had still been borrowing on the credit lines and increasing my debt without even thinking about it.

I needed to earn five thousand dollars more each year just to keep my head above water. But five thousand dollars would be a big increase in my salary, nearly 25 percent. I couldn't ask for such a raise. I could always look for another job, as long as the new job had health insurance. But why would a new boss pay me more than the old one? I didn't have any special skills. The other possibility would be to spend less. I tried to pare five thousand dollars off the list of expenses. The only way to pay less rent would be to take another roommate, but that didn't seem possible. Moving wouldn't do me any good, because this apartment had been the cheapest I could find. If I cut back on my clothing, I'd be wearing rags before long, but maybe I could save a few hundred dollars there. I could give up ever eating out, not that I had done very much of that. Quite frankly, after I had gone down the whole list, I didn't see a solution. And I felt lousy. It was like the story of the emperor and his new clothes; I had been living my life thinking everything was fine, but it hadn't been. It made me feel crazy. How could it have seemed to be all right until I looked at it?

I felt trapped. I wished that I had never looked at these papers, but what choice did I have? At least I understood now that I was running five thousand dollars in the red every year. It made me angry. After all, I had nothing. I didn't ask for very much. I wasn't eating at fancy restaurants. I opened the door to the closet to prove I wasn't shopping in pricey boutiques. I hardly had any clothes at all, just my signature black slacks and the blouses I made from patterns. My sewing machine (it had been my mom's and she taught me) sat on a shelf at one end of the closet. The closet overflowed with Tina's wardrobe. She had at least a dozen designer dresses. I don't know how she did it, but she always had money for shopping.

I certainly wasn't jetting to vacation spots like St. Barts or St. Tropez and rubbing tanned shoulders with the rich and famous. All I wanted to do was dance. I wasn't even doing that. Viewed objectively, I was a receptionist who couldn't live within her means. I didn't like that very much. In fact, it hurt. I closed my eyes so I wouldn't see the papers on the floor, lowered my head, and let my chest heave until hot and salty tears squirted on my cheeks. I couldn't believe I had come to such a dead end. If I spent nothing on living expenses and everything on my debt, it would take me three years to pay off what I owed. But I couldn't do that. After all, I had to live. I had to eat and have a roof over my head. My first problem wasn't how to pay the debt, it was how to avoid getting in deeper.

Tina came back from her date and found me slumped over with depression. I should have stuffed the papers back in the plastic trash bag and hidden it under my bed, but I was in a stupor. I must have been sitting on that floor for three or four hours, my mind frozen with all those numbers.

"Hey, Iris, what are you doing?" Tina stood at the edge of the expanse of papers, wondering how to get across to her side of the bedroom. When she saw my face, she bent for a better look, "What's wrong? Are you all right?"

Tina was a real blond, a breezy, cheery sort of person who kept her feelings concealed most of the time. She looked even more like a dancer than I did, with her tight-waisted slenderness and elegant height. She had grown up with money—her dad was big in investment banking, whatever that meant exactly, but she was on the outs with him because he wanted her to study finance and stop dancing. Her mom and dad had divorced when she was a kid, and I found that she often thought people were criticizing her when they weren't. In any event, she and I had gotten through the surface stuff and we were really buddies. I wiped my cheeks and tried to stop crying, but the tears had a mind of their own.

Tina sat on my bed and massaged between my shoulders. "What's the problem?" she asked.

"I feel so upset." More tears sprang from my eyes. "I'm so miserable."

"Why?"

"I'm broke."

"So that's it," Tina accepted the news calmly. "Join the club."

Her hand on my neck relaxed me, but I didn't think she understood what I meant by broke.

"I'm in debt. I owe for my credit cards, my student loans, department stores. I'm never going to be able to pay it off."

"Me too," Tina agreed. "And Rachel, too."

I knew they were both in debt. Of course, Tina might reconcile with her father someday and he could wipe out her debts with his pocket money. I thought about Doug, whom I had met at the dance studio before my skating accident. We'd had several dates over the last two months and we hung out sometimes. I really liked him, so I kept wondering if the relationship might grow. He had played goalie on the all-star Canadian hockey team and come to the city about a year earlier to start his dance career. He had student loans and credit card debts, too. I wasn't sure if I knew anyone my age who didn't.

"Why are we all in debt?" I asked.

Tina grinned. "It's the American way."

"I don't get it." I waved a hand at the piles of papers. "I don't understand it."

"When I was talking to my dad, he used to say that I didn't see the big picture. Lenders make a lot of profit from debt. I think that was his point."

I shook my head. "I don't see how it's going to get any better." Even though I was close to Tina, I didn't feel able to tell her that I was spending more each month than I earned. For one thing, I didn't want her worrying about whether I would pay my share of the rent. I didn't want her to think of me as someone who couldn't be trusted about money.

"You hungry?" Tina glanced at her watch. "I bought some pizza. Also, the news should be on soon."

The reason it was important to watch the news was to see whether or not we had won the lottery. She, Rachel, and I always bought tickets if we had any money, especially when the jackpots grew bigger and bigger. Almost every night we'd watch the TV news and wait for the numbered ping-pong balls to pop out of that canister. Some nights we would joke about what we planned to do with the millions of dollars that would soon be ours. Pert, little, dark-haired Rachel wanted to buy a sculpture of a ballerina by Degas, while Tina thought a maid to clean once a week would be a blessing. The list went on and on. Money to the rescue. Money to do this and to do that. I thought that money would let me dance. I could pay off all my debts, go to as many classes as I wanted, focus completely on the creative life.

The three of us glued our eyes to the television. Tina and I sat at the dining table with wedges of pizza topped with melted cheese and vegetables drooping over our hands. The paperwork had nauseated me to the point where I didn't want to eat, but waiting with Tina and Rachel for the lottery numbers made me feel a little hope again. The usual news stories flashed across the screen—a building on fire, a car totaled in an accident, a murder, a drug bust, a dog show. Who decided whether to run this story or that one? It seemed like a rerun every night, new faces suffering the same old stories. Unfortunately, the same could be said for the lottery. We never had any real drama. Once Rachel had the first three numbers. That would have been enough to win at a one-armed bandit, but the lottery has six numbers. Six ping-pong balls popping out of that big canister. I thought the ceremony should be more solemn, not just a lot of ridiculous balls deciding who would be rich and who would stay on the treadmill.

We all had our tickets out, but by the second number we were groaning in disappointment and tearing our tickets into confetti.

"There's always tomorrow," Rachel observed, dragging the coffee table to one side so she could open the bed in the convertible couch.

"We won't win tomorrow," I said.

"Come on, Iris," Tina said. "If it can't get any worse, it's gotta get better. Right?"

"Sure," I agreed listlessly. After we had cleaned up the remains of the pizza, I went back to the bedroom floor and put a rubber band around each pile of papers, then quickly shoved the piles back into the trash bag. It didn't look as if it would fit under my bed. The neat piles seemed to rise higher than the disorderly mass of papers with which I had started. But I sat on the bag as hard as I could and wriggled my rear end back and forth until the bag deflated a bit. Then I raised up the box spring of the twin bed a few extra inches, and shoved the plastic bag into the darkness where it should have stayed.

Later, after we had queued for the bathroom and finally turned out the lights, I lay on my bed and stared up at the ceiling. Thoughts raced through my mind, but all these thoughts ended with my being a failure. Five thousand dollars in the red, five thousand times a failure.

Every year for the rest of my life, not earning enough, owing more and more. Every day at the office I saw people who seemed to have it together. They earned more than I did, had spouses, houses in the suburbs, children. Why couldn't I measure up to them? Why had they been able to manage their money wisely while I had spent too much?

Tears flowed from the corners of my eyes, wetting my hair and the pillow under my head. I cried silently in the dark, not wanting to disturb Tina whom I could see dimly bundled in her blankets a few feet away. I felt that curious sensation that came to me at different moments throughout my life. On my left side I was missing something. There should be something there, but I didn't know what. It didn't make sense, because I had everything that a person should have— a left arm, a left shoulder, a left hip. But I was feeling it ever so intensely, like a person you can't quite see out of the corner of your eye. There should be something there, and its absence made me even more lonely. Had Jim and Mary thought about how, when they died, I would be left without a family? I'd never know, but I felt the loneliness. I had no one to whom I could turn.

The image of Saidah floated into my thoughts. She would be on the park bench. The idea that I had to seek the comfort of strangers made me feel diminished. Wasn't it bad enough that I couldn't earn a living? Did I also have to expose my inadequacies to people I hardly knew? It was a hellish night; a dark night of the soul, as the poets say. I couldn't see a solution, except to buy some more lottery tickets tomorrow during my lunch break. So I saw the cycle of my days, the miserable hope that chance might free me from my debt followed by the inevitable disappointment when my tickets proved worthless. What could be better than this? Truly, I didn't know.

CHAPTER 5

The Seven Wonders of the World

One wonderful aspect of being a receptionist was that I had very little responsibility. I could think my own thoughts, fantasize about whatever I wanted, daydream to my heart's content. On a typical day, I might see myself on the great stages of the world, dancing in New York, Paris, or Moscow to the applause swelling in waves from enraptured audiences, excited, passionate men and women who had glimpsed the great artistry to which I had aspired and, after overcoming innumerable obstacles, attained.

This particular day, however, my thoughts followed a less pleasant trajectory. I still could see no way out of my predicament. Sitting at my computer, pretending to be busy, I felt fear. Whenever the telephone rang, I would put on my cheerful voice and say, "Good morning, Castle Advertising," but I felt that same block of ice in my stomach. I thought that it might be that time of the month, but a check of my date book showed me this had nothing to do with hormonal flows, just flows of money. A couple of times I took out my wallet and studied my credit cards as if they might reveal some secret, but my perplexity remained.

At last, when I was feeling like I might jump out of my skin, I recalled what Saidah had said about the Seven Wonders of the World.

If I wanted to see her again, and I was thinking I might like to go by the park bench when I got off work, I had to find out what those seven wonders had been. Actually, I was curious about it.

During my lunch hour I walked over to the library. I used several of the encyclopedias from the reference shelves and then went on-line to look for extra information. I learned that the seven wonders had been built centuries before Jesus lived and included:

The Pyramids of Egypt. I had never been to Egypt. In fact, I had never left the United States since my parents adopted me as a baby, but I had seen the pyramids in television documentaries and photographs. Of the seven wonders, only the pyramids had survived into modern times, so for the rest I used my imagination.

The Hanging Gardens of Babylon. These had been beautiful ter-raced gardens built by King Nebuchadnezzar beside his royal palace on the banks of the Euphrates River.

The Temple of Artemis at Ephesus. This huge temple in what now is part of Turkey had been built of marble.

The Statue of Zeus at Olympia in Greece. Crafted of gold and ivory by famed sculptor Phidias, this enormous statue dominated the tem-ple at the site of the earliest Olympic Games.

The Mausoleum of Halicarnassus. Constructed on the Aegean coast to the south of Ephesus, this huge tomb with ornate sculptures had been built for the ruler Mausoleus. His wife Artemisia loved him so much that after his death she mixed his ashes with wine and drank this potion to have him forever with her.

The Colossus of Rhodes. This statue of the sun god, more than one hundred feet tall, guarded the harbor of the island of Rhodes.

The Pharos of Alexandria in Egypt. A lighthouse, four hundred and fifty feet high, stood at the entrance of the city's harbor. I guessed this might have been as tall as a forty-story building, truly a wonder in a world where most buildings would be one or two stories.

When I returned from my lunch hour, I tried to understand why Saidah had wanted me to find out about the seven wonders. As I answered the telephone and typed a few memos, I tried to see what they had in common. For example, why hadn't the seven wonders included the wonders of nature? In addition to the pyramids, why not include the Nile with its annual flooding that turned desert into fertile farmland? But the wonders of nature survived, the rivers, the mountains, the deserts, the seas. The seven wonders had all been built by people and, except for the pyramids, had vanished with hardly a trace. As I thought more about them, I realized that in antiquity these wonders must have seemed almost impossible to build—impossible in some cases because of sheer size and in others because of the artistry of the construction. That impossibility might have made these creations appear to be divine, or at least divinely inspired.

After a while I pretty much ran out of ideas about what Saidah might have wanted. I did notice that thinking about the seven wonders had made me stop worrying about my financial troubles. When I thought about death or even temples built for worship, I felt that I gained a better perspective on my money issues. I remembered those T-shirts that joked, "Whoever dies with the most, wins," but I was living and had real concerns about money. Why hadn't I started taking dance classes again? My arm had healed enough. Then I daydreamed about auditions where the choreographer would single me out to join the company and dance the lead.

I also wondered about Doug. Might we someday love each other with an imperishable love? If he were hit in the head by a puck speeding so fast that it knocked him all the way to heaven, would I mix his ashes with wine—or some blended fruit-and-vegetable health drink, since I didn't actually drink alcohol—and ingest what remained of him so that our spirits would forever be joined? He was cute, big, and kind of funny with a frozen, far-north humor that melted ever so slowly, but I couldn't stomach the idea of sprinkling his ashes on pizza while I watched television. I wanted to move beyond where we were to the joy of love, but maybe he wasn't the one. Or maybe I didn't have the right stuff. Probably I hadn't met the right person. I could switch back and forth on this topic a million times.

Five o'clock at last. I headed for the park, which filled the center of the city. I kept seeing Saidah's face. She had no reason to feel concern for me, yet she had. She could have just kept reading her newspaper or walked away. I recalled her warmth like a touch. It drew me back to her. "Financial planning from the heart." It was another beautiful April day and, like the day before, there were so many people sitting on the benches and strolling along the paths. Why should I have sat next to Saidah out of so many people?

I saw the bench ahead, beside the macadam walk snaking through a grassy field bounded by oaks and maples. I could see the white pages of a newspaper spread open. As I came closer, I saw that the reader was Saidah. I felt a bit breathless as I sat beside her.

"Hi."

Her head tilted quizzically and she gave a sidelong glance, then smiled, "Hello, Iris. Nice to see you again."

We got to talking. I told her about my roommates and how we always watched the ping-pong balls and hoped to win the lottery. She nodded and asked about the tickets I had bought the day before.

"No luck." I said.

As I felt more comfortable, I began to tell her how I had gotten the trash bag out from under my bed. What I really wanted to tell her was how upset I felt. I made a big deal about organizing the piles of papers and figuring out what I earned and what I spent, but when I got to the deficit I admitted that it made me feel really bad.

"Five thousand a year," she repeated after me, "Who wouldn't feel bad? And then did you add up the other things, the things that don't have price tags?"

It was only at that moment that I realized I had forgotten completely about that part of what she said. I hadn't valued friendship, love, creativity. Maybe I forgot because it seemed impossible to value, at least in terms of money, and I said as much to her.

"It will help you," she admonished me. "I know how upsetting it is when the numbers don't balance. When you're upset, it helps to see a larger perspective in which money is only one aspect. Give it a chance."

"But what should I do?"

"You're doing it. Think how much more you know now."

"Sure, I know I'm between a rock and a hard place."

Saidah smiled. "That's a place to start from."

"Start where?" I asked. "Where am I going?"

"You're going where you have to go." Seeing me about to protest, she raised a hand to silence me, "This isn't about my telling you what to do. I'll give you what practical advice I can, but you have to make this your journey."

I wanted to argue more, but then thought better of it. "When you make a financial plan for someone, what do you do?" I asked.

"I don't make their financial plan, they do."

"But you're the expert. You have the graduate degrees."

"There's no cookie-cutter solution to money, just like there's no right answer to how to live your life. I help people develop the plans that suit their deepest needs. Maybe there are a few people in the world who only want money, but I haven't met too many. My work is to let people speak about money from their hearts, so that whatever the shape of their financial plan, it comes from their heart's necessity."

I realized that I had misunderstood Saidah's card. When the card said "Financial Planning from the Heart," I thought she meant from her heart. I would certainly have called her warm-hearted, but now I saw that she meant financial planning from the hearts of her clients. How different that seemed to me from the calculating, objective mental process that I had imagined set people like robots on a course for wealth.

"By the way," Saidah continued, handing me a slender, spiral-bound booklet, "I want to give you this. These are what I call 'The Money Exercises.' I use them when I give talks about planning. You may find them helpful." Saidah later gave me permission to include the Money Exercises at the back of this book, which I've done because I did find the exercises clarifying, stimulating, and sometimes provoking. Skimming through the text and forms in the booklet for the first time, though, I felt overwhelmed by how much it covered—Your Financial Attitudes, Your Money Priorities, Your Financial Education, Your Financial IQ, Your Spiritual Assets, What You Own, What You Owe, What You Earn, What You Spend, Your Money Ledger, Your

Spending Plan, Your Debts and Interest Payments, Your Plan for Creditors, Your Financial Future, Your Important Papers, and Further Reading about Money.

"Thanks." I didn't want her to see that I was wondering if I could handle all this, so I skipped over to the next topic that I wanted to tell her about. "I checked out the Seven Wonders of the World."

"Really? You have been busy. What did you think of them?"

"They all sound amazing, especially compared to what else existed so long ago. It was like daring to imagine the impossible, then doing it."

"If we can't imagine what we want to create," Saidah replied, "it's unlikely we'll ever create it. I sometimes think of imagination as the mirror of the soul; it reflects back to us our spiritual yearnings and possibilities. It lets us reach new levels. To reject imagination, the dreams of where our potentials may carry us, is to be trapped and limited by fear."

"I felt so much fear last night," I said. "And at work this morning when I thought about not earning enough. Why should money make me feel that fearful?"

"I think it's because we know money is a survival tool. When we don't have enough, we feel that our lives are threatened. Perhaps we also judge ourselves to be inadequate, just the way that we worry other people might judge us. But if you step back, you can see something valuable about the fear that you felt."

"What?" I really couldn't see it at all. It had felt awful and I didn't see any reason why I wouldn't be fearful all over again as soon as I confronted my money scenario.

"Fear lets loose our demons, but those demons have a lot of energy. They can make us worry, see illusions, feel so depressed we wish we could sleep forever. But if we get them to work for us, then we can accomplish near miracles." Her eyes shined as she spoke. "Then we can imagine an eighth wonder of the world of our own making. What would yours be?"

"To be debt-free," I answered.

"What else?" she prompted.

"To dance."

"And?"

"Isn't that enough?"

"We have a choice between fear and play, the play of creativity and joy. When you feel fear, capture its energy for play. Put those demons to work so they can't get into any more mischief. Always keep a sense of wonder, the kind of wonder that let the ancients dream and build the Seven Wonders of the World."

"But," I had been turning over in my mind a certain puzzlement, "why were there only seven wonders?"

Saidah chuckled, "What other wonders should there have been?" she asked.

"People were dreaming and building all over the world. What about the Great Wall of China? Or the pyramids of the Mayans? Or the caves in India, with all the Buddhas chiseled into the stone?"

"That's good, Iris."

"Isn't nature filled with wonder?" I raised the point I had been thinking about earlier.

"It is," Saidah agreed. "And so are people. Every person has that spark of the divine. We have to trust in that. No point thinking about what we can't be. Just be all that we can."

Listening to her, I felt for a moment as if I were flying, floating above the landscape of my everyday life. Then I thought about my financial predicament and immediately seemed to have feet of lead that plummeted me back to earth and my worries.

"But what about the five thousand dollars? And the debt? Thirty-seven thousand dollars." I intoned the words with awe. How had I, Iris Cassidy, run up such a debt?

"You know what they say," Saidah smiled her easy smile. "The Great Wall of China wasn't built in a day, nor were the vast stone castles of Great Zimbabwe. You didn't get into debt in a day and you won't get rid of it overnight. You've started, that's what's important. The greatest danger is before the adventure begins. It's the danger that we will never start, never discover our full potentials."

"Adventure?" I echoed. "I don't see being in debt as an adventure."

"But it is a challenge. Every challenge forces us to change, to develop ourselves. It may not be an adventure with knights in armor and fire-breathing dragons, but it requires courage to face our debts."

I gave a deep, long, wistful sigh. Saidah observed me for a few moments.

"I want to tell you a story. It's from western Africa, the area that my own ancestors lived in before they were brought as slaves to North America. Want to hear it?"

"Yes."

Saidah bowed her head a moment to collect her thoughts, then began speaking in a voice as mesmerizing as any that ever spoke the words, "Once upon a time…"

"One day a hunter named Soko came to the great tribe known as the Ashanti. He came with a debt, although he never said and no one knew how this debt had been created. Soko said that he wanted to live among the Ashanti. When the elders of the tribe considered his request, they were fearful because none of them had ever heard of debt. There was no such thing among the Ashanti. So the elders told Soko that he could live among them only if he rid himself of his debt.

"Soko didn't know how to do this, but the spider god Anansi heard about his predicament. Now Anansi is very smart, but he can also be a trickster. When he found Soko making palm wine, he told Soko that in exchange for the palm wine, he would take the debt. Soko agreed, so Anansi drank the wine and took the debt.

"Anansi planted his fields and said that whoever ate from his harvest would take the debt. A bird ate from the crops and took the debt. And the bird laid eggs in its nest in a tree and said that whoever broke the eggs would take the debt. A falling branch broke the eggs and the tree took the debt. The tree said that whoever ate its blossoms would take the debt. When a monkey ate the blossoms, the monkey took the debt. The monkey said that whoever ate him would take the debt. A lion ate the monkey and so took the debt. Then the lion said that whoever ate him would take the debt.

"One day Soko was hunting in the forest when he saw the lion. He shot an arrow through the lion's heart and brought the lion back to the village to share as a feast with all the villagers. And that is the story of how Soko the hunter and Anansi the trickster god brought debt to the land of Ashanti."

I liked the story, especially the impish humor with which Saidah recounted it, but I didn't understand it.

"Why was Soko in debt?" I asked.

"Why do you think?" Saidah asked me in return.

I shook my head. The story had a paradox that baffled me. Soko is told to get rid of the debt, but instead, the debt keeps moving until finally the whole tribe shares the debt. So Soko did get rid of the debt, but then he ended up with part of it again and also gave it to everyone in the tribe. Surely that hadn't been what the elders intended.

"Was he allowed to stay?"

Saidah shrugged, "That's where the story ends."

"What do you make of the story?" I asked her.

"Debt is a form of circulation," she replied. "We have to see that aspect of debt, the way debt connects us to other people."

"Is that good?"

"Like all connections, it can be good or bad. If we circulate our love and friendship to others, that's certainly good. If we use debt to better ourselves and others, that must also be good. If debt is entered into in ignorance and imprisons us, then how can it be good? I think of debt like fire. It can be immensely useful or immensely destructive. We have to learn how to control it. We have to circulate it wisely."

"How do you know what's wise?" I asked.

"A person should be able to repay debts without feeling fear or a heavy burden. If that's not going to be possible, the person shouldn't borrow and the lender shouldn't lend."

"But don't they check your credit before they offer you credit cards?"

Saidah looked like I'd surprised her. "Say that again?" she said, "I'm not sure I heard you correctly."

I repeated myself, keeping my voice nearly inaudible since I knew she didn't agree with me.

"This wood bench is feeling mighty hard and," Saidah shifted on the bench and looked at her watch, "I have to start for home. You want to walk a little ways with me?'

We started ambling through the park. After we walked a few minutes into the trees and then past a restaurant on a pond with rowboats that people could rent, she spoke again.

"Maybe you should retain me as your financial adviser."

I checked to see if she was joking, but she was serious. In fact, she looked thoughtful and rather concerned.

"But I couldn't afford that," I said, which was the first thing that came into my mind. Saidah had two graduate degrees and ran a business. How could I possibly afford her when the first thing I needed to do was cut back on my expenses?

"You sure?"

I considered this for a moment. "You must charge a lot," I said, realizing that I didn't know and adding, to cover myself, "and I should be spending less, not more."

"Is that right?"

"I think so. Or I could earn more, but I don't see how."

"Sounds like you need a financial planner."

"All right," I had to laugh. "How much do you charge?"

"I'm glad you asked, because if you don't ask you'll never find out. I happen to have a sliding rate scale. Once, when I was a very idealistic young woman, I charged people whatever they wanted to pay. That was an interesting experiment, and I'm lucky that my husband is a good man with a good job. So I've learned not to be very idealistic—just idealistic. I charge most people my standard fee, but I let people I like and think have special potential pay what they can afford. I'd put you in that group."

I was surprised that she thought I had special potential, and touched that she liked me. If I understood her correctly, she was saying that I could pay whatever I wanted. Considering that I had never worried much about money before, it was odd that I felt like I couldn't afford anything. I didn't want to insult her, but paying her would still be an outlay when I ought to be spending less and less. So I hesitated.

Saidah walked like a breeze, flowing comfortably over the paths. I thought about her ancestors in the land of Ashanti. At least she knew where she came from. It troubled me that I didn't know that about myself.

"What would be fair to pay you?" I asked to avoid giving her an answer.

"You have to decide that. I only require that you pay something, but if you want to pay a penny, then I'm happy to receive that penny. Who knows," she smiled, "it might be a lucky penny and make me rich."

"What if," I started, "a wealthy person only wanted to pay a penny?"

"A truly wealthy person will want to pay more than my standard fee. But that's really a whole different subject. So are you going to be my client?"

Saidah had such an unperturbed air about her. I especially liked the way her eyes played across her surroundings. Because I was a dancer, I was very aware of how a lot of people, especially in the city, kept their eyes straight ahead in a tight focus. That was how they walked, too, a single idea leading them forward in a direct line. Saidah, I could tell, had a vision that encompassed everything about her, from left to right and near to far. She would be aware of a movement at the farthest peripheries of her vision. I recalled one of my dance teachers saying how a good dancer can sense where the other dancers are on the floor. It's like intuition in our flesh. Saidah had something like this. It made me trust her, even if I didn't understand her, and I had no real choice in my reply.

"Yes."

"Good, because I need a lucky penny."

"So," I returned to my question, "don't they do a credit check before giving credit cards to people?"

"Iris," Saidah paused as we reached the edge of the park. "You and I have a lot to talk about. Now that you've retained me, we can make an appointment to meet. Then I've got to head for home."

"Tomorrow?" I asked, not sure where she would want to meet. "Same place, same time?"

Saidah smiled her infectious smile. I grinned back at her. I don't know exactly why I felt so cheerful, but Saidah made me feel I could accomplish the impossible.

"See you then," she said, calling as she started across the street. "You made a wise decision."

I stood on the sidewalk that circled the park and watched her walk away. I couldn't afford a financial adviser, but I had one nonetheless. I marveled at the strangeness of life. What unlikely odds had been over-come to let me meet Saidah and have her be my adviser. It made me think that this might be a miraculous day, a day when all the long shots pay off. I rummaged in my handbag and pulled out my purse. I had three tattered dollar bills and a little over two dollars in change. Except for emergencies, I had decided not to use my credit cards anymore, so this cash had to last me another two days until I got paid on Friday. Also, I had to pay Saidah tomorrow. If I ate canned food—I thought I had a can of tuna fish and a can of stewed tomatoes at the apartment—and walked to work, I could get to Friday without having to spend any money. I just felt lucky. I was thinking about combinations of numbers involving the date that I met Saidah and my birth date. Carefully I put a dollar aside for Saidah, and headed for the newsstand to buy lottery tickets with the other four dollars.

CHAPTER 6

Lucky Numbers

I liked Doug enough to feel disappointed our relationship didn't move beyond an occasional date and some evenings shared with friends. He had the physique of a god from one of those old statues, a face that was rugged and warm and trustworthy, and a lot of curly dark hair that must have been magnetized, the way my fingers were drawn to touch it. I even felt a little jealous of him, because so few men wanted to be dancers that Doug was already getting to perform. If he tired of dancing, he could probably play professional hockey.

Everybody was home, so Doug and I had crawled through the bedroom window and spread a blanket on the roof. Our neighbors could look out and see us, but it made the apartment seem a little larger and we had a great view of the sunset. I liked being close to Doug, and getting out on the roof gave me the curious feeling that I had left everything behind. After all, windows are a barrier to the outside world, so if you use one like a door, you end up someplace out of the ordinary. I can't say that the roof really was out of the ordinary, but it felt that way, to be watching the setting sun spread its red glow over the rooftops and look in occasionally and see Tina reading in the bedroom.

"Do you ever feel lucky?" I asked Doug. I was still upbeat about the lottery tickets.

"Sure," he answered.

"What about?"

"Lots of things."

"I mean lucky about something that you might not expect would ever happen but then it did. Or you might have thought it could happen but the odds were against it."

He lay on his back and looked up at the darkening sky. "When I was a kid, I dreamed about playing hockey in the Olympics. The odds were against that, but it did happen. I guess that's lucky."

"If I told you I was going to win the lottery tonight, would you think I was crazy?"

He rolled on his side to look into my eyes in the fading light. "I already know you're crazy, but how much did you spend on the tickets?"

"Four dollars."

"What's the jackpot now?" he frowned, trying to remember.

No one had won in over a week and the jackpot had been growing more enormous each day. "Thirty-six million dollars."

He whistled. "You're going to have trouble spending it all."

"Well, they don't pay it to you all at once. First, they take out the taxes, then they pay it in installments for twenty years. If the taxes are fifty percent, I'll only get about a million dollars a year."

"In that case," he smiled, "spending it won't be so hard."

The sun vanished behind the silhouetted buildings. Doug and I chattered about nothing at all, just dreamy ideas about the future—where we would go, where we would dance. We had been visible to everyone in the apartment buildings around us, but with nightfall we vanished in the darkness and they became visible in their well-lit apartments. I liked this feeling of the world turned inside out. It made me all the more certain that anything is possible. At last Tina rapped on the window.

"The news is on."

Doug and I slipped back through the window and gathered with Tina and Rachel in front of the television. It held my attention the way a mouse might hold a cat's. I was just waiting for those ping-pong balls to turn up my numbers. The glass canister spun and agitated the balls until the first rolled out and the announcer, in her excited voice, called out the number:

"Four."

I had my tickets out. I had met Saidah in April, the fourth month, so I had picked four as my first number. "I've got it," I said.

No sooner had I spoken than the second ball rolled out beside the first.

"Eleven," the announcer called.

I had eleven on both tickets, because I had met Saidah on April 11th. "I've got that, too," I said, wondering if I should pinch myself to wake up.

"One."

Everybody else had turned to watch me, but I found I couldn't say anything because I had met Saidah on Monday after that traumatic visit to Dr. Testa. Monday is the first day of the week, so I had one as my third number. If only the last three numbers would match my birth date, I'd have accomplished the impossible. I had a flash, a vision of all my debts paid and a generous income to let me do what I pleased.

"Thirty-three."

I started crying. Doug came and put his muscular arm around my heaving shoulders.

"I had three numbers," I said finally. "I thought I would win."

"I thought I would win, too," Tina said, "and I didn't get any numbers."

"It's nothing to get upset over. Those are long odds." Doug meant well, but I felt inconsolable.

"And you can try again," Tina chimed in. "Tomorrow it'll probably be fifty million. You'll be happy you didn't win today, if you win tomorrow and it's fifty million."

I got up and went to the bathroom for a few moments of privacy. I washed my face, but the tears kept coming. I couldn't understand it. I had been hoping I'd win, but I had been hopeful before. Only this time I had used the magic of meeting Saidah to win. I had used those special numbers that came from the date that I met her. I kept bending over the sink, splashing my face with cold water, and looking at myself in the mirror only to see puffy eyes and more tears. I felt I had betrayed Saidah. That was the truth. I had spent my last dollars on lottery tickets instead of paying her the most that I could, not that five dollars would have been enough. But it wasn't about amounts of money. It was the spirit from which I had acted that disturbed me. I could have been generous toward Saidah and shown my thanks for her concern for me, and her advice. Instead I spent most of it selfishly on the lottery tickets, and I hadn't even won.

At last my tears stopped. I didn't bother to redo my makeup, just patted my face dry with the towel, and went back to the living room.

"You OK?" Doug asked.

"Sure."

"Really?" Tina studied my face.

"Sure, really." I knew if I talked about how bad I felt, I'd probably start crying again. "I think I'm overtired. I'm going to turn in."

Doug received this news with equanimity. He and I went into the hallway to say good night.

"What is it?" he asked.

"Nothing." I couldn't tell him that I was upset about money. I thought that he'd judge me and care about me less.

"Why don't I believe you?"

"If I had an emergency," I don't know why I said what I did, but the words came out and I was too upset to stop them, "and I needed to borrow money, would you lend me some?"

"Of course I would. How big an emergency? How much would you need?"

"Maybe a thousand dollars," I knew I was crazy to say the words as soon as I had spoken them. Doug did a double take and studied me in a way that made me uncomfortable. I must have still been caught up in the fantasy of the lottery. I would have liked to say forty thousand dollars. Then I could pay off my debts and still have a few thousand dollars left over to live on until I got my income and expenses in balance, but even a thousand dollars would give me some space to try and figure out a solution.

"I could scrape together a hundred, maybe. I..." He stopped and thought for another moment, then asked abruptly, "You're not doing drugs, are you? I mean, people aren't after you for money?"

He said it with concern, but I saw my predicament as laughable. I was humiliating myself in front of Doug, a guy I'd have given a lot to fall in love with, and he didn't have any more money than I did. Did I dare tell him that I wasn't being pursued by gangsters? If he thought I was a drug fiend, I figured I'd better be honest.

"No," I was able to smile. "The mafia isn't after me, but the credit card companies are. Or will be pretty soon, when I can't pay. I don't understand how I ran up so much debt."

"Join the club," Doug shrugged to show he had no solution. "Who isn't in debt? If you think it's bad for you, what about people who are a little older than we are and have kids? All of my brothers are in debt. The paycheck comes in, and out it goes. Last time we all got together, at Thanksgiving, we were talking about it. Al, he's my oldest brother, said the best time of his life had been college, when all he had to do was worry about grades and hang out at the frat house. Everybody agreed, and I'm starting to feel that way, too. I don't know how long I'm going to be dancing. I keep thinking, maybe I should borrow some more and go to law school. At least someday I might earn enough to pay off my debts."

"What about hockey?"

He shook his head. "I don't want to play hockey. I want to dance. If I can't, I might as well prepare for a good career."

I hadn't known this about Doug. Once he told me, I realized that it should have been obvious. Doug did carpentry and odd jobs that didn't keep him in an office from nine to five, so he could get to dance classes and rehearsals. He lived on the outskirts of the city with four roommates. I knew he had debts, too. Unless he came from a wealthy family, why would I have thought he had money to lend me?

Our good-night kiss wasn't passionate; in fact, our quick embrace struck me as being compassionate for our shared troubles. As soon as Doug had left, I went in my bedroom and took out the pad with the summary I had made of my income and expenses. For at least an hour, until Tina came to bed, I studied the numbers. I had felt a little better after talking to Doug, but my spirits started sinking again. The numbers were like a closed system that wouldn't let in anything new. At least I didn't see any way to change them. I didn't usually observe myself, but I noticed how I was getting upset over numbers on a piece of paper. The numbers had been the same before I put them down on the piece of paper, only I hadn't known about them, so they hadn't upset me. Maybe I had been better off that way.

"You want me to turn off the light?" I asked Tina, who had slipped into bed.

"Thanks."

I went into the bathroom so I could keep the light on without disturbing anybody. Except myself, because the more I looked at the numbers the worse I felt. I was sitting on the floor, my back against the white porcelain of the bathtub and the pad on my lap. I kept trying to figure a way out of the annual shortfall of five thousand dollars. Suddenly I had a scary thought. Once you got into debt far enough, the only way to keep going was to get into debt further. For me to go on, I had to figure out a way to borrow five thousand dollars more this year. If I could do that this year, then next year I would have to borrow more than five thousand and so on. How could anyone do it? How could I turn it around?

I could skip one meal a day, walk everywhere I went, and never go to a movie or a dance performance. That would save at least a thousand dollars a year. So why don't I skip three meals a day, I wondered miserably. When I didn't come up with anything practical, my thoughts started drifting. I began thinking about the perfect crime. If I could commit the perfect crime, I would pay off everything and no one would ever know. But how can there be a crime if no one knows about it? At least the victim has to know. What if I could steal something from someone's mind? A great idea that the person hadn't even realized. Maybe a patent for an invention that would free humanity from its laborious toil. Only how would I be able to get inside the mind of someone else? How could I know what they didn't know?

I returned to the hardness of the tub and floor tiles. If the fantasy of a perfect crime didn't work, what about marrying a rich husband?

In the daylight hours, I would never have admitted such a thought to my mind, but this was the midnight hour, or past that, and I was tired and feeling pretty bad. The plan to marry a rich husband was a lot like committing a perfect crime. I would sacrifice myself to a man who had money, but in every other way was unattractive. Gradually, like *Beauty and the Beast,* I would reform him by my own nature until he would be transformed to a radiant, handsome, loving man. Whatever my original motives (didn't Beauty go to the Beast to help out her father?), I would soon be wealthy and happily married.

There were a few small problems with this fantasy, too. I didn't know any rich men, I didn't want to marry someone just because they had money, and I didn't think that if I did marry someone for the wrong reasons I would ever be able to change them for the better. Maybe they would change me for the worse. Or maybe I was bad even to think about such demeaning and improbable solutions.

I'd cried too much earlier to cry anymore, but when the silver-lined clouds of my fantasies evaporated I felt very tired and miserable. I rested my face in my palms. Where to turn? Then I saw Saidah, her easy walk and quick smile. I had forgotten to do what she had told me. Add into my budget the things that had value other than money. I considered this, at first drawing a blank, but finally writing under the income side of my sheet: (1) knowing a guy like Doug; (2) having friends like Tina and Rachel; (3) loving to dance; and (4) meeting Saidah. But how can you attach a money value to friendship, caring, or respect? I didn't know, but I must say that the possibility of getting my numbers to balance made me willing to think new thoughts.

What if my relationship with Doug were worth one thousand dollars? I asked myself whether I'd give up seeing Doug for a thousand dollars. Since my answer was no, it had to be worth at least that much. In fact, I wouldn't stop seeing my friends for any amount of money. So even though I seemed to be mixing apples and oranges, and I felt kind of naughty to be doing what I was doing (nice people don't value relationships in terms of money), I put five thousand dollars next to Doug's name and three thousand dollars each next to Tina's and Rachel's. I was surprised that when I got to Saidah I wanted to write ten thousand dollars, but I went right ahead and did it. Not that these relationships couldn't be worth more, I thought to myself, but that they were certainly worth at least this much. When I got to my love for dance, also priceless, I figured fifty thousand dollars and wrote it with a flourish. Before I broke my arm and had to get a nine-to-five job, I had been volunteering to teach dance to preschoolers on Tuesday mornings. Even though I didn't get paid, I enjoyed that a lot and wrote down four thousand dollars next to it. During the blood shortage a few months earlier, I had volunteered to donate. Especially since I hate needles, I thought it would be fair to value that around one thousand dollars. And there were other things as well, little good acts that I had done and never valued. When I started adding up these new assets, I was really impressed. I had almost one hundred thousand dollars!

I knew this was all crazy, because money is money, but it made me feel better. I liked it more than the fantasy of the perfect crime or the rich husband. At least I was trying to place a value on what was really happening in my life. It occurred to me that maybe there was another whole way to look at money. Maybe money should be evaluated in terms of things that can't be valued. If the Beatles were right—that money can't buy love—and I sure thought they were, then maybe money wasn't the end all and be all. The Almighty Dollar. Jesus said, "You cannot serve God and Mammon." When I was a kid, the Bible at Sunday school had pictures that showed Mammon like an unbelievably enormous and ugly bull standing upright on his hind legs, but we were told that Mammon really represented money and all the worldly distractions that keep us from our own spirit.

I think I began to nod off, but I was feeling almost cheerful, as if a burden had been lifted off my shoulders, when Tina pushed open the door of the bathroom. She looked like a sleepwalker, squinting at the brightness of the light as she asked in a disbelieving voice, "It's the middle of the night. Aren't you tired?"

"Now I am," I said, standing so I could give her privacy.

"What's on the pad?" she asked.

"My money stuff. It makes me a little crazy, but I'm trying to understand it better."

"You should think about credit counseling," she said. "They check out what you owe and consolidate your loans at a lower interest rate."

"How did you hear about that?" I asked.

"On TV."

"But where would I find a place like that?"

"The Yellow Pages."

I exited and crawled into my bed. I was so tired I felt numb, which was all right because at least I didn't feel bad. Credit counseling. I knew I needed help. It was nice to feel like I had assets that couldn't be measured in terms of money, but I still had to deal with paying the rent. From what Tina said, it sounded like the credit counselors might step in and take charge. Tell me what to do to get out of this mess. It made me hopeful. It seemed safer and more realistic than the lottery. When I saw Saidah the next day, I would definitely ask her about it.

CHAPTER 7

Acts of Faith

I wouldn't want anyone to think that I was always depressed, because most of my life I've been pretty happy. I liked growing up with my parents. I had my share of unhappy moments, but they were mostly about things like not having a date for a high-school dance or getting a B- instead of B+ in my college biology course when I had studied hard. Most upsetting was the death of my parents, but those times came and I grieved and went on with my life. Owing money, however, belonged in a class by itself. It didn't happen and then go away. It happened and then kept happening; if anything, it was growing worse and worse.

The realization that I couldn't see a way out of my struggle with debt never left my mind. Once I recognized the problem, it affected me all the time. Especially after having high hopes for the lottery, I felt depressed at work the next day. It was a relief to join Saidah at the end of the afternoon. I was beginning to think of this park bench as our special place.

"How are you?" she asked.

"OK, I guess."

"If you're guessing, it's not OK," she said.

That was all I needed to pour out the latest episode of my problems, starting with how close I had come to winning the lottery and ending with how my numbers would never balance. I would be in debt forever. Somewhere toward the end of the middle I told her about Tina's idea of credit counseling. When I finished, Saidah was shaking her head with a little smile and looking at me like she knew something I didn't know.

"We have a lot to talk about today," she said. "Maybe we should start with the lottery. Why do you play, if losing upsets you?"

"I think I started because it was fun, like gambling."

"It *is* gambling," Saidah corrected, "but why should it be fun?"

I shrugged. "Watching the numbers come up. There's something exciting about it."

"You know the odds are against you."

"Sure," I answered. "But I'm betting a few dollars and I could win millions. A few dollars isn't going to make any difference to me, but millions would change my life."

Saidah frowned, like a conductor who hears an instrument off-key. "Iris, I think you have it backwards. Those few dollars you spend every day add up to a lot of money. How much did you spend yesterday?"

"Four dollars." I was embarrassed because I only had one dollar to pay her and she'd know I could have paid her more.

"If you gamble every day, that's three hundred and sixty-five times four," she multiplied quickly in her head, "fourteen hundred and sixty dollars. That would be a good start on that five thousand dollar deficit you're worrying about."

"But I don't play the lottery every day." Some days I couldn't afford it, but I didn't tell Saidah this or that on other days I spent more than four dollars.

"How much did you spend on the lottery last month?"

I shook my head because I didn't know. In my budget it must have fallen under "Miscellaneous," which had been a big number that I hadn't been able to break down.

"Whatever you think it is, it's more. And it's the small things that are important. Like the Chinese water torture. Maybe it's only a drop of water falling on your forehead, but if those tiny drops keep falling, you go crazy after a while. That money spent on the lottery is like those drops of water. Enough drops will fill a bucket or a bank account. The big picture is in the details. You have to be willing to look."

"But I could win."

"If you saved that money instead of gambling, you would definitely win. It would be in your bank account. If somebody wanted to bet you on the toss of a coin, but he got thirty cents from you if he won and you only got twenty cents if you won, would you do it?"

"No, it's not fair."

"Then why would you play the lottery when only 65 percent of the money that people bet is paid out as prizes for the winners? It means you're just giving away one-third of all the money that you spend on tickets."

"But if I won," I protested, "it could change my life."

Saidah shook her head. "It already *is* changing your life. It's like letting somebody steal from you. No, it's like helping them to steal. If every dollar you spent on the lottery was in a bank account, I'll wager you could pay off a significant part of those credit card bills."

"Now you're wagering, too." I picked up her word play and kidded her back.

"Most of the people who win the lottery are pretty miserable. Money doesn't solve all their problems. There are exceptions, of course, but a lot of people blame money because it's a way they can avoid taking responsibility. It isn't my fault, I'd be OK if it weren't for my bad boss, my mean spouse, the unfair system, what my parents did to me as a kid, my lousy job, and, of course, the fact that I'm broke. Viewing yourself as a victim may give you a lot of excuses, but it's not going to help you get ahead in life. It's better to take responsibility for your own situation."

"I do," I said, feeling hurt by the implication that I was some kind of whiner or quitter.

"What the lottery winners don't understand is that they have chosen the lives they lead. Money didn't make the choices. What makes you happy is part of every moment, it's not in your bank account. After they win the lottery, they go on making the same choices. Habits are hard to change, especially the habit of how we see ourselves in the world. Money is seldom powerful enough to change that."

I kept wanting to protest that I would be different, I would be one of the few who could win the lottery and change her life for the better. Yet I understood what she was saying about how people see the world. I could picture myself through her eyes. I didn't want to be always blaming somebody or something for why I couldn't do what I wanted.

"You with me?" Saidah asked when I didn't answer.

"Not everybody's the same."

"That's true, but people don't change all of a sudden. Not most people anyway. We become who we are by a whole lot of small steps and decisions over many years. That isn't going to be changed by whether we get a lot of money or not. But there's more that I want to say. When you hope you're going to win, why do you think you should beat the odds instead of someone else?"

"I don't know. I never thought about it that way."

"A psychiatrist who did a lot of research said gambling was an expression of the need for religious faith."

I smiled in disbelief. "I don't see how it could be."

"He said that people who go against the odds are hoping that God will intervene and take their side. Why else would you expect to win when the odds are against you? If God helps you win money, then you'll be reassured about your self-worth. If God chooses you as special, then you must be worthwhile."

"I don't think that."

"It's not what we're aware of thinking that guides our lives, but what we are unaware of. Our task is to become more and more aware, to bring light where there was darkness. Gambling is an act of faith. It's faith that you can beat the odds. But faith should be used in prayer and good deeds. Otherwise it's like demanding that God reassure you by allowing you to win."

"That's all a theory."

"If I'm wrong, explain why and I'll change my mind. But you stay open-minded, too. You do have the power to change your life, but you have to exercise it. You can't be wasting your energy on false hopes and ships that don't come in. In fact, I have something you can try that may be as good as that fantasy about winning the lottery ever was."

"What's that?" I asked.

"Prayer." She nodded her head to affirm her words, her brown eyes glowing with the light of an inner lantern. "You don't have to gamble to find out if God loves you. I don't care if you're Christian, Jewish, Muslim, or Hindu. There's great strength in prayer, in faith. And another thing."

"What?" I asked, wondering about the strange way that Saidah jumped back and forth from the lottery to faith. I looked her over, just to reassure myself that she was all there. But she looked as imperturbable and happy as ever, elegant today in her royal-purple suit tailored perfectly for her rounded edges and height, her white pearls bright about her neck and a pair of golden earrings like small chandeliers glittering beneath her ears.

"The gambling business—yes, it is a business, you mustn't forget that—is a lot like the banking business."

"No."

"Why do you say no?" she asked.

"Because it's so different. There's no chance in banking."

"Let me interrupt," Saidah waived a hand to halt me, "because there's no chance in gambling either."

"But you just finished talking about the odds. Isn't that chance?"

"I'm talking about the business. The gambler faces odds and loses in the long run. But gambling is big business, just the way banking is. Companies that manage gambling are publicly traded on the stock exchanges just like the big banks and credit card companies. Gambling and banking are like highways. You pay a toll to get on the road. In the case of gambling, it's that 35 percent that won't be paid out as winnings. With banking, it's all of the fees plus that old siren, interest. They're always trying to get you to borrow for this or that. Checking accounts with credit lines, home improvement loans, automobile financing, home equity lines of credit, one product after another, to get you to pay interest."

"What's wrong with that?" I asked. "People wouldn't borrow if they didn't need the money."

"Iris," Saidah looked at me severely. "People are borrowing all the time for what they don't need. Folks who grew up in the thirties had a whole different attitude—frugality. I could repeat that word two or three times. It's like an old lesson that people don't want to learn anymore. Save. Earn before you spend. Now it's consume before you earn. Borrow first and worry about paying later. Credit for common folk didn't even exist before mass production, like the assembly line Henry Ford designed to make cars. Once you had mass production, you needed mass consumption. Only people didn't have money, so they democratized credit. Consume, consume, consume. And borrow, borrow, borrow. Once you start, you're on a treadmill that's hard to get off."

"Last night, when I was looking at my numbers, I thought that once you're in debt you need to keep borrowing more and more." I explained to her how each year the deficit had to be financed but that only led to larger and larger deficits.

"That's a good insight, Iris, but it's even worse than it sounds. When you borrow, you don't pay taxes on what you borrow. But when you earn money to pay back your debts, you do have to pay taxes on your earnings."

"I don't get it." Much as I had appreciated Saidah's praise a moment before, I wasn't following her now.

"If you borrow one hundred dollars, you get to spend one hundred dollars. But how much do you have to earn when you want to pay back that hundred dollars? If you're in the 33 percent tax bracket, you have to earn one hundred and fifty dollars, because after taxes you're only going to have one hundred dollars left."

I felt numbed and fearful to hear her. If I thought that I had to scale an impossible mountain, she was telling me the mountain was a lot steeper than I had thought.

"It sounds worse and worse," I said. "I don't understand how to get the numbers in balance. How am I ever going to reverse the treadmill and get out of debt?"

"It takes patience. You have to plan, have goals for the short run and the long run. It takes a lot of attention to small amounts, because small amounts add up to big amounts sooner than you might imagine. Let's get back to the banking system. Do you have a checking account?"

"Of course," I replied, ruffled that she would even ask me.

"Why of course?"

"Everybody has a bank account, except maybe poor people who use check cashing services."

"Are you rich or poor?"

She had me there. I would have said middle class, because my parents always had a nice house and a new car. My idea of poor had always been people who owned nothing and couldn't borrow to get anything. On the other hand, if they couldn't borrow they wouldn't owe anything, so they might be better off than I was. Like my idea of the poor, I didn't own anything, but unlike the poor, I did owe a lot of money. I didn't think owing a lot of money could make me middle class, so it was confusing.

"Right now I'm pretty poor," I finally answered.

"We're only talking about finances, because you're rich in other ways—your love of dance, for example," Saidah said, then asked, "Can you afford a checking account?"

"What do you mean?" I couldn't conceive of not having a bank account.

"What does it cost you?"

I wanted to say, "Not much," but I didn't dare lie to Saidah because she was too sharp. I didn't know and said so.

"Do you pay a monthly charge to have the account?" she bored on resolutely.

I shrugged unhappily. I knew that I did, because some months when I didn't write any checks my tiny balance would still be reduced.

"I think so."

"How much is it?"

"Fifteen dollars a month."

"There's one hundred and eighty dollars a year. What do you pay for each check?"

"Thirty-five cents."

"How many checks do you write a month?"

"Maybe six or seven."

"It's only a little bit, but it all adds up."

"Do you mean that I shouldn't have a checking account?" I felt indignant.

"I mean that you have to look at everything that you spend. Nothing is too little to look at. You probably need a checking account, although you might consider whether it would be cheaper to do without it. Pay your bills with money orders and cash your checks at a check cashing service or your employer's bank. If you're going to have it, though, you need to do comparison shopping. You have to look for banks that are offering free checking or lower charges. That attention to detail can save you money. Most millionaires, by the way, are frugal. They didn't buy into consumerism. They have what they need, but they aren't wearing flashy watches, driving foreign cars with names you can't pronounce, and living in mansions. They're ordinary people who earn and save enough so that they don't have to worry about paying the bills. They didn't become millionaires overnight, either, but by saving regularly day after day and year after year."

She was discouraging me, and I had to tell her that. "But I can't save. I'm going deeper in debt every day."

"Remember what I told you: I am a good and loving person."

I nodded and repeated her words to myself. It made me think of the good things that I had done, like teaching dance to the four-year-olds, and I felt a little better.

"You have to go one step at a time," she said. "If you try to solve everything at once, it will seem overwhelming. First you understand, then you plan, and finally you act. Let's finish up with the banks and go on to credit cards. Do you have an ATM card?"

"Sure."

"What does it cost each time you use it?"

"Fifty cents."

"How many times a month do you use that?"

"Probably eight or ten times." I had to get access to the money in my account somehow, and often I didn't have time to go to the bank.

"You ever use an ATM at a bank outside of your neighborhood?"

"Sure."

"Did it give you a message saying you'd be charged a fee?"

"Sometimes."

"How much?"

"A dollar, maybe a dollar fifty."

"Did you pay?"

"I had to," I said, feeling embarrassed. "I needed the money."

"How much money were you getting?"

"Usually forty or sixty dollars. Maybe twenty dollars if I didn't have a lot in my account."

"If you paid a one-dollar fee to get twenty dollars, what percentage was the fee in relation to the money you got?"

"About 5 percent. I know it's bad, but . . ."

"If you'd just planned a little, you could have gone to your own bank and used the ATM without paying that extra fee. If you pay a dollar to the bank that has the ATM and fifty cents to your own bank, and you're getting fifty dollars on average, you're losing 3 percent of every transaction."

"You're right." I couldn't deny it, although the truth made me feel something of a fool.

"But even paying that fee at your own bank adds up, especially when you compare it to the amount of money that you're getting." She shook her head. "You're letting them make you part of their system. It's like you're working for them, but you don't even know it."

"Who are they?" I asked.

"It's not a big conspiracy. They're companies doing business. They are working hard to make profits and benefit their shareholders. If they can charge you more for it, often they will. Fifteen or twenty-five dollars for a late payment, thirty-five cents for a check, fifty cents for using their ATM, an extra dollar or dollar fifty for using ATMs at some other banks—these charges can add up to a lot of money. It's found money for them. That means it's lost money to you. It might as well have fallen out of your purse."

"What can you do about it?" I got what she was saying, but I was puzzled at what choice there might be. If I went comparison-shopping for a bank, which seemed presumptuous to me considering my balance, I doubted if I'd find anything better.

"The first step is understanding," Saidah replied. "Don't take anything for granted, especially don't assume that you have to do what everybody else seems to be doing. Everybody else may not be doing whatever you think it is, and in any case, you can always strike out on your own. We're just beginning to understand how some things work, so let's go back to where we left off yesterday."

"You mean about who they offer credit cards to?"

"Yes. You thought they would do a thorough credit check and offer cards to the people who could afford to pay. Imagine that you were issuing credit cards. Who would you want to accept the cards?"

"People who could pay back whatever they borrowed. And pay it back on time."

Saidah shook her head. "You would have been a great banker—about a hundred years ago. That was when the banks didn't lend to working people. They just kept money on deposit and hardly paid any interest at all. Of course, there weren't any credit cards then. Credit cards came into wide use in the 1950s, after the Depression and the war, when people used credit to make up for lost time. Iris, listen to what I'm going to tell you, because it's important. People who pay back credit cards on time are called 'free riders' by the credit card issuers. They take the convenience of the card but they never pay for it. They might as well be thieves, robbing the issuers of monthly interest payments."

I was almost as surprised by the expression "free riders" as by the idea that the credit card issuers didn't want such people to have the cards. "What about the annual fee?"

"You're right. If the card has an annual fee, the 'free riders' pay that, but they aren't paying interest at fifteen to twenty percent. That's what the issuers want, because that's where the profit is. So the ideal customer is someone who earns enough to make the minimum payment every month and not go bankrupt, but doesn't earn enough to pay off the debt on the credit line."

"There's something wrong with that," I said.

"What?" Saidah asked.

"I really thought they offered cards to people who are good risks."

"Now you know differently. The issuers don't care if 3 or 4 percent of the cardholders never pay and might go bankrupt. They don't worry about how much those people in the 3 or 4 percent may suffer. They've built the risk of loss in as a write-off on their P&L."

"P&L?"

"Profit-and-loss statement."

"But that's wrong!" I exclaimed, upset that the lenders seemed so uncaring about their borrowers.

"That's not all that's wrong. Did you ever pay late?"

I nodded with some shame. "When I was trying to pay the full balance every month. Once I gave up on that and only paid the minimum monthly charges, I found it much easier to pay on time."

"When you paid late, did you get charged a fee?"

"I think so."

"How much?"

"Maybe twenty-five dollars."

"How many hours do you have to work for twenty-five dollars?"

I calculated this. "Almost three hours."

"You think that's fair?"

"I did pay late."

Saidah gave me a how-can-you-be-that-way look, like why wasn't I more spunky.

"You have to see, it's a system. People are little wheels in the big machine, and the big machine makes profits. It's not about people. If you want it to be about people, you have to make it that way. You can't trust the banks and the credit card companies to worry about you. Because they don't. You have to make sure you get treated like a human being and not a wheel in the big profit machine."

I was thinking about paying taxes on money that I earned to pay back debt. It made everything seem impossible. My posture must have given away my thoughts, because Saidah patted me on the shoulder.

"Don't worry, because worrying doesn't do any good. It can be done. I've seen lots of people do it. What are you going to do to cheer yourself up?" she asked.

I recalled the night before when I added up all the things that had no value in terms of money. I told Saidah about how that did make me feel better.

"Good. That's very good. You keep doing that. When are we going to get together again? I can see that you need to hear a success story."

"Day after tomorrow?" I asked. I wanted to see Saidah the next day, Thursday, but I realized that I was about to give her my last dollar. Friday was payday, but my deposit wouldn't clear until Monday. I'd have to borrow money from someone to carry me through the weekend, and I would need a day to make sure I found someone from whom I could borrow. That way I'd have the money to pay Saidah.

"Sounds good to me. Our usual spot after work?"

I nodded, feeling embarrassed as I opened my purse. "Saidah, I'm sorry this isn't more," I said as I handed her the dollar. I thought she might chastise me for spending the four dollars on the lottery.

She surprised me, because all of a sudden her eyes filled with tears and she shook her head. "Iris, you're paying me what you can afford. I thank you for that. Because I see this dollar as a ticket for a journey that not everyone is brave enough to begin. When I see someone step aboard that ship sailing for unknown waters, I feel God at work. I'm the witness to a miracle beginning, and I feel humility and gratitude."

I had never met anyone like Saidah. My perplexity must have showed, because Saidah brightened with a smile and asked, "Any questions?"

I remembered what Tina had said about credit counseling. "I was thinking of going for credit counseling. My friend said they look over your numbers and help you put all your loans together at a lower interest rate. Do you think it's a good idea?"

Saidah frowned for a moment, then said, "If it seems like a good idea to you, you should explore it. The goodness or badness is always in the details. At least you've got the numbers now to show them."

I took what she said as encouragement to give it a try.

"One more thing," she said. "Would you believe me if I told you a president of the United States was in the same fix you're in today?"

I shook my head, because I had never thought of presidents as even thinking about money except in the big sense, like the national budget, much less having any personal money problems.

"Are you going to ask me who?" she teased as she gathered herself to go.

"Who?" I asked.

"Abraham Lincoln," she answered. "We'll talk more about it on Friday."

"Thanks, Saidah," I called after her, surprised that a great man like Lincoln struggled under the burdens of debt. I was already thinking about the lottery. Nobody had won, so it had gone to sixty million dollars. I didn't know if they had lotteries in Lincoln's day, but if he had played and won it would have been an easy way out of his financial problems. I wanted to buy some tickets, but I didn't have a cent. I wondered how late the credit counseling agencies stayed open. If I went home and called, I might be able to make an appointment for the next day. By the time I met Saidah again, I could have my financial problems solved. So I planned an exciting evening opening the cans of tuna fish and stewed tomatoes for dinner, then catching up on my laundry, and finally seeking to balance my numbers like acrobats on the perilous high wire.

CHAPTER 8

A Free Consultation

That night I took my notepad and the Yellow Pages down to the laundry room. I had at least two loads, a dark and a light, so I got the washer going and settled in for a quiet evening. Doug hadn't called since my request to borrow the thousand dollars and, in a way, I couldn't really blame him. I wanted to call him. Only he was probably at rehearsal and might need time to remember how much fun I can be, so I thought it would be better to bury my head in the sand.

I started with the Yellow Pages, because that promised a complete solution to all my problems. I went first to "Counseling," which, I quickly realized, wasn't the right place. It offered "Partners in Psychotherapy" for "depression, stress management, anxiety, recovery from trauma, sexual dysfunction, infertility, parenting, adoption, and eating disorders," or, on a more personal note, I could go to Isis O'Sullivan who offered "energy field healing for body, mind, and spirit." Moving on to "Credit Counseling," I didn't find any listings at all, but instead stumbled on "Credit & Debt Counseling Svces." I wondered who made up their abbreviations, especially since the word "Services" would easily have fit on the same line without being abbreviated.

Obviously I wasn't the first person to seek this kind of help, because there were several pages filled with listings and display ads. The AAAA Credit Redemption Alliance headed their ad with "Debt Repayment

Plans" and went on to say "•Licensed •Accredited •Non-Profit •Confidential •Bankruptcy Alternatives •Financial Counseling •Available in Person, by Phone, or Mail," all of which sounded good to me, although what I really wanted to know was whether their toll-free number had somebody answering it after regular business hours so I could call right away and have them explain their slogan, "The Way Out of Debt."

Or, I could try Trust-in-Us Credit Counseling Services, which asked "Do You Have Any of These Problems: •Bankruptcy •Judgment •Foreclosure •Tax Lien •Late Payments •Repossession •Bad Debt •Student Loan." There was no question mark in the ad, and I could see myself falling into several of their categories, such as late payments, bad debt, and student loan. Not only did Trust-in-Us promise "Price and Service Can't Be Beat," but also "Free Consultation at Your Convenience," as well as "Collector Harassment Stopped" and "Credit Card Debts Consolidated into One Low Affordable Monthly Payment." That sounded very good to me. I wrote down the phone numbers for AAAA Credit Redemption Alliance, Trust-in-Us, and four or five others so I could call as soon as I got back upstairs. Whoever answered the phone first would be my credit counselors. I liked to think of this as fate working its mysterious magic.

I shifted the light load to a dryer and started the dark load in the washer, then picked up my notepad and began working to break down the "Miscellaneous" number, which amounted to almost 20 percent of my expenses. I had started carrying a pocket notebook in my purse so I could write down everything that I spent. So far I had recorded "4/12 Lottery $4" and "4/13 Saidah $1," but at least I was starting to look for the details Saidah said were so important. As long as I was moving numbers around and trying to figure out what was going on, I felt like I was accomplishing something. When I stopped trying to solve my problem, my spirits might quickly fall, but then I would add to my already substantial income from what I had begun to think of as the "good life." The good life included not only what I could buy with money, but also everything that had a value not usually expressed in money. It might be small things, like the fact that I was doing some of Tina's laundry at this very moment, or that at work I had given up my lunch hour so the other receptionist could take care of some errands for her parents' twenty-fifth wedding anniversary. Of course, I should admit that Tina had supplied the quarters for the washer and dryer.

When I burst into the apartment with my arms wrapped around two baskets of clean laundry, I was delighted that nobody was home. It wasn't that Tina didn't know about my debt problem—after all, she suggested the credit counseling agencies—but I didn't want her to witness every humiliating detail of my inability to handle my financial life. It made me feel like a failure, and I preferred to keep those feelings to myself. I started calling the credit-counseling companies, but nobody answered and I realized I'd have to wait until the morning.

Later that night I watched Tina and Rachel grimace in disgust at the ping-pong balls, and shred their lottery tickets. This evening ritual, like so many things that happen again and again, was getting boring. In bed I felt excited that I had managed to break down the "Miscellaneous" number. I had to make estimates, because I couldn't be sure, but I had added a lot of categories like cosmetics, hair styling, hair coloring, manicures, pedicures, facials, electrolysis, and body piercing (the silver rings in my nose and navel had been recent changes and I had been considering doing more, including maybe a small tattoo of a rose on my hip just below the top of my underwear)—all this added up to a lot, considering my salary.

I realized that I had to keep track of every dollar that I spent. Close wouldn't be good enough, it had to be exact. If I tracked my outgo of dollars as I planned in my notebook, soon I would have a precise record of all the categories and amounts. But I could see already that comparison shopping among beauty salons and taking care of some of my needs at home would save a significant amount of money. Also, Saidah had been right about how much I spent on the lottery. Maybe not as much as she guessed, but it could be eight hundred dollars a year. On my income, that was a large sum that I couldn't afford. Immediately I contradicted myself by arguing that I could afford it if I won. That was the key, winning. But when I saw my total income and the negative five thousand dollars that I had to overcome each year, I didn't want odds. I wanted to give myself a chance to break even and then get ahead. As I drifted nearer to sleep, half dreaming, I imagined myself living in such a harmonious way that all my numbers would balance, I would be free of debt, and my participation in the good life would grow and grow.

The next morning at the office I started calling as soon as I had a chance. Nobody was in the waiting room, and I had caught up on my work. I decided that Trust-in-Us deserved my first try, because I kept seeing the image of George Washington from the front of the dollar bill. Maybe Trust-in-Us reminded me of "In God We Trust," and also it was closest to my office, so I could walk there. After two rings, I heard a man's voice at the other end.

"Good morning, thank you for calling Trust-in-Us. How may I direct your call?"

"I wanted to make an appointment to come in."

"How did you hear about Trust-in-Us?"

"I let my fingers do the walking," I answered dryly.

"Ah, the Yellow Pages."

"It says the first consultation is free."

"That's correct. Absolutely no charge." The man spoke in that mechanical and friendly tone that I, too, had perfected working for the ad agency. "How might we be able to help you?"

"I want to consolidate my debts and get on a budget."

"When would you like an appointment?"

"Maybe for 1:15 or 5:15 today? I could also make 1:15 tomorrow."

"Let me check the schedule," he said, after which there was a brief silence on the other end, then he came back on sounding pleased. "Yes, I see that Mr. Goode is available at 1:15 tomorrow."

"How long does the first meeting take?"

"No more than half an hour. It's a very preliminary evaluation. We have you fill in some forms about your finances, then give you a sense of your options."

"But you do consolidate loans at a lower interest rate and put people on a budget?" I asked.

"Yes, we certainly do that for many people."

I gave him my name, but as soon as I hung up I felt dissatisfied. I wanted to solve my debt problem immediately, but tomorrow would have to do. I didn't have a lot to look forward to at home that evening. I had finished the last cans of tuna and stewed tomatoes, so tonight I had a choice between a box of prunes and mooching off Tina and Rachel. Much as I liked prunes, mooching seemed worth a try.

I also considered asking Tina for a loan of ten or twenty dollars until Monday, but I didn't want to do it. Tina could be touchy about money. It probably had to do with her relationship with her father. The more I thought about how I had asked Doug for a loan, the more I thought it had to do with asking him how he felt about me. Not a very good way to ask, but did he care for me enough? Enough to what, I asked myself, since I hadn't known him very long. Enough to have the potential of becoming a romance, I answered myself. He had offered to lend me what he could raise, so maybe that was a good sign.

I wavered as to whether to call Doug and ask to borrow forty dollars to get me through the weekend. Because I was always short of money, I had moved my checking account to my employer's bank. This meant that my check would clear in one working day instead of three, but I still wouldn't have any money until Monday. On Fridays, the lines at the bank were so long with people cashing their paychecks that I had learned not to waste my time. I had to be back at the office on time, and I couldn't risk losing my job. I still didn't think I should ask Doug for a loan, because it might complicate things. On the other hand, he had offered to lend to me when I asked him, and I did need the money. Head in the sand or not, I figured I'd better give him a call. The appointment with Trust-in-Us made me feel I was on my way to paying off my debts, and I would certainly have the money to pay him on Monday. Calling would also be a chance to check out his plans for the weekend.

"Hi, Doug." I was surprised to get him at the apartment that he shared with his roommates, since I had guessed he would be at rehearsal. In fact, I had been hoping to get his answering machine and had a cute message all ready to leave on it.

"'Lo, Iris." Doug sounded sleepy or something, kind of distant.

"How are you doing?" I asked.

"OK."

I tried talking about the weekend, but he wasn't very communicative and said he would be busy with rehearsals and work. I liked dancing with Doug at the clubs, so maybe I pushed it a little bit, but in the end I felt my impulsive request for that thousand-dollar loan had chilled our relationship for a while. I had a foreboding feeling about asking for even a small loan, but I also felt like a bat flying without radar and crashing into all sorts of things that I couldn't see were there. So I pushed on ahead.

"Doug, could you lend me a little money tomorrow? I need it until Monday. My paycheck will clear and I'll pay it right back."

It felt demeaning to be asking, like saying to someone whom I wanted to admire me that I couldn't take care of myself, that in some way I was a failure. Doug hesitated, and in the pause I reassured myself by repeating what Saidah told me: I am a good and loving person. It struck me as curious that borrowing and debt would bring into question whether I was good and loving, but it did undermine my self-worth.

"I could lend you twenty dollars," Doug finally said.

I didn't hear any enthusiasm in his voice, but I had made my bed and now I had to lie in it. "Thanks, I really appreciate it."

We talked a bit more and he agreed to drop the twenty dollars off at the office in the morning. After I hung up I had a moment of feeling like crying, tears came to my eyes, but then I thought maybe Doug was meant to be a friend and not a romance. Only that didn't make me feel any better.

Much later, after caging a bit of dinner from Tina by reminding her about the laundry the night before and promising to do her share of cleaning the apartment, I remembered what Saidah had said about prayer. I hadn't prayed since high school, when I lived at home and went to services every Sunday with my parents. Thinking about the pastness of all that, and how time goes by and changes happen, I had that ghostly feeling of missing something on my left side. Often this feeling made me wonder about my birth parents. Who had they been? Were they still alive today? And where? Did I have brothers and sisters, nieces and nephews? Was I part of a large family that might welcome my return? Thinking of this gave me the guilty sensation that I was betraying my mother and father. But I felt annoyed with them as well. Why hadn't they left me some link that I could follow and find my birth parents? Why hadn't they seen that their death would leave me without a family, except for the family that I might create by marrying and having children of my own?

I felt embarrassed to let Tina see me pray, but once the lights were out, I sat up in bed and pressed my hands together. My first thought was to be thankful, and I expressed this thankfulness in my prayer. I felt thankful to be alive, thankful to Jim and Mary for adopting me and saving me from whatever hardship had broken apart my birth family and made it impossible for them to keep and raise me. I asked that I be allowed to become as good and loving as I had the potential to be, and that however small my contribution might be, that I have the opportunity to help make the world a better and happier place. Praying did make me feel better, and I fell asleep wanting to pray more often and looking forward to my visit the next day to Trust-in-Us where my debt problems would be solved. It would make seeing Saidah at the end of the day even more of a pleasure, a little celebration that I had so quickly overcome my debts.

On Friday I rushed out of the office right at one o'clock when my lunch hour started. Ten minutes later I was filling out forms in the waiting room at Trust-in-Us. As soon as I turned in the forms, I was taken to a small office where Mr. Goode sat behind a desk that looked like every paper clip was in its proper place.

"Please be seated," Mr. Goode gestured to one of the seats facing his desk and I sat. I studied him while he studied the forms that I had been proud to be able to fill out. Mr. Goode had a pasty face, stringy, long, blond hair, and looked like he didn't eat very much. When he finished with the forms and glanced up, his grey eyes appeared watery in his narrow face. I had been looking at the walls. No diplomas. I had no idea what Mr. Goode's credentials might be.

"You'd like us to consolidate your loans."

I nodded. He looked again at the forms, shaking his head a few times.

"We'd like to help, but your numbers don't really merit it."

"What do you mean?" I didn't understand, but it sounded like he was insulting the numbers I had worked so hard to figure out.

"Even if we consolidate your credit card debt at a lower interest rate, you're still going to be in the red. You're negative five thousand dollars a year. Maybe we could save you fifteen hundred of that. Personally, if I were you, I'd declare bankruptcy. That would get you out from under these credit cards."

"You can't help me?" I asked, dazed and kind of shaken.

He stood up. "I'm truly sorry, but after we consolidated your loans you would simply go more deeply into debt. We have to be careful to help people who can get out of debt once some of the interest burden is removed and they get on a budget. With your salary, I don't see that as a good prospect."

I left his office in confusion. I had revealed everything about myself to him. Or, at least, everything about my earnings and financial life. He had rejected me. Like some guy not asking me out for a second date. He didn't want to see me again. I started to feel angry, but what was the point? Mr. Goode just applied guidelines. I hadn't fit his criteria. I didn't earn enough and I had too much of the wrong kind of debt. Far too quickly the anger changed to fear. What was I going to do?

The visit to Trust-in-Us (now, the very name made me mad) had taken ten minutes to fill in the forms and five minutes to be deemed unworthy by Mr. Goode. I rushed to my bank to deposit my paycheck in the ATM and also checked my balance. The bank had charged its monthly fees and I had minus ten dollars. It was interesting that this bank, which wouldn't give me a line of credit because I already had too many credit cards, was willing to let its fees put me into the negative. It would pay itself back from my deposit.

Being at the bank, I thought I might as well pick up their fee schedule. I didn't see it with the well-designed brochures in the display rack, those were all about different kinds of loans, but when I asked at the information desk, I was given a typed sheet with all the fees listed. It was exactly as Saidah had said. I was paying a lot of different fees: a monthly charge to have the account, a fee for each check, a fee for each use of the bank's ATM, a larger fee when I used ATMs outside the bank's system and, to my surprise, there was also a fee for doing business with a teller at the bank. It made me think that they wanted to do everything without employees. Customers should interact with machines. Whatever the machines cost, not having to pay employees must save them a lot of money in the long run.

I had about fifteen minutes left on my lunch hour, so I decided to go to all the banks that I knew were in the neighborhood. Why not compare the fees of the banks? It would be like comparing the fees of the beauty salons, except that I might really like one salon because I came out looking awesome. I didn't have loyalty like that to any bank. At the same time, I thought that I would go to all the beauty salons and get their price schedules, too. If I was going for it, why not go all the way? Also, I could certainly give up any more body piercing as well as the little tattoo until my finances improved. It didn't feel like a big sacrifice and it would cut back a bit on my expenses.

When I returned to my chair at the reception desk, I felt rattled. Why bother to save on bank fees when my bucket had a thousand leaks in it? Why didn't I just kick it over and declare bankruptcy, like the man said? What struck me as unreal was the way I must look behind the reception desk—fit, smiling, dressed well enough in my black slacks and black blouse. What about me suggested that I was different from everybody else? That I was in debt and on the road to bankruptcy? While I acted my role, speaking cheerfully on the telephone and graciously attending to visitors and messengers, I kept seeing an image of myself alone and in tears. The image looked like me as a grown woman, but I felt like a little girl lost in a nightmare. I couldn't wait for work to end so I could visit with Saidah. At least I had the twenty dollars Doug had given me, so that today I could pay her more than one dollar.

CHAPTER 9

Honest Abe and the National Debt

wish I had a rich uncle," I complained to Saidah, after I told her what had happened at Trust-in-Us. When I said this, I realized that I wished I had an uncle whether or not he was rich.

"Credit counseling can help a lot of people, especially if they spend lavishly and owe a lot on credit cards," Saidah said.

"I owe a lot on credit cards," I said miserably.

"But after the credit card interest rates are replaced with a lower rate through the loan consolidation, there has to be a spending plan that works," she replied. "In your case, they didn't think that over a reasonable period of time you would get out of debt. You could try other agencies. In fact, if you were going to use an agency you should certainly compare fees and services just like you're doing for the bank. A lot of these agencies also charge high interest rates. They make your monthly payments less by spreading them out over a longer period, but this locks in your debt and interest payments for a long time, too. Perhaps it's just as well."

"It's like a life sentence."

"Maybe it is." Saidah didn't seem to smile as much today and I felt something weighing on her mind. "They used to imprison people who couldn't pay their debts. Once in debtor's prison, a person had no way to earn the money to repay what was owed and be set free. It was cruel and wrong, but it did illustrate the imprisoning power of debt."

"When did that stop?"

"By the 1840s for the most part," Saidah said. "Today debt, especially credit card debt, demands so much energy to pay the interest that it can sap away life. It makes debtors constantly have to run faster, work harder, to keep their heads above water. Everyone knows that African-Americans came to this country as slaves, but far fewer people realize how many Europeans came as indentured servants in colonial times. They would go into debt to pay for the transatlantic passage, then contract to pay off the debt by working for three or five or seven years for masters who could treat them harshly. In the amendment that banned slavery, indentured servitude was also outlawed."

"But that was a long time ago," I protested.

"Credit card debt is servitude with a smiling face," Saidah said severely. Seeing my uncomprehending expression, she changed her tack. "Let's imagine that you had a rich uncle."

"OK."

"He wants to help you and offers to pay off all the debt on your credit cards."

"Sounds good to me."

"I actually had this happen with a client. Her father offered to pay off her credit card debt. She didn't want him to, because she was a little older than you are and wanted to feel she stood on her own. But he convinced her that it didn't make sense for her to pay such high interest rates. It would be better if he lent her the money at a much lower rate. Both my client and her father thought that if they made it a loan rather than a gift, she would be showing her financial responsibility."

"What happened?"

"As soon as the father paid off the credit cards, the daughter went on a spending spree. Now she's maxed out all her credit cards again, so she's paying the highest interest rates. But she also owes her father. She doubled her debt. Since she was having trouble paying the credit cards off in the first place, she can't pay anything to her father."

"He's angry?"

"Actually, he's disappointed in himself and in her. He feels he failed her as a father; she feels she's back in the dependent position of a child."

"That's heavy."

"Going to a credit counseling agency can be like having your father try to bail you out of debtor's prison. It can help some people, but it can also be a way of passing the buck. You throw your hands up in the air and say, 'I can't do this, I need someone to do this for me.' Daddy appears in the form of something outside of you that will solve your debt problem. Maybe it's the lottery, or maybe it's a credit counseling agency that can consolidate your debts and put you on a budget, but you don't have the benefit of taking charge, of saying, 'I got myself into this and I'm going to get myself out. And here's how I'm going to do it.'"

"I could go bankrupt."

Saidah shook her head. "Bankruptcy is another version of saying someone else should solve your problem. Also, you did benefit from whatever goods and services you bought using the credit card."

"But it's unfair. You said yourself that it's like being in prison. The interest rates are so high they should be illegal."

"There are state laws against usury, which is charging interest that is too high. The credit card companies are careful not to violate any of those laws."

"Maybe the laws should lower the rate that's allowed."

Saidah smiled, but she seemed faded today, not her usual vibrant self. "That was proposed in Congress a while ago and actually passed in the Senate. Then you should have heard the howling. If they had to lower the interest rates, the credit card companies said, they would stop lending to the riskiest people. The government economists got worried because those high-risk people spend a lot of money using credit cards. Two-thirds of our economy is based on consumer spending, so they thought contracting credit would contract the economy and cause a recession. An election was coming up, and a recession was the last thing the politicians wanted. Of course, there's always some election or other coming up. Needless to say, the bill never became law."

"But I feel defrauded," I complained. "Those big companies came to me in college and made me feel I could afford a credit card. If they know how much people in credit card debt can suffer, and how likely we are to get in trouble, why didn't they warn us? You know, like 'Cigarette smoking is hazardous to your health.' Anyway, they're just big companies. If I go bankrupt, it won't mean a thing to them. You already said they expect a certain percentage of people to go bankrupt and build that into their accounting."

"I'm concerned about you, not about them. If you go bankrupt, you won't have learned how to pay your way out of debt. That learning is what is important. You have to learn to save in order to pay debt. You must have a spending plan, in which your expenses are less than your income. Do you know the novelist Charles Dickens?"

"Sure, he wrote *A Christmas Carol*."

"His father went to debtor's prison. Charles, who was a boy of nine or ten, visited his father there, in a prison called Marshalsea in London. He said the misery of having his father in debtor's prison stayed with him his entire life, even after he became a famous author. In his memoirs he recounted how he and his father wept when they visited in prison. His father told him, 'If a man had twenty pounds a year and spent nineteen pounds nineteen shillings and sixpence, he would be happy; but that a shilling spent the other way would make him wretched.' Dickens wrote a fictionalized version of the story in *Little Dorrit*. You might enjoy reading it. In fact, reading about debt is a way to get a larger perspective about it. Another good book is *The House of Mirth* by Edith Wharton. When you read about the financial struggles of someone else, it's easier to see your own situation in a new light."

"It's still wrong to charge such high interest rates."

"But two wrongs don't make a right, especially when not paying what you owe is harmful to you as well as the credit card company's bottom line. You have to understand what bankruptcy means."

"It means you owe more than you have and you can't pay."

"That's a narrow definition. In the larger view, it means that you've taken goods and services from the people around you, other members of the community. When you took these things you wanted, you agreed to work your fair share and give back. The fact that big companies are involved makes it easy to blame those companies and some of their unfair tactics, but you have to decide whether your word has meaning. It's about your integrity, whether you're going to give back at least as much as you receive."

"Of course, I want to…"

She waved her hand to silence me before I could add "but."

"Let me tell you a story about someone who didn't pay his debts. It's a folk tale from Tibet about a poor man who lived next door to a rich man. One day the poor man found a baby sparrow that had fallen from its nest and broken its leg. The poor man nursed the bird back to health and, one day, the sparrow returned with a few morsels of grain in its beak and told the man to plant them."

"A talking sparrow?"

"Yes," Saidah smiled and repeated emphatically, "a talking sparrow. So the poor man planted the grain, and each plant blossomed with jewels that gave the poor man great wealth. Now the rich neighbor felt jealous of the prosperity of the man who had been poor. The neighbor went on his own roof and pushed a baby sparrow from its nest so that it fell and broke its leg."

"Nice guy," I said sarcastically.

"Then he nursed it back to health. Sure enough, the sparrow came back with grain for the rich man to plant. But when this crop grew, it produced a fierce-looking man with a bundle of papers under his arm. This man said he had been a creditor of the rich man in a former life, and the rich man had left his debts unpaid. The creditor had come back with all the papers necessary to take everything the rich man owned—his house, his cattle, his lands, everything. So the poor man became rich, and the rich man became poor."

"That's a great story, but credit card companies can't collect if you die."

"If you die and have no assets, you'd be right. But is that desirable?" Saidah studied me a few moments before continuing. "The story isn't really about living or dying. It's about the burden that debt makes us carry. Even if you escape paying the debt, you continue to carry the burden because you haven't created a harmonious way of being. In the ancient Hindu law, a man's debt survived him and passed on to his sons. We might call this a karmic view of the spiritual consequences of unpaid debt. In fact, in ancient Egypt, creditors would sometimes seize a mummy to shame the heirs into paying the debts of the person who had died. Today, of course, 'He that dies pays all debts,' as Shakespeare wrote in *The Tempest*."

"It's depressing," I said, "to think that dying is a way out of debt. Unless you take a karmic view, and then even death isn't enough."

"Let me tell you how Abraham Lincoln paid his way out of debt."

"Like George Washington and the cherry tree?" I couldn't help myself. Why did Saidah use a hero for her example? Whatever Abe Lincoln had done, I would be unlikely to be able to match.

"Maybe," she said, looking me over in that way she had. "After all, he was called 'Honest Abe.'"

"But he was Abe Lincoln," I protested, hardly able to believe that such a legendary figure had ever been in debt anyway.

"What are you afraid of?" Saidah asked sharply.

She surprised me. I didn't know what to answer.

"Why?" I asked.

"You keep resisting me. It's like you can't bear to imagine a life without debt. It takes courage to change. The familiar, no matter how unpleasant, may seem safer than what we don't know. But we're talking about your freedom. Or you can stay in the narrow confines of your debtor's prison. It's a choice. Your choice, not mine."

I felt like getting up and walking away. Yet I knew that she was right. I was resisting her, I was afraid. Not of getting free of debt, but more of admitting that I had been inadequate, failed really, and needed to change. Hadn't Saidah told me about using the negative energy in fear to take positive steps?

"I'm sorry," I said, "I really do want to hear about Abe Lincoln."

"Let me digress for a moment. Did you know that the first mention of a credit card was in a utopian novel published in 1888?"

"No, I didn't."

"*Looking Backward* by Edward Bellamy. He saw the credit card as a device for a fair sharing of the wealth produced by society. His kind of credit card was really what we would call a debit card, that is a card that draws against assets you already own. Bellamy's utopian society didn't use money, but today debit cards can be used like checks to draw money out of your checking account. They're a good idea, because no borrowing is involved, and they have a lot of the convenient features of credit cards."

"Should I get a debit card?" I asked.

"It could be part of your plan to pay for everything on a current basis, without borrowing," Saidah answered. "But you have to be careful. There are fees charged for having a debit card. Also, sometimes a line of credit comes with the debit card. That makes it a lot like a credit card and you end up borrowing if you exceed your cash in the bank. Some merchants charge you a fee for using a debit card, and they may also put a hold on your bank account if you use the card when the total bill isn't certain right away—like staying in a hotel. If a debit card gets stolen, you don't have as much protection as you would with a credit card. That's not a recommendation to get credit cards, but a warning that debit cards have to be scrutinized very carefully."

"I see." I felt disappointed that debit cards had these potential problems.

"What's interesting," Saidah continued, "is that the first federal bankruptcy laws were enacted in 1898, a decade after the idea for the credit card. It's the point that I was trying to make before. Mass production, especially of automobiles, required mass consumption. Since people weren't wealthy, consumption required credit. Soon after 1900, banks started to lend to ordinary people, relying on their wages and good character for repayment. A lot of that early credit was used to buy the cars coming off the assembly lines of the auto manufacturers. Do you see how the pieces fit together? Mass production, mass consumption, consumer lending, credit cards, and bankruptcy are all steps on the way to the consumer culture we live in today."

"But I thought you said credit cards didn't become popular until the 1950s."

"That's true, but I'm trying to show you the ideas that were in the air, that shaped business and people's lives in the twentieth century and will be at least as important in the twenty-first."

"If the first bankruptcy law wasn't enacted until 1898, then Abe Lincoln certainly didn't go bankrupt," I said.

"You're right," Saidah agreed, "but he was bankrupt in the sense that he owed more than he owned. You have to remember that he wasn't always Abe Lincoln, the President of the United States. In 1832, when he was in his twenties and only beginning to study law, he went into debt as a partner in a retail store. When the store failed, he and his partner owed eleven hundred dollars, a large amount in those days. Then his partner died and Lincoln became responsible for the entire debt. He had no assets and no way to pay it off. He couldn't declare bankruptcy, because there were no bankruptcy laws. At least he had a sense of humor about it. He called it 'the National Debt.'"

"What did he do?"

"He worked at what jobs he could, got a license to practice law in 1837, and slowly paid down what he owed until, by 1844, he was in the clear."

"It sounds hard."

"But he did it. He took responsibility for it. One of my favorite stories is how he met his best friend. In 1837, on the day that Lincoln got his license to practice law, he rode into Springfield, Illinois, on a borrowed horse and went to the country store. He wanted to buy bedding, blankets, sheets, and a pillow. When the store owner, a man named Joshua Speed, told Lincoln that these items would cost seventeen dollars, Lincoln said that was perhaps cheap enough but, small as the sum was, he was unable to pay it. If he could be given credit until Christmas, and if his attempt to practice law were a success, he would be able to pay it back then. Looking immensely sad, Lincoln went on to say that if his law practice failed, he didn't know if he could ever pay this small debt. Instead of going through with the sale, Joshua Speed offered Lincoln a place to sleep. Lincoln was delighted. Rather than becoming debtor and creditor, they became friends."

"Is it possible for me to do what Lincoln did? My debt keeps increasing."

"It's true that his debt was different from yours. He went into debt to finance a business, which could have succeeded and supported him. Most wealthy people today are entrepreneurs who run their own businesses. But the important thing is to see how any of us can persevere and overcome a debt problem. Lincoln wasn't much older than you are when he got into his debt troubles. He couldn't have known that he would become a successful lawyer. You have no idea what you may become. Each of us has so much potential, but we have to plan wisely and not let fear limit what we strive to be. You are surrounded by success stories of people who have overcome debt."

"How do you know?" I looked around the park. I only saw ordinary people, a man in a suit hurrying home after work, a mother with a baby in stroller, a woman about my age jogging with a golden retriever a few paces ahead of her.

Saidah answered me with a question. "Are you aware that more than one million people are going bankrupt every year? There used to be a feeling of shame about bankruptcy, but consumerism has eroded that. You can only go bankrupt every seven years, so that means one million *new* people go bankrupt each of the seven years. To say it another way, more than seven million people will go bankrupt in the next seven years. Unless the number of bankruptcies changes for the better, but I think it's going to change for the worse. If you figure that each person going bankrupt is part of a household with an average of 2.5 people in it, then more than seventeen million people are affected by bankruptcy in any seven-year cycle. That's a lot of people, about seven percent of the people in the country. Practically every group of people you meet has someone hurt by bankruptcy. Then think of all the people who are in debt and also suffering, but manage to eke it out year after year. Not a pretty picture."

"But you think it's going to get worse?"

"I do."

"Why?"

"Because the number of bankruptcies increases roughly in proportion to the amount of consumer debt. And consumer debt keeps going up and up. So does each household's overall debt burden. A generation ago, the debt of a household, including its mortgage, might have been 35 percent of disposable annual income. Today that figure is more like 90 percent and closing in on 100 percent. In a society that encourages more and more consumer debt, an ever-increasing number of bankruptcies is inevitable. Unless…"

"What?"

"Unless people defend themselves with information and planning, so they don't end up as statistics."

"But where are the success stories? It's great that Abraham Lincoln got out of debt, but that was a long time ago and he was not an ordinary kind of guy. It doesn't make me feel like *I* can get out of debt."

Saidah reached in her handbag and brought out her business card and her pen. Suddenly I remembered that she had done this once before. Carefully she wrote a phone number on the card and handed it to me.

"I'll give you this number again."

I had forgotten about the phone number.

"What is it?" I asked.

"That group for people in debt. I gave you the number the day we met." Looking at me, Saidah must have seen my doubt. I didn't feel comfortable telling a group of strangers that I was in debt. She cajoled me. "It's just a phone call. I think you'll find it helpful."

"All right." I put the card in my pocket, making a mental note to remember this time.

"Iris, I'm going to be leaving on a trip for a while."

"Business?" I asked. I saw the lines of worry rising at the inner edges of Saidah's eyebrows, and the pained tightness about her mouth. What I had been sensing all night suddenly became visible in her face.

"Not really," she paused. "My teacher is ill. I have to go and be with her."

I realized that I knew almost nothing about Saidah. I had told her all sorts of stuff about myself, but except that she did "Financial Planning from the Heart," had two graduate degrees, charged her fees in a funny way, and was married to a good man, I didn't know anything about her. I had never imagined that she might have a teacher. Silly of me, because everybody has to learn from somebody else.

"Where is she?" I asked.

"I'll have to fly to the coast."

"Is it serious?"

"She's very old. This may be the end." Saidah caught the last word in her throat, like a muffled cry, and tears flowed down her cheeks. "I love her."

I put my arms around Saidah and held her trembling shoulders with her face nestled on my neck. When she straightened and fished a white handkerchief from her handbag to dry her eyes, I saw that her focus had returned to me.

"Are you OK?" I asked.

She nodded. "I feel bad about leaving you now. We're just getting started."

"I'll be fine," I said, not really believing myself. I didn't want her to go, but what choice did I have?

"There's so much more that I want to tell you," Saidah said. "But everything has to wait for the right time. Too much can be discouraging."

"I have plenty to work with." I was keeping a stiff upper lip.

"What are you doing now?" Saidah glanced at her watch. "Want to get some dinner?"

"It has to be cheap," I said, "but I'd love to."

She pulled a cell phone from her handbag and dialed.

"Honey, I'm going to be home a little late tonight."

She chatted another minute or so, then said good-bye and shut off the phone.

"Is that your husband?" I asked.

"Yes, he's home alone. The boys are away at school. Shall we?"

Saidah and I rose and began walking.

"How many sons do you have?" I asked.

"Two: Jesse and Alton. Jesse's away at college, Alton's in his last year in private school."

"What's your husband do?" I felt like my questions might be intrusive. Was there a taboo about asking Saidah to tell me more of her personal life? It had something to do with the way she was my adviser. I think I created the taboo myself, so I wouldn't find out that she was human like everybody else.

"Cedric? He coaches baseball."

"In the majors?"

"That's right. He played for a couple of teams, but he's over forty and that's old in professional sports. He made a good transition. His ambition is to be a manager."

I wasn't a baseball fan, but I did feel awe for anybody who succeeded in such a competitive field.

"And your teacher? How did you meet her?"

"You want to go to Lakeside?" Saidah asked.

"Sure." Lakeside was the restaurant beside the boating lake in the park.

"You know that old saw: When the student is ready, the teacher will come."

"I guess." Actually, I wasn't sure that I had heard it before and it sent a shiver up my spine. "You were in debt?" I asked, feeling a kind of horror.

She laughed like I was a child.

"And you think you have problems! I was as mule-headed as you—excuse me—and I don't know why my poor teacher hung in there with me. But she did. You want to see a success story? You're looking at one right here. What do you think made me want to be a financial adviser in the first place? My own suffering, knowing how bad it hurts people to be in debt and not see a way out."

For some reason, I wanted to cry. First I thought it was her honesty, then I realized that it was her generosity. She didn't have to tell me the truth. She could have stayed high and mighty in her role of financial adviser and never told me or anybody about her struggles. But she had overcome her debt and I felt that I could overcome mine. I didn't know exactly how, but I felt reassured to be walking with Saidah at my side.

CHAPTER 10

Of Time and Money

S aidah and I settled into a table by the lake as the sun began to set. The clouds swirled up in a big spiral of pink and scarlet. On the lake the people in the rowboats seemed without destinations and drifted in the calm of dusk. The waiter lit a candle on the table and we each looked at the menus. After we ordered, I asked her a question that had been on my mind.

"What if someone already has gone bankrupt? Is it really so terrible? Can't they get their life back on track? That story about the creditor from a past life makes it sound like that's impossible."

"No, I didn't mean it that way. Everyone has their own path. For some people bankruptcy may be necessary. After they go bankrupt, they'll find the way to have a spending plan and prosper. But for many people, it will be a lost opportunity to learn self-sufficiency."

"So you're not always against it?"

"There are exceptions to most rules."

"Because it seems like a big price if you don't go bankrupt. Paying off all your debts."

"In your case," Saidah smiled, "it's a price worth paying. Of course, it's not a price at all, you already spent the money. But it reminds me of a story. Do you know Nasrudin?"

"No, should I?"

She shook her head. "He's a character in a lot of Sufi stories, sort of a wise fool. In the story that I'm thinking of, Nasrudin tells a group of spiritual seekers that they will have to pay to hear his teachings. One of the seekers asks, 'But why should we have to pay for something like truth?' To which Nasrudin answers, 'Haven't you noticed that the scarcity of a thing determines its value?' That's what we're really talking about here, the price for truth."

"I'm willing to make the effort, but I'm not sure I know how. And if I figure out how, it seems like it's going to take forever."

"The fact that it's slow recommends it."

"I don't understand."

"You're upset because the goal appears far away. You want to be debt-free immediately. You have to distinguish the goal from the process. Once you create a spending plan that works, you'll be on your way. That process will relieve your anxieties and give you a sense of power over your own life, because you'll know that some-day you'll be debt-free and able to save."

Suddenly I had an idea that I wanted to think over before I talked to Saidah about it. What if I waitressed one or two nights a week? That might give me enough income to make my spending plan a success. The idea excited me and made me listen more intently to Saidah.

"If the process is slow," Saidah continued, "you'll learn it all the more thoroughly. I think speed is one of the great failings of the times we live in. You see it all around us—automobiles, airplanes, the Internet, the cell phone that I used to call Cedric. Consumerism is about speed, too, immediate gratification. It's too bad we can't keep the good and discard the bad."

"What would you discard?"

"The way debt is used to make everything move more quickly. If people had to save in order to buy, we would have a far slower world."

"But wouldn't people be unemployed? If consumers don't buy, then companies aren't going to hire workers to make products."

"Think of it as a plea for moderation. There are a lot of connec-tions between time and money."

"What do you mean?"

"Most obviously, that the time we work has a value in money."

I couldn't imagine how else our time could be valued. "Is something wrong with that?"

"Not wrong perhaps, but dangerous. Maybe our work should be valued another way. For example, if we're borrowing money, we're really borrowing time. That is, we're borrowing the time in the future that we will have to work to pay back the money. If we borrow too much time, we end up with a sense of imprisonment. We don't literally go to debtor's prison, but our lives are restricted."

"But most people live that way," I ventured. My impression was that as people got older and earned more, they also had more debt. I hadn't seen anything wrong with that.

"People are moving more and more quickly, but are their lives better? Paying the interest on debt is one reason why we have to keep moving so fast. Why should someone who lends money get back more than he or she has lent?"

I considered this. If Rachel or Tina borrowed something like a book from me, I would expect them to return the book, not the book plus some extra pages. Even if we lent each other small sums of money, we just paid back what we had borrowed. We never paid interest.

"I wouldn't charge interest to my friends," I said, knowing I didn't have an adequate answer. "But for banks and credit card companies, that's the way it works."

"Why?" Saidah insisted.

I recalled about the 3 or 4 percent of borrowers who didn't pay the credit card companies. "Because of the risk of losing the money?"

"That's a part of it, but the most important aspect is time. If money can be used in a productive enterprise that will earn a profit, then giving up money has an opportunity cost."

"You mean the lost opportunity to make a profit?"

"Exactly. So interest is paid for that lost opportunity. The longer the period of time, the greater the lost opportunity."

"So interest is all right," I said.

"What opportunity for profit does a consumer gain?" Saidah responded.

She perplexed me. What was she getting at? I hadn't studied economics in college. When she didn't reach a conclusion quickly, I began to feel in a race where the finish line is constantly moving away from the runners.

"Consumers don't make profits," I answered. "They buy things they need or maybe think they need."

"Then what should be the reward for someone who lends to a consumer? There is no profit in what the consumer does." Seeing that I wasn't about to reply, Saidah continued, "I want you to see how beliefs and laws change. The medieval church believed that exchange should be used to perfect relationships among people. Interest violates this goal by pitting people against each other, the profit of the lender against the well-being of the borrower. Starting with the Enlightenment, economists proposed that the rational marketplace should govern exchanges. In the market, money would have a price, which would be interest, and there would be nothing wrong with a person paying that. Except, of course, that the marketplace lacks any human connection between people. There's no Golden Rule in the marketplace."

"It's complicated," I said. "What would you do about it? Would you change the laws, if you could?"

"Actually, I would. I would distinguish between loans to businesses and loans to consumers. For loans to consumers I would lower the interest rate to 12 percent and not allow interest to be charged on interest. It would be hard on some people who wouldn't be able to borrow so much and on some businesses that profit from lending as much as possible. But in the long run, I think, it would be better for people and for the society. As fast as people are borrowing, the credit-card companies are giving them bigger and bigger credit lines. If a recession comes along, and a lot of people who have borrowed as much as they could go bankrupt, the banks may get in trouble."

"But you said legislation like that didn't pass."

"That's right, so you have to legislate for yourself. You can decide whether or not you'll pay interest. In fact, you can decide whether or not love will affect your exchanges with people, even if the exchanges are in the marketplace."

"When I buy something at a store," I said, "I always like to exchange a smile and a few words with the person at the checkout counter."

"That's a start. And, of course, there are two sides to these issues. Some people argue that restricting the interest rate would just give an opportunity to loan sharks who charge exorbitant interest rates to desperate people. I would outlaw the lotteries and gambling casinos, too, even though it might encourage illegal gambling. Actually, changing how we think is at least as important as changing the laws. Once we think differently, we can change our behavior. I had a client who went out and bought clothing every time she was depressed. She couldn't afford it on a secretary's salary, but she used her credit cards. She told me that buying the clothing made her feel better for a little while. Or it could be the same problem with eating to feel better. But the secretary's closets were bursting with beautiful dresses, skirts, and blouses, and she kept feeling depressed."

"Sort of like me and the lottery. I feel better when I can fantasize about winning, then I feel bad because I didn't really win."

"I still say gambling is asking for approval from God, to be chosen as the lucky one, the special one." Saidah took a long drink from her glass of water, then continued. "By the way, another objection the medieval church had to interest was that God created time. Since interest is the price of borrowing money for a certain amount of time, the taking of interest stole the time that God had freely given humanity."

"That's kind of iffy," I said.

"Medieval people didn't think the way we do."

The waiter came with our pizza and set the platter in the center of the table.

Saidah paused and smiled at her penchant for storytelling. "It brings a story to mind. Are you ready for another story?"

"Sure."

"The Romans worshiped a god named Mercury, who was the god of commerce among other things. In this story, a merchant carved a statue of Mercury and tried to sell it in the marketplace. He kept calling out, 'A god for sale, a god for sale, one that will bring you good fortune and wealth.' Finally, a passerby demanded, 'If your statue will bring good fortune and wealth, why don't you just keep it?' To which the merchant answered, 'It's true that Mercury will someday bring fortune and wealth, but I want money at once.' I think that story says a lot about people today. We want everything at once. I've had clients tell me that they thought of credit cards as free money. So I think it's worthwhile to know that in another time people saw the world quite differently. They wouldn't have valued speed for its own sake. They saw usury as the sinful stealing of time from God."

"But who doesn't pay interest today?" I asked.

"Of course, a lot of people pay interest, but not everyone. My point isn't for us to roll back the clock to the Middle Ages, but to see that our attitudes about money and debt could be different. Mercury, by the way, wore a winged helmet so that he could move instantaneously from heaven to earth or the underworld. He was the god of speed, travel, communication, and trade. He guided people to new territories."

"He does sound modern," I agreed. "He could be the god of the Internet."

"So it's important," Saidah said with her hallmark smile, "to keep in mind that Mercury was also the god of thieves. Just as the consumers want money at once and imagine there is such a thing as free money, so companies are ruled by the bottom line and also want money at once in the form of profits. If the money hunger lacks boundaries, it can easily cause sharp practices and thievery. Like that credit card commercial that calls the card 'smart money,' when obviously credit cards are about debt, not money. So much advertising encourages us to live with illusions. In fact, it's worth thinking about whether time itself isn't an illusion."

"Time?" I echoed. I would never in a million years have thought of most of this stuff that Saidah liked to talk about.

"I want to make a simple point. We imagine time as a straight road going from the past to the future. Of course, that's not what Einstein theorized, but it is how ordinary people have been taught to experience time. Because money can be translated into time, we can fantasize that enough money will buy us extra time, extra life. That's why some people hoard."

"Not one of my vices."

"What if time isn't really a straight road at all? For example, what if time is cyclic, and inevitably ends where it once began? I'm talking about what people in the past have believed. Or what if time doesn't move at all? What if there is no road? We don't walk forward from the past to the future, but rather the past, present, and future are wrapped around us like space. So that our ancestors live in the same moment in which we live. They aren't older that we are, but are our contemporaries, as our unborn children already exist in this same embrace of time."

"It's hard to imagine."

"But if you could imagine it, would it make any sense to charge interest?"

Saidah always came back to her point.

"The straight road of time kind of sounds like the assembly line in a factory," I said.

"The assembly line is based on a rational use of time and labor, just as the marketplace is based on the rational use of exchange. But so much of importance is irrational, even passionate, such as love. All I'm saying is be open to seeing the world differently. Advertising, consumerism, money at once—we learn so much that may not be true. We have to examine what we've been taught and feel free to find our own truths."

With that, Saidah took a big bite of her pizza. I followed suit with mine, the crust hot on my fingers.

"Your older son, Jesse, he must be almost my age," I said.

"He's nineteen."

I might have been thinking that Saidah could have been my mother, but I don't know that I exactly thought that. It was more a feeling of being cared about and nourished by an older woman. What she said would make me look more closely at money. But I would miss her, too.

"And Alton?"

"He's fifteen."

We ate in silence for a little while. The sun hung like a red lantern on the rim of the sky.

"I'm sorry you're going," I said. "It's hard to believe that I just met you this week. It feels like so much has happened. But if you look on the outside, nothing has changed at all."

"Thanks." Saidah took another bite and rested the crust on her plate. "You're really talking about psychological time. It's true, only a few days have passed, but for some reason, you've been moving inside, absorbing new ideas and imagining new possibilities for your life. I wish I didn't have to go, because I see what's happening with you. But you'll do fine without me."

I wanted to say that it wasn't only the financial advice that I would miss, but I didn't.

"Who's going to take care of your office?" I asked.

"I call in for my messages. I've postponed as much as I can, the rest I'll try to handle by phone."

"Do you know when you'll be back?"

She shook her head.

"How did you meet your teacher?" I asked and took my last mouthful of the pizza.

"Sort of the way you met me," Saidah answered. "I needed some help and a greater power brought me to my teacher. You have to trust in that."

"On a park bench?"

"No," she smiled, "don't be so literal."

"She must have been awesome," I said, imagining this angel-like figure descending in flowing robes to lead Saidah out of the darkness.

"She's an ordinary person," Saidah said. "Just like I am. You may respect or even love your teachers, but don't idealize them. If you idealize them, you don't really know them. Worse, you imagine that they are the solution to what troubles you. They may help you learn about yourself, but your potentials and energy will bring you to your own solutions."

"What you said about time, or the history of the medieval church, or the god of commerce—that doesn't sound ordinary."

"Maybe ordinary isn't the best word, but you have to rely on yourself, not the lottery, credit-consolidation companies, bankruptcy, or even the finest teachers. I'm offering you information that will help you think differently about debt, but what you use and what you discard is up to you."

I had an odd double vision when she said this. I wasn't certain if I was standing alone, or if I was with a force of immense power that both was me and would lead me wherever I might have to go.

"When are you leaving?" I asked.

"Tomorrow afternoon. Call and leave a message if you need to be in touch. I'll get back to you as soon as I can."

"Will you send me a postcard?" I asked.

"Sure."

I reached in my purse and brought out a five-dollar bill, which I pushed across the table to Saidah.

"It's not much for your services, but it's better than last time." I only had the twenty dollars Doug had lent me and I still had to pay for my share of the dinner and get through the rest of the weekend.

"Don't apologize for last time or this time. Remember," Saidah smiled at me, "a price doesn't always have to be rational. Sometimes it's affected by respect, hope, or even love."

"Thanks," I answered, thinking that as soon as I got home I would start working again on my spending plan. Even as I felt sad to say good-bye to Saidah, I wanted to return to those columns of numbers. I really did want to change my life and find a solution.

CHAPTER 11

Fools Rush In

found myself with a lot of energy on the weekend that Saidah left. That idea that I had at dinner with Saidah kept growing and growing in my mind. I could go back to work as a waitress and keep my job as a receptionist. Since Doug was busy all weekend and I didn't have much money to spend, nothing distracted me from filling page after page of my yellow notepad with possible spending plans. I vacuumed and dusted the apartment, used Windex on the windows, and cleaned the bathroom so everything gleamed. Hope gave me a lot of energy. I can get out of this, I kept thinking. I can do it by myself. I felt like a cartoon character who takes off her day-to-day clothes and discovers a superwoman outfit underneath. I could do it without any help. The only blemish on the beautiful face of the weekend was the fact that I would have to visit Dr. Testa again after work on Monday.

It took some tough calculating, but I figured that each night during the week that I worked as a waitress would earn me almost three thousand dollars a year after taxes were taken out. Saidah had alerted me to the taxes, which made me regret my borrowing even more. Why didn't they lend people dollars that had already been taxed? It would make it a lot easier to pay off the loans. But that wasn't how the system worked. Anyway, I made good money as a waitress. I could work shorter hours and earn about what I was earning as a receptionist. So if I worked eight hours a day at Castle Advertising and then worked another five hours at the restaurant, I would only have to work two nights a week to cover my five-thousand-dollars-a-year shortfall.

In my enthusiasm that weekend, however, covering the shortfall didn't seem good enough. I wanted to wipe out my debt. If I worked four nights a week at the restaurant, I could clear twelve thousand dollars a year and apply seven thousand a year to reduce my debt. I might even be able to do better if I could reduce my expenses. Then I looked closely at all the credit card bills to see which ones had the highest rate of interest. I put them in a pile with the lowest interest rate on the bottom and the highest on the top. If I could go down the pile, paying off the balance on the cards with the highest interest rate first, I would actually start to reduce my annual interest expense.

It's curious how you can be home all weekend with hardly any money to go anywhere and be so excited about something that hasn't even started to happen yet. But that's how I felt. I was Super Dancer, the whirlwind woman whose secret powers allow her to work five full days at her 9-to-5 job and then work another four nights as a glamorous hostess in an exotic food emporium. I figured that I would waitress Thursday, Friday, Saturday, and Sunday nights, because the weekend was always good for tips. That would also leave me some free time. I'd have Monday, Tuesday, and Wednesday evenings, plus most of Saturday and Sunday. Doug would hardly mind if I was a bit unavailable. In fact, maybe he'd notice I wasn't around and want to see me more. I'd have to cross that bridge when I came to it, but I had the picture clear in my mind: Doug on his knees, pleading with me to take a night off so we could go out to the clubs.

Looking at the numbers, I realized a curious fact. If I could get this whole process started, it would gain its own momentum. If I could pay off seven thousand dollars in a year, then my interest payments would fall by about thirteen hundred dollars. So my shortfall the following year would only be thirty-seven hundred dollars instead of five thousand, but I would still have the twelve thousand extra that I was earning as a waitress. After I paid off another eighty-three hundred dollars, my interest payments would fall by another fifteen hundred dollars as I began to pay off cards with lower interest rates. Suddenly my shortfall would only be twenty-two hundred dollars a year, but my being a waitress would still earn me another twelve thousand for a surplus of almost ten thousand dollars. In other words, within three years I could wipe out my credit card debt and start paying off my student loans. Once I began to reduce the debt, the interest payments would fall and make it even easier to pay off the rest of the debt.

I was enthralled, but I didn't stop there. Some planning demon took me over. I had enjoyed teaching dance to the four-year-olds on Tuesday mornings, but couldn't continue after I broke my arm and took the day job at Castle Advertising. It would be fun to go back and do that again. Now that I understood Saidah's way of figuring income, it would also bolster my numbers. True, I didn't get paid for it, but it did some good in the world. Maybe I could do it on Saturday morning. I also wanted to have time set aside for prayer and being quiet. Sunday plus three evenings struck me as plenty of time for that. I wouldn't have to waste a lot of time on personal errands, since I would be cutting back on as many of my expenditures as possible. That might get me out of debt even faster.

I realized that I was stepping off one treadmill onto another that moved a lot faster. This new treadmill, however, promised that one day I would be free of debt. It's strange how quickly I moved from my fears about not having enough money now to feeling good about where I would be in a couple of years. All that interrupted my mood was an occasional nagging thought about my dancing. When would I take lessons? When would I go to auditions? If it was going to take me five years of this nonstop work to get completely out of debt, I would be twenty-eight before I could stop working either as a receptionist or as a waitress. That struck me as pretty old, particularly for anybody who wanted to dance as badly as I wanted to. Look at

Cedric, Saidah's husband. He had been a pro ball player; now he was in his forties and his playing career was long over. Still, at least he had had a career. I had a bad feeling that I might make it to my thirties without ever getting a chance to perform.

Fools rush in, they say, and I sure didn't hesitate. I called my old boss at the restaurant and he was happy to hear my arm was better. He needed waitresses and told me I could start the next week. I called the woman who ran the nursery school where I had taught dance. She wasn't too sure about Saturdays, because most of the moms dropped their kids off to go to work on weekdays, but she said she'd check into it and get back to me. Monday I cruised through work, cashed my paycheck, saw Doug for about a minute when he dropped in to get his twenty dollars, and headed off for Dr. Testa's office with a happy springtime bounce in my stride. I was really doing it. I was taking the energy of those demons and using it to make my life better. Saidah would have been proud of me.

Dr. Testa also seemed to have turned over a new leaf.

"Good afternoon," he said with a smile that I wouldn't have expected after the way he lectured me on my last visit. I felt a bit bad to have to use my credit card for this visit, but it would be my last visit and I didn't have any other way to pay him. After this, I was putting my credit cards away. Period. No more emergencies. Every time I charged something, no matter how much I needed it, I just extended the time before I could get out of debt. I understood in a way I never had before that this extended time was like a sentence in a debtor's prison. I was on parole so I could work, but dollars equaled days that I would be laboring for my freedom.

"Hi." I answered without much enthusiasm. I certainly hadn't forgotten my last session when he tortured me with his dental tools and endless talk.

"I noticed that your credit card went through on the first try this week."

"Uh-huh," I agreed as I walked past him and slipped into the padded chair that adjusted in so many different ways.

Unfortunately, Dr. Testa proved himself to be a lot like Dr. Jekyll and Mr. Hyde—he was nice as long as I was able to talk back, but immediately broke into his monologue, once he had my mouth stuffed with cotton and tubes. I was thankful that he didn't use the long needle this time. Maybe the humane society had gotten them outlawed in the week that had passed since my last visit. He jabbed my gum with a shorter needle to shoot Novocaine around the tooth and then started in with his monologue.

"Maybe I talked about debt too much last week," he said.

"Um." I hoped this meant that he would work in silence, but that wasn't to be.

"It's important to keep your eye on your money. You have to know where you are all the time. Do you ever think about being old? What you're going to do for retirement?"

I didn't even try to answer, but I would have said no. I had been living from paycheck to paycheck. Even that wasn't really true, because debt had been lending me a helping hand. To me being old was getting to thirty without dancing.

"It's really simple. You don't even have to make a lot of money. What you must do, however, is set something aside from every dollar you earn. Say 15 percent of your after-tax income. Pay yourself first. That's the secret. You put that 15 percent or 8 percent or 10 percent, whatever works for you, into a long-term investment. You leave it there and let it grow. Then the eighth wonder of the world, compound interest, works its magic in your favor.

"Let me tell you something unbelievable. If you put two hundred dollars a month away in savings, you'll probably be worth a million dollars by the time you're ready to retire. Why? It's the miracle of compound interest. It's working for you every day, every hour, every minute. Whatever you have, compound interest makes it worth more and more."

I wanted to interrupt and tell him about the Seven Wonders of the World, but I had to keep my mouth open as he removed my temporary filling.

"You're probably wondering what to do with the money. Put it in the bank? Buy bonds? Maybe buy stocks? Hard question, simple answer. Don't loan your money out, because over the long run you won't earn as high a rate of return. That means you don't leave it in the bank and you don't buy bonds. It's much better to own a piece of the companies that make the American economy the strongest in the world. Equity, own equity. Open wider."

I realized that Dr. Testa didn't really communicate with people. He spoke words and these words had a certain meaning, but the point of communication is to go back and forth. Sort of like tennis or dancing with a partner. You don't hit more and more balls across the net while the other player takes a siesta. The ball gets hit back and forth. He couldn't communicate with me because he had no idea of my response to all this. For example, he didn't know that I was thinking about getting out of debt, which made his secrets of building wealth irrelevant. Also, I wanted to ask him why he kept talking about money. What was its fascination for him?

"My solution is to buy mutual funds. You check out the fund, do the research. Be sure it has a solid rate of return. Make certain the fund manager who got that rate of return is still there. Buy a fund that invests in stocks across many industries and countries, so you have diversification. Watch out for the commissions, or load, that you have to pay. In fact, you might only want no-load funds, those that charge no commission at all. And reinvest your dividends. That's crucial, because that's the way you make certain to maximize the rewards of compound interest. After you have some savings in your mutual funds, then you might think about buying a home. One step leads to another. Owning your own home is a good feeling, and it can be a good way to save. It has tax advantages, too. Open wide. Deductible real estate taxes, deductible mortgage interest. And real estate has been a good investment, although you have to compare rates of return carefully to see whether real estate beats the stock market. There's not much point in generalizing either, since real estate is always location, location, location. Plus you need a place to live. You just have to be careful about home-equity lines of credit, because they can be abused like credit cards. Getting a mortgage with a good interest rate and paying it down over the years is a great way to save.

"You need a good accountant. You've got to plan for retirement the right way. Put your money in tax-deductible retirement accounts, if you can. If you can't do that, consider putting it in a retirement account anyway. At least its increase in value won't be taxed. A little wider. That's good."

He had a small black square of paper that he put on my molar.

"Grind your teeth together."

I did and he took out the paper and looked. He began working lightly on the surface of the inlay with the drill.

"Benjamin Franklin had a lot of great sayings about money. Old-time wisdom. I don't think you can beat it today. *The Way to Wealth* was a great book of his. 'If you would be wealthy, think of saving, as well as getting.' When I read that, it made an impression on me. Or, 'Creditors have better memories than debtors.' A lot of truth there." He put another square of the paper on my molar. "Grind again, please."

I rubbed my teeth back and forth. I didn't know if the lecture on money was distracting him from his dentistry or his dentistry was distracting him from his lecture on money. Maybe he had perfected doing both at the same time. I paid attention when he said that he had read what Ben Franklin said about money. It hadn't occurred to me that perhaps everything he knew came from books. I could read those same books.

"Looking good." He surveyed his work with pleasure. Now he inserted a small wooden stick, like a pencil, and had me bite down a few times. "How does it feel?"

"Fine."

"OK." He removed everything from my mouth and I rinsed a few times. "So you're finished. Mission accomplished. You may have a little sensitivity to hot and cold, but that should go away soon enough."

"Can I ask you something?" I don't know what made me bold, but I couldn't let it pass. "Why do you talk so much about debt and money? Do you do that with everybody, or was it a special lecture for me?"

"Did I talk that much?"

"The whole time through both my visits here."

"You should have told me to stop."

I pointed to my mouth. "It's a little hard to say anything."

"I'm sorry if I annoyed you. Nothing could have been further from my intention. Maybe I was just thinking about how it's a struggle, all the creative fields. In college I wanted to be a potter. Making beautiful vases and plates and so on. My parents convinced me to give that up. It wasn't practical enough. You make a good living as a dentist."

"It must be more than enough to support a family," I put in.

"Yes, it is, but I'm planning to get back to pottery."

"When?" I asked.

"When I retire."

"How long will that be?"

The pained look in his eyes made me wish I hadn't asked.

"Another fifteen years, the way it's planned."

When he said that I felt like a hand of ice took hold of my heart. He was talking about waiting to live his life. These hours in his office, doing his work, earning his money, weren't really living. That would come in the future, when he retired. It made me think of my own plan to work my way out of debt. What was living, anyway? Would I be alive if I weren't dancing?

"Thanks." I felt awkward and edged past him to the door.

In a few moments I was outside with his face still haunting me. Why did everything have to be flawed? I couldn't help but see a parallel between Dr. Testa and myself. By working the way I intended, I, too, planned for a future that seemed so far away. After I paid off my debts, then I would dance. After I worked two jobs for years, then I would fall in love. When I was stashing 10 or 15 percent of my earnings in a retirement plan, then I would be ready to marry and have a family of my own. What about this moment? Right now?

I ran my tongue over the surface of the inlay, its peaks and indentations like my other teeth. My bite felt perfect. Dr. Testa might not be a potter, but he had the skills of an artist. I thought I would buy that book by Benjamin Franklin, *The Way to Wealth.* On second thought, I would take a look at it in the library. I tried to skip a few times on the pavement, but the visit with Dr. Testa had knocked that bubbling feeling of spring right out of me. Was I really like him, about to give up everything that made life worth living for me? The evening opened its empty arms to embrace me. I wondered what was happening with Saidah's visit. Wouldn't her husband and sons be lonely for her? Was her presence comfort for a dying woman? I had only known her a week, but she had made her impression on me. I wished she were still here so that I could visit with her on that green bench in the park, but I would have to find something else to do tonight.

CHAPTER 12

The Accident

didn't want to go to the apartment, because I didn't want to be alone there. Not only did I not want to be alone, but I also didn't feel like having Rachel or Tina around. I wanted people, but sort of in the background. Nobody who would be talking to me. Maybe I'd had enough of Dr. Testa's talking or I simply needed some quiet.

Anyway, I meandered in the park until I noticed that my feet were taking me in the direction of the library, which wasn't far away and stayed open until 8 P.M. on weekday evenings. I loved the library, especially the collection of video tapes of dance concerts that could be watched in a special room where you were assigned a TV set and headphones. Tonight, however, I used the computer to search for *The Way to Wealth*. In a minute I had the call number and left a slip requesting the book with one of the librarians.

I sat in one of the wooden carrels and waited for my call number to come up on the electronic board. Dr. Testa had given me so much information, but I felt like he had been talking to the wrong person. What use is it to give someone skis if they're at the bottom of the mountain and have no way to get to the top? Of course, the only way you'd know they wanted to go to the top was by asking them. Unlike Saidah, who listened to me, I didn't think Dr. Testa was a very good teacher. I made a little joke to myself about him: Whether or not the student is ready, the teacher will come. And talk about something irrelevant. Not to my entire life, because someday I hoped to be earning money and paying myself first by regularly saving a portion of what I earned. Right now, however, I was facing the fact that my debt seemed overwhelming. I needed all my energy to win this battle with debt; I didn't feel that I had any energy left over to give to saving. In fact, I told myself that paying off debt really was like saving. It was moving in a positive direction.

Finally my call number came up and I went to the desk to get the book. It was slender, more like a pamphlet than a book, and its cracked and yellowed pages were in tatters. It might have been printed by Ben Franklin on his own presses. How many hands must have opened this copy over the years? How many people had sought advice from this teacher who passed away two centuries earlier?

The book's introduction offered some background about Franklin's own life. I found out that he left school at the age of ten to help his father's business. At the age of twelve he was indentured to his older brother, James, who had a printing business. He didn't get along with his brother and, after five years in which he learned to be a printer, he broke the indenture and secretly left Boston for New York. Aged seventeen, he couldn't find work in New York and went on to Philadelphia where he eventually made his fortune not only by his frugality and hard work, but also by carefully showing these aspects of his character to others and gaining their trust.

As I leafed through the crimped and battered pages, I felt that I walked on a road that many others had already taken. An elderly man, named Father Abraham, was quoting from *Poor Richard* to a crowd that waited for an auction to begin. I began to write some of these quotations, as follows:

"God helps them that helps themselves."

"But dost thou love life, then do not squander time, for that is the stuff life is made of."

"Drive thy business, let not that drive thee; and early to bed, and early to rise, makes a man healthy, wealthy, and wise."

"Industry pays debts, while despair increaseth them."

"Employ thy time well, if thou meanest to gain leisure; and, since thou are not sure of a minute, throw not away an hour."

"What maintains one vice, would bring up two children."

"If you would know the value of money, go and try to borrow some; for he that goes a borrowing, goes a sorrowing."

"But ah! Think what you do when you run into debt; you give to another power over your liberty."

"The second vice is lying, the first is running in debt."

"Rather go to bed supperless, than rise in debt."

It couldn't have taken me more than half an hour to read the little book. When I finished it, I sat quietly in my wooden chair. I liked the library, its calm, the books on the shelves filled with bright thoughts like the minds of old friends. I hadn't known much about Benjamin Franklin, but he inspired me the way he had inspired generations before me. He had started as an indentured servant; he had been in debt. His own efforts, his willingness to sacrifice and work hard, had let him move up in the world and become a wealthy man and a respected philanthropist. His education had stopped at the age of ten, but he had still become a statesman and an inventor. I found it difficult to understand how anyone could be so prolific, but it made me think that I was on the right track. To have a plan, a budget, to pare my expenses, increase my income.

I began to daydream. The wonderful thing about daydreaming is that it's not reality. I didn't have to deal with all the hours of work that faced me. I could simply imagine that I was debt-free. I felt like I was floating, the way pleasurable dreams of flying sometimes liberate me from the gravity-bound sensations that I know. Then the flying became soaring, the leaps of dancers in some ballet of beauty and spirit. The klieg lights dazed our eyes, so that the audience remained hidden in darkness, but on the stage we moved with an energetic grace that made me think how every human is created in the shape of the divine.

Intense daydreams! But I was in that frame of mind, gearing myself up for what was ahead. I sat there almost until closing time, then rushed to find the books that Saidah had recommended, *Little*

Dorrit by Charles Dickens and *The House of Mirth* by Edith Wharton. I checked them out and, over the next couple of weeks, as I read the books, I felt comforted because they reminded me of Saidah. I missed her. I thought she must be busy with a lot of worries and didn't need me bothering her right now. I did call her, but I only got her answering machine.

"Hi, Saidah, it's Iris. You don't have to call me back, but I hope everything is going OK for you. I hope we'll talk soon."

In the meantime I got back to waitressing. I can't say that I was happy about it, but it did feel good to know that my arm had healed. I could balance a full platter on my palm almost as easily as I had before. Being young and doing my squeezing exercises with the rubber ball in my hand probably helped me heal. I realized how much my day job tied me in one place behind the receptionist's desk. I liked moving back and forth between the customers at their tables in the dining room and the staff in the kitchen. It was two worlds, but I could experience both of them. After the meals, I would gather up the tips with a glowing sense that the future was coming closer and closer.

You'll probably think I was crazy, but I also wanted to continue my in-line skating. Only this time, I planned to take lessons. At Castle Advertising everything went along fine. If I was a little tired at work on Friday and Monday mornings because I had waitressed the nights before, all I really had to do was stay awake. I was able to manage that and be pleasant to everyone. At the apartment everything seemed fine with Rachel and Tina.

Chalma Akerson from the Little Folks Nursery finally called me back and I went down to see her on the second Saturday in May. I remember the date because the next day was Mother's Day. I liked Chalma; she was willowy, about thirty, and had a good sense of humor that the kids liked.

"We do have a number of parents who bring their children on Saturday mornings, but I can't say for sure how large the dance class would be," Chalma said

"That's not a problem." After all, I wanted to teach because I loved dance. It's always fun to teach a large class, but having fewer students would allow me to give more attention to each. Especially with the four-year-olds, a smaller group was easier to keep focused.

"And we don't have any budget," Chalma added apologetically.

"Don't worry about it. I'm not doing it for the money."

"But you should be paid."

I shook my head. Maybe I seemed a generous fool, barely able to pay my bills and yet giving my services for nothing. I didn't think Chalma knew anything about my financial situation, but I appreciated her concern anyway.

When I told Doug I would be working so much he didn't seem upset. Then I asked him what might have been a fatal question. I say might have been, because I don't think we were really headed anywhere.

"How would you describe our relationship?" I asked.

Doug paused to give this his full consideration.

"People joined by strong mutual attraction," he answered.

"To each other?"

"No," he was serious, "to dance."

"But Doug, what about you and me?"

"Look, Iris, you and I love dance. There's no mystery about the lives that dancers lead. They don't have any money. They risk injuries. They probably have no insurance. If they're lucky, they end up touring in the sticks. What do we really have to offer each other?"

If I didn't have anything to offer to Doug, I didn't have anything to offer to anybody. His logic chilled me, because I didn't think that logic belonged in the discussion. People fall in love and do the best they can with whatever circumstances they face. Yet I did understand him. If our connection deepened into love, where would that lead? To marry and have children would be the end of dancing. We'd have to settle down, plan careers, stop sacrificing for the love of an art that would never reward us with a living wage. I wasn't ready for that, but I still felt there could be something else, somewhere between everything and nothing, where love might grow.

I backed off, because I really liked Doug. Who could be certain what would happen between us? Maybe we needed to get to know each other a little longer. Or maybe I was foolish to keep alive my hope when his logic struck me as so clear and cold. Anyway, I had to get to the restaurant, so I took off.

Mother's Day always made me lonely. I took my books and in-line skates and headed for the park. At the outdoor rink I took a skating lesson, wobbling around for an hour and learning how to stop and how to fall. If only I had taken that class before my first outing on the skates, I might never have broken my arm. As I unstrapped my knee, elbow, and wrist guards and took off my helmet, I followed this line of thought a little further. If I never broke my arm, I would never have found out the danger of not having health insurance. I wouldn't have had to run up the balances on so many of the credit lines for my credit cards. And when I saw Dr. Testa for the first time, I wouldn't have given him four cards that were already maxed out. So I might never have felt depressed and sat groaning on that bench in the park. In which case I would never have met Saidah. And only after meeting Saidah did I see a way out of the financial pit that I had dug for myself with debt, a way that would give me back my freedom.

So was I saying that I was happy I broke my arm because that led me to Saidah? No, but I was certainly happy that I had met Saidah and I missed her, especially today, when everyone was doing something for Mom. I thought about my parents, Jim and Mary, who had adopted me late in life. Over my years growing up I had asked them a lot of questions about my adoption. While I think it pained them for me to ask, they spoke freely of why they had adopted me, but they gave me no information about the family of my birth. The love between them had been so great that they had wanted to share it with a child. And I felt that love in their home, beneath the minor quarrels or discomforts; it soothed everything with its gentling hands. But that very love made me miss them. On a holiday like Mother's Day I didn't have any other family with whom to share. Then I would start to wonder about the woman who had given birth to me in a far-off land where the people looked like me and spoke some foreign tongue. Who had been my father? Did I have brothers and sisters whom I would never meet? My left side began its aching, that yearning for something unknowable. I would never find that family and, if I did, they would not be my family because I would come to them as a stranger.

The following Saturday I started teaching the dance class at Little Folks. It wasn't part of the regular schedule but an extra hour that could be added to the morning. The parents or babysitter had to come to the class, so that helped a lot. I had four girls and two boys, and soon they were hopping across the room to the frog dance, bounding to the antelope dance, and cantering to the horse dance. I showed them some basic movements like the *plié* and *jeté*, although I called them "bending knees" and "jumping over the moon." Everybody had fun, including the parents who watched proudly from the chairs along the side of the room.

In my free moments, which were few and far between, I began reading *The House of Mirth.* I quickly learned that the reference to mirth was ironic; it was a sad tale of a young woman named Lily Bart who lived in New York City around 1900. She moved with the upper classes but was always in need of money and borrowed where she could. I could relate to many of the descriptions of Lily's troubles with money, such as, "Her head was throbbing with fatigue and she had to go over the figures again and again; but at last it became clear that she had lost three hundred dollars at cards. She took out her cheque-book to see if her balance was larger than she remembered, but found she had erred in the other direction. Then she returned to her calculations; but figure as she would, she could not conjure back the vanished three hundred dollars."

Lily began going down, both in spirit and in living conditions. I kept hoping for her to marry Selden, the man she loved and who loved her, but instead she fell on worse and worse times. They didn't have credit cards for borrowing then, but she borrowed from a man who wanted to gain power over her by the debt. At last she received a small inheritance, paid all her debts and then, by mistake, took too large a dose of sleeping potion and died. When Selden realized that her last act was to pay back all that she had borrowed, although it left her penniless, he kneeled by her lifeless body and, at last, told her of his love. Wow. What a depressing book, but it definitely held my interest. I kept hoping that Lily would find a way out, but I should have known better. And I could feel in my gut the way debt gave Lily "a paralyzing sense of insignificance." I had that feeling myself, whenever I thought about the imbalance in my numbers without also thinking about my plan for financial redemption.

After almost six weeks on my plan, I was beginning to see results. I had perfect records, so I was starting to be able to account for a lot of the expenses that I had labeled "Miscellaneous" before. Also, keeping track of my expenses cut down on them. If I knew that I would have to write it down, I thought twice before spending it. And there was no problem on the income side either. The extra income as a waitress had put me over the top in terms of balancing my budget. Not only did I have a surplus, but it was a bit larger than I had thought it would be. Why was I disheartened?

It wasn't about Doug not being romantic or Saidah being gone such a long time. It had to do with waking up on Monday morning and feeling tired. Physically, Friday morning was worse because I felt tired from a whole week in the office plus from waitressing the night before. But emotionally, Monday was the hardest. I didn't want the week to start. In fact, I wanted everything to stop. I wanted to rest and not think about working. One night I had a terrible nightmare about a rattlesnake that kept striking at my legs. Finally, I bit off its head and chewed it until I had venomous pouches in my own cheeks. I, too, had become poisonous. What could a dream like this be about in the real world? I could feel my anger, but at what?

That's when I wished that I had Saidah to talk to. June had come with its big bright days that stretched on and on as if to last right through until dawn. She had been gone almost two months. I did receive two postcards, but I needed more than that. I wondered how Cedric and Alton were getting along without her. I had actually reduced my debt by almost one thousand dollars. I would find myself lying in bed on Sunday morning thinking that I could take care of it all myself. I could go the whole way and pay off my debt completely. At the same time I felt too heavy with misery to get out of bed. I didn't think that I would live long enough to pay it all back, and if I did, what good would it be when I seemed to have lost my life? I resented having to do the dishes, the laundry, clean the apartment. It was too much. It couldn't possibly get any worse than this. Of course, I was wrong. It could get worse, and it did.

In the meantime, I managed to start reading *Little Dorrit*. What a complicated plot! And so many characters. Little Dorrit was a beautiful girl who was born in the debtor's prison of Marshalsea in London and whose father remained a prisoner there for more than two decades until she was a grown woman. I recalled that Saidah told me that Dickens's own father had been imprisoned in Marshalsea. When Little Dorrit's father is finally freed and restored to the fortune that had been wrongfully taken from him, Little Dorrit tells Arthur Clennam, the man she loves, that "It seems to me hard that he should have lost so many years and suffered so much, and at last pay all the debts as well. It seems to me hard that he should pay in life and money both." Later in the book, Arthur Clennam ends up in Marshalsea and refuses to take from Little Dorrit the money that would allow him to go free. Unlike *The House of Mirth*, however, after a lot of twists and turns Little Dorrit and Arthur Clennam marry and live happily ever after. That was the kind of ending that I liked.

Expectations and endings. The good thing, or maybe the problem, is that after the ending there's always another day. Maybe that's the beginning. Only books have the certainty of endings, everything else goes flowing along. More like a river than a book. Maybe it will rain and the river will swell, or maybe it won't and the river will trickle. But it's life nonetheless. Or maybe it will feel like a big dam suddenly bursts and what pours out is a lot more than I ever imagined. Anyway, the next thing that happened wasn't so good.

It was late on a Saturday night, nearly midnight, and I was finishing work at The Golden Plate. Bertrand, the owner, came to get me. He's wiry, very Gallic, with a thin face and sad brown beagle eyes. A nice man except for every once in a while, and he looked worried.

"Phone call for you, Iris," he said with his accent like a French sauce that enhances the flavor of all that it touches.

I followed him to the office and he left me by myself.

"Hello?"

"Iris, it's Doug."

"Doug, are you OK?" I asked because he didn't sound OK.

"I'm at the hospital."

"What happened?"

"I hurt myself."

"How?"

"It was the last number. I came down wrong from a jump and I heard something crack. It was like a gunshot. I had pain in my knee that I couldn't believe. I managed to get off stage, but I can't walk. I need some help, Iris. Can you come down here?"

"Sure. I'll get a taxi and be there as soon as I can."

I got the directions from him and hurried out of the restaurant. I was thinking how terrible it was that Doug had suffered this accident. I felt compassion for his pain and sorrow for the recovery that would stop him from dancing just as my broken arm had stopped me. But I have to admit that wasn't all I felt. He had called me to come and help him. Could this be the signal that I had been waiting for? That I was special in his life, as the marriage vow said, "to have and to hold, in sickness and in health…"? The way my broken arm had led me to Saidah and my attempts to get on firm financial ground, could this unfortunate accident lead to something hard to imagine, some unexpected new beginning that would be good and bring Doug closer to me?

CHAPTER 13

A Difficult Decision

The emergency room wasn't crowded, and I found Doug in a small ward with six beds. Three of the other beds were occupied, but out of a combination of wanting to respect their privacy and not see their suffering I kept my focus on Doug. The back of his bed had been raised, so he was sitting up with a mound of ice packs and towels supporting and covering his right knee. He was still wearing his black leotard under the blue gown that the hospital had given him. His pants and shirt must have been thrown on over his dance clothes before he was raced to the hospital.

"Hi." I hesitated, not quite sure how to approach him. I sat in the chair beside the bed and took his hand in both of mine.

"Thanks for coming, Iris, I really appreciate it." Doug's pupils looked large and had a dull glow, a contradictory look of expansiveness and not quite being there.

"Are you OK?"

Doug shook his head. "The doctor says I may have torn a ligament in my knee. It hurt unbelievably."

"Is the ice helping?"

"They gave me painkillers. I feel kind of light-headed."

"What happened?"

"I came down from an air turn and it was like my knee wasn't under me. It buckled and I fell. At least I had been headed off-stage right, so I managed to crawl into the wings. I would have screamed if they hadn't still been performing. I was in contortions with the pain. I can't stand on the leg."

"What's the doctor say?"

"He's not sure. He's an intern. A knee specialist has to look at it. But if it's a ligament, the way he says, it could be the end of my dancing."

"What?" I was shocked. I squeezed Doug's hand between mine, but his hand felt curiously unresponsive, flaccid.

"He's not a specialist, but he said it was pretty likely."

"That's a terrible thing to say," I felt angry, "when he can't know for sure."

Doug shrugged. "He's telling me what he thinks it could be. He didn't say definitely, but maybe. Ohhh."

Doug squinted and tightened his lips in pain.

"Can I do anything?" I didn't know how to help him.

He shook his head. We talked some more about his knee, but he didn't know anything definite. Then we talked about the accident and a little bit about the performance. I asked Doug what he planned to do.

"Get better." He smiled weakly, looking disoriented and sleepy. "Iris, I have to ask you something."

For some reason his words excited me. To be asked. That ancient formula in which the man lovingly asks for the woman's hand in marriage. Or gives her a diamond engagement ring. I didn't think these thoughts as much as they cascaded into my mind on their own.

"I hate to ask you this, but do you think I could borrow some money?"

I was let down. And, as if someone plucked a guitar string, a tremor of fear vibrated in me. I didn't have money to lend.

"I don't know," I answered. I couldn't focus on money when I was concerned about Doug.

"I've been thinking about it. I don't have any medical insurance."

"What about the dance group?"

"Maybe they'll be able to help, but I doubt it. There's rent, food, getting around town."

"I'm having trouble dealing with this," I said. "I mean, I'm really worried about you. It's hard to think about money too."

"But it's all part of the same picture. I'd probably need a couple of thousand dollars until I'm back on my feet," he smiled because "back on my feet" was too apt an expression. "Even if you just lend me part of it, maybe a thousand dollars, it would be a huge help. Will you think about it?"

Unlike the doctor who might or might not be right about his knee, I didn't want to give Doug any bad news. Not tonight, he didn't need any more.

"Sure," I replied, "I'll think it over."

"And let me know?"

I nodded. "Yes."

"I'll see the specialist in the morning. Will you come visit me tomorrow?"

"Of course."

"It's so strange," he said, "to make one mistake. It didn't even feel like a mistake until I landed."

I could see that he was falling asleep. I got up and smoothed his forehead with my palm. I felt bad for him, but I had another feeling I would have been ashamed to admit. I had trouble accepting his injury, seeing this handsome man with his easy smile lying on a hospital bed. As I walked down the corridor and wondered why, I imagined that Doug had meant dancing to me. That had been the image I carried of him in my heart. To see him injured made me feel that the wonder had gone out of my life, as if his dancing had been my dancing. I'd had a long day, with the class for the kids in the morning and waitressing all night. Suddenly I felt more than tired; I felt depleted, at the bottom of a dark pit. The elevator gaped open. I stepped in and descended downward.

When the phone rang in the morning, it sounded far away and muffled. I turned in my bed and pulled the covers over my head.

"It's for you," Tina poked her head in the doorway.

"Who is it?" I had been dreaming about something, but I couldn't quite remember what. It had been about needing. Had I been need-ing or had someone else in the dream? I wanted to sleep again and let the dream finish. It couldn't help but be better than this reality of Doug in the hospital and wanting to borrow money.

"She didn't say."

That got me out of bed. I went right to the phone in the long T-shirt and underwear that I always slept in. Rachel was ironing by the window, so I sat on the couch.

"Hello?"

"It's Saidah. How are you?"

The warmth of her voice made my heart leap.

"Where are you?" I asked, not wanting to answer her question to me.

"I'm at home. Arrived last night."

"I'm glad you're back. Is your teacher OK?"

There was a short pause, then Saidah spoke more quietly. "She passed on."

"Oh, I'm sorry."

"Thanks, I appreciate that."

"What are you doing today?" I blurted out the words. I wanted to see her and ask her what to do about Doug. I had so much to tell her. She had been gone almost two months.

"Getting reacquainted with my family. Jesse came home from col-lege so we could all get together."

"So you're probably not free to visit," I said.

"Is everything all right?"

I was aware of Rachel nearby, but I wanted to talk to Saidah. Not caring if Rachel heard or not, I told Saidah about how Doug had been hurt and wanted to borrow money. That would be news to Rachel, because she'd been asleep when I stumbled in long after midnight, but I knew she'd be sympathetic.

"You don't have to decide today," Saidah said. "Any time you're feeling urgency to make a decision is a good time to take a deep breath and reflect some more before doing anything."

"I'm not sure when he needs the money."

"Can it wait until after work tomorrow?"

"Yes, sure."

"Let's meet then. Our usual place. That would be better for me. Keep in mind that you don't have to do anything; certainly not anything in a hurry."

"Thanks, Saidah. I'm glad you're home."

"Me too," she said emphatically. "See you tomorrow."

After I hung up, I talked a bit with Rachel.

"How much does he want to borrow?" she asked.

"A couple of thousand."

"Is that two or three?"

I shrugged. "I don't know."

"Do you have any cash?"

I shook my head. "None."

"So there's not much to talk about."

Rachel kept ironing the cotton blouses that she wore to her temp jobs. We all had strategies to survive and be able to dance. Rachel figured that temp jobs were best because you got paid well and had no hope of advancement. No possibility of building a career that would distract from dancing. She could keyboard an incredible number of words per minute. More than one hundred. And she was unerring. Law offices welcomed her. Sometimes she even worked the night shift because that paid the most.

"If I didn't like him a lot, I wouldn't be worrying about it."

"You can't give what you haven't got."

Rachel meant her words to be supportive, but I kept thinking that Doug's asking me showed that I was special to him. As soon as I could, with a stop in the bathroom to brush my teeth and splash water on my face to wake up, I pulled out my yellow notepad and looked at the credit lines for each of the credit cards. My eight credit cards allowed me to borrow nineteen thousand seven hundred eighty dollars in total. I had owed about seventeen thousand dollars two months earlier, but then I had added another dental bill and paid off some of the balances, so now I owed sixteen thousand eight hundred thirty-two. I could lend Doug almost three thousand dollars if I was willing to max out all the credit lines on all the cards.

Thinking about doing that made me panicky. If I gave him the full amount, or even part of it, I would be adding steps to that treadmill. Where was the joy in it? Steps to pay back what I borrowed, steeper steps to pay back the interest on what I borrowed, and finally the steepest steps to pay the interest compounding on the interest. The Eighth Wonder of the World. But what kind of world? Did I want to live in it? A world of prisons, built with bricks of fear? No one forced me to work two jobs. I was doing it because I wanted to respect myself. I walked to walk so fast on the treadmill that the terrible machine would at last fall apart and I would be free.

What of romance? That dreamy life whose geography fit the warm contours of Doug's muscular body, whose sky had a brightness like his smile? I couldn't continue, because Doug and I didn't have that kind of a relationship. Not truly. I had hoped it would become like that, but we hadn't been seeing much of each other and my working a lot hadn't drawn any loud complaints from him. Sure, I thought he was a nice guy. Maybe he felt like the brother I didn't have. But I wasn't likely to mix his ashes in wine and gulp him down. Not even with carrot juice.

I closed the yellow notepad and stuck it under my bed for safe-keeping. Taking a deep breath, I realized how odd I felt. It was like not knowing where my skin ended and the air surrounding me began. I kept thinking that I could give Doug the money. Then I would think of the hours, the endless work necessary to pay for that money. Immediately I would see Doug lying in the hospital bed with that look of pain on his face. Not knowing if he would dance again. What a place to be in! My heart would go out to him and I would want to give him the money. But then I would think of the numbers. How one or two or three thousand dollars would keep me in debt that much longer. And what if something happened to me? Who could I turn to for money? Yet Doug was such a lovable guy. I cared for him, for the goodness of him whether or not he would be my boyfriend, my lover, my husband. Why did everything have to be about possession—mine, his, yours? I wanted to be generous and helpful, but the idea of giving the money to Doug made me fearful. In turn, the fear made me want to cling to what little I had and not make a bad situation any worse.

My sense of myself was caught up in these thoughts. I seemed to be shrinking and swelling, thinking I can and then I can't, I will and then I won't. My mind was a perpetual motion machine of yes and no. I wanted to reach inside my head and stop the spinning gears. Why hadn't Doug asked me to cook for him? Or run errands? Or keep him company while he recuperated, gently tucking in his blankets and offering agile witticisms to lift his spirits? Instead he wanted money. When I had so much to offer him, he wanted what I didn't have.

That afternoon I visited Doug in the hospital again. He still looked like he was on painkillers, his eyes dulled and slow to focus.

"'Lo, Iris."

"Hey, how're you doing?" I bent and kissed him. He hadn't shaved and his whiskers rasped my face.

"OK."

I sat in the armchair next to his bed. "They treating you good?"

"They've been fine, but I'm leaving today."

"Are you sure?"

"The doctor said I could. He's given me a prescription for the pain. Two prescriptions actually—one for now, with codeine, and another for later, when it doesn't hurt so bad. But I can't run up a big bill here. Anyway, there's no reason to stay. I can lie around my apartment."

When he mentioned not running up a big bill, my fear came back and didn't leave as we talked more about his injury. I kept expecting him to ask for money again.

"I tore the anterior cruciate ligament," Doug said. "It's like a big rubber band that holds the knee in place. The sound I heard when I landed was the ligament tearing."

"How does it heal?"

"Not too well. I have a choice. If I want to dance, I need an operation. They take some tendon to repair the ligament. Then I have a long rehabilitation with a lot of pain and work."

"What's the alternative?"

"No operation, but I'll have to be rigorous about rehabilitation anyway. I'll probably never dance again. I'd certainly never perform again. And it's unlikely that I'll be able to play hockey or ski or jog." His eyes had filled with tears, not from the pain in his knee but from the thought that he might lose these vibrant joys.

Gently I reached up to rest my hand on his. He held my hand between his and pressed with a warmth that made me feel connected to him. The fear left me. I understood his dilemma; maybe I felt his emotions. I wanted to comfort him, which made me feel useful and pushed my fear down. We talked awhile, not about much of anything. I enjoyed being near him and feeling that my presence soothed his pain and worry.

"Did you think about the loan?" he eventually asked. "I'm sorry to bring it up, but I have to buy crutches, pay my rent, all the daily things plus the medical expenses."

"I don't know if I can do anything. You know I owe money too."

If he had pushed me at that moment, I would have been able to say no to him and have a clear conscience. About what? That's harder to answer, but I would feel guilty not to help him. I had access to that credit line. I was healthy and could pay it off sooner or later. Actually, it would be later, but I could do it. Only he didn't put any pressure on me.

"I know. Of course I know. I certainly understand if you can't. I was barely able to lend you twenty bucks. I really appreciate your coming last night and today."

He told me that his roomies would be coming to take him home from the hospital, so I didn't stay too much longer. Walking back to my apartment, I thought how he didn't have to say that he appreciated my coming. Why didn't he assume that I would come? Thinking this way, I felt lonely. He didn't assume it because we didn't have a close enough relationship. He certainly didn't feel that we did. It was so like me, trying to make him into someone he wasn't. Adding the money to that, I didn't know what to do. I wanted to do the right thing. The fact that he hadn't pressed for the money made me want to help him. And I felt his suffering and his predicament. I kept thinking about him all night at The Golden Plate, where I seemed to be constantly forgetting what the customers wanted. Monday at Castle Advertising was the same. I could hardly remember the name of the person calling long enough to tell the person who was being called. After work I rushed toward the park, only to find the green bench empty.

I sat by myself. The park looked the same in that different way: different people and more light, as every day in June lasted longer than the one before, but the same feeling of peacefulness that I always felt when I saw the sloping lawns and the paths vanishing among the elms, birches, oaks, and willows. It's strange to want to help someone and also believe that it would be wisest not to. I took a deep breath, but my thoughts didn't change. I wanted to help Doug. What could explain the insistence of this feeling? My reason told me that I didn't have the money. If I borrowed to loan to him, I would pay with more hard work over a longer period of time. I already felt like I could barely bring myself to do both jobs. It wasn't exactly physical exhaustion, because I had plenty of energy to do fun things. When I thought about working, especially on Thursdays and Fridays when I had to go from the agency to the restaurant, I would suddenly feel exhausted and irritable. I didn't want to. Against all this was my feeling that Doug deserved my help. He needed me.

After ten or fifteen minutes I saw Saidah coming toward me. She smiled and raised a hand to wave, but I noticed how slowly she walked. She looked slightly bent over and, when she came within ten paces of me, I could see that her face looked different—more deeply lined, solemn. I stood from respect and the realization that what I saw in her was grief for the passing of her teacher. With barely a thought I opened my arms and welcomed her with a big hug. She hugged me back and I smelled that scent that she wore—a sweet honeysuckle that became merely a hint of itself as soon as we separated and sat on our bench.

I didn't know how to start, because I wanted to talk about myself and also find out about her.

"It's good to see you," I said.

"You too," Saidah answered.

"You were gone a long time. Almost two months."

"It was important for me to be there."

"What happened?"

Saidah scanned the landscape of the park. I was wearing my usual uniform of a blouse, this one ecru, and black slacks; she had abandoned her two-piece suits for a flowing, African garment made with a beautiful fabric of blue and gold. She looked to have come from another land, like the Magi must have looked strange and holy to the townspeople in Bethlehem.

"I'm still trying to understand what happened. There was so much more than I would have imagined and on so many levels. Of course, Elizabeth died."

That was the first time that I had heard Saidah call her teacher by name.

"What caused it?"

Saidah shrugged with perplexity. "She was in her early nineties and she just stopped eating. I don't know why. She was finished here and ready to leave. And determined—Elizabeth was a very determined woman."

"How long had you known her?"

"Sixteen, nearly seventeen years. I met her when I was about your age. I was working as a flight attendant. This older woman gets on the plane. I gave her the same attention that I gave everyone else. Got her a pillow, magazines. Then I found myself talking to her. She was spry, alert. Looking in her eyes and listening, I forgot all about her age. We didn't talk about my problem with credit cards, not that day, but we kept in touch."

That Saidah had been a flight attendant surprised me. I guess that I think everything has always been the way that it is now. I hadn't thought about what Saidah might have done before she began "Financial Planning from the Heart."

"You got to talk to her."

"Yes, that was good." Saidah looked at me. "We didn't leave anything unsaid. The last night I sat on the end of her bed and we talked for hours. How could it be? That she was dying and had the strength to talk. All her life seemed to be right before her. She had reconciled herself to what had happened, and to leaving. To me she was like an angel. She made me feel that we may all be angels, waiting to let things fall away and reveal us. She wasn't old anymore. She wasn't any age. Just in her readiness to go, she had surpassed aging. They say the spirit leaves the body at death, but I never understood how large it could become. It grew in her like love that had to burst into the world. Sitting there on that bed I felt that spirit enter me. Just a little of it was enough to fill me completely."

Tears had filled Saidah's eyes and rolled slowly on her cheeks. She smiled at me through the tears.

"It's so good you were there," I said, putting my hand on her shoulder. "For her and you."

Saidah nodded. She found a handkerchief in her purse and patted away the tracks of her tears. "It made me think a lot about my debt to her. Not money, I never borrowed from her, but the debt that a student owes to a teacher. Elizabeth shaped my life. If I hadn't met her, I would have been a different person. Maybe I would have gotten out of debt anyway and still become a financial planner. But we only live one life, and she was so influential for me. That kind of debt can't be repaid. Not to the person you owe it to. Maybe because you don't really owe it to them."

"What do you mean?"

"Elizabeth had a teacher, too. She repaid that teacher by becoming a teacher. It's like that story about the debt that keeps flowing—from the wine to the grain, the egg, the branch, the blossoms, and eventually back to people. It's like quicksilver, splitting, flowing, rejoining. The debt is larger than a person. It's more like a tradition. The gift of the teacher, the debt of the student who becomes a teacher and passes the gift and the debt along to the young ones."

"That's what you're doing," I said with admiration.

"Maybe someday you'll do it, too," Saidah replied to me.

We talked a lot more, about Elizabeth and how Saidah's family—
we called them "the men"—had managed to get by without her.
Apparently, Cedric had been a master sergeant in the army and
could cook with the best of them, so he and Alton had been fine at
home. We finally got around to my story about Doug. Saidah was
sympathetic until the part about his wanting to borrow money,
when she straightened and grew intent.

"I want to lend him the money, but I don't have any."

"So you can't," Saidah said.

"I have just enough left on my credit lines," I said, feeling a bit
foolish to admit that I would consider using credit at this point.

"Why do you want to lend to him?"

"He needs it. He's not the kind of person who would ask if he
didn't."

"What do you hope would happen because of your loan?"

"It would help him as he gets better."

"And?"

"He would know that I care about him."

"Anything else?"

I felt embarrassed, but I added, "Maybe his feelings for me would
deepen."

"Because you were there for him."

"Uh-huh."

"What about his paying back the loan?"

She caught me by surprise, because I had never thought about
that.

"Of course he would."

"Did he offer you some security?"

I frowned. "Security."

"Did he say that he'd give you something valuable of his to keep
until he paid you back?"

"No."

"Did he say when he'd pay you back?"

"He probably doesn't know."

Saidah nodded and thought for a moment. I wanted to say something, fill the silence, defend myself or Doug, but I didn't know what to say.

"Usually I counsel people not to make loans to friends. If they have to, I advise them to treat the loan as a gift. In fact, only loan what you can afford to give. That's a good rule."

"But why? Friends pay each other back."

Saidah shook her head. "My advice is never to loan. Make a gift, but don't expect repayment. If one day that person wants to pay you back, wonderful. It's a nice surprise. People can find so many reasons for not paying back loans. Whatever caused them to have to borrow in the first place may not go away. It may get worse. What if Doug decides on that operation? Will you loan him more money?"

"I wouldn't be able to. I'd have used up all my credit."

"You have to know where to draw the line for yourself. If you can afford to give money to Doug, then you can make him a loan—or even call it a gift. If you can't afford to make that gift, then you shouldn't make a loan. And, Iris, don't expect anything more than a thank you."

We talked some more, but it was this part of our conversation that I kept returning to later in the evening as I rustled through my budgets and lists of debts. It made me sad. I knew that I didn't have enough to lend anything to anyone, but I wanted to help Doug from the bottom of my heart. Even if he would never love me, I wanted to help him. That he called me from the hospital made me like family. If this familial bond were slender or illusory, still it touched me. A brother, not a lover. What I wouldn't give to have a brother in my life. If it had only been about love, I'm sure that Saidah would have convinced me that a loan was a bad idea. But to me it was about something far more elusive that had a lot to do with me and not so much to do with Doug. It was about standing up for someone, about caring enough to be there, about giving generously without worrying whether you could afford it. Hadn't Saidah quoted to me from the letters of St. Paul? "Owe no debt to anyone, except the debt to love." That debt I could feel. The world might be filled with millions or billions of people suffering. I couldn't help them all, but Doug I knew. Doug had touched my life. I saw the treadmill turning, turn-ing, turning. It began to gather speed, step after step, quicker and quicker. Was my desire to help Doug goodness or madness? On the edge of sleep, I hoped for clarity in the morning that would make me see the foolishness of my yearning to lend to him. I couldn't afford to give. Of that I was certain. Yet, paradoxically, I felt that I couldn't afford the failure to give. My mind kept going back and forth. For-tunately, what with everything going on, I was exhausted and at last sleep knocked me out like an anaesthetic.

CHAPTER 14

Loans and Gifts

ometimes I think that if you take a step in any direction, the fates rush you forward another two or three steps. Who are the fates? That's a tough question. Maybe they're a part of ourselves we haven't been introduced to yet, pushing us faster and faster in whatever direction we choose. Then there's the divine. Maybe that's inside us, too, but up at the top of the mountain, more important than anything but also hard to find and harder to recognize.

I noticed something important that next day, Tuesday, while I was working at the agency. The only credit line where I could get money also had a lot of small print. In this block of light-blue type, I read that cash advances were charged an extra fee of 3 percent. So the thousand dollars that I planned to lend to Doug would actually cost me one thousand and thirty dollars. That made me mad. I figured that if every month you borrowed cash of one thousand dollars and then paid it back the next month, you'd end up paying one thousand three hundred and sixty dollars to have a loan of a thousand dollars for the year. That would be 36 percent interest, which would be usury except that they didn't call it interest. Of course, you didn't have to pay back the thousand dollars every month, but then you'd be paying nearly twenty percent interest on the balance on the credit line. That way the thousand dollars would cost about twelve hundred and thirty dollars to borrow for a year and then pay back. I tried to imagine what kind of people had created a system like this. I kept seeing men with soft, sweaty hands that would cling to money, faceless men whose blubbery torsos were covered by expensive suits accented by the colorful silk of designer ties.

That detail, that extra fee that struck me like the straw to break the camel's humped back, made me sweat and feel fear. These bankers or credit card moguls had created a maze to trap people like me. When I blindly stumbled inside this maze and knew nothing, I felt fine. Ignorance is a kind of bliss. But knowing what I knew now, I could hardly bear the idea of going further into the maze, further into debt. It was like losing myself, not knowing if I would ever come out. When I thought about the people who had created this system, I realized how ghastly crimes can be committed by ordinary men and women following orders. Probably no one had thought to entrap people into debt. The inventors of the first card might have been dreamers who wanted to help everyone by the convenience of the card. Then other people had ideas about how to make more money, and bigger and bigger companies got involved. Once the cards had caught on, there was no one who remembered the dream or could see how it had been corrupted and used to hurt people.

That's what I was thinking when I went to see Doug with the thousand dollars in my purse. I figured I'd better go as soon as work got out on Tuesday, because once Thursday rolled around I would be working both jobs. I had to take a bus to Doug's, and I kept trying to forget my fear. I also tried not to think about Saidah, because I knew she wouldn't want me to loan him the money. Not unless I could afford a gift, which I couldn't.

Doug had found his share in a rickety tenement building on a street that might have been called a slum except everybody seemed happy to be living there. The front door to the building was unlocked, so I walked in and up the stairs. When I rang Doug's bell, he yelled from inside.

"Door's open. Come on in."

I pushed open the door and stepped into the chaos of Doug's apartment. I won't go into the details, except to say that it looked like the five of them had just been moving in when, in fact, they had lived there more than a year. Boxes and duffel bags were piled around the living room, and Doug lay on the shabby brown couch with his back propped up at one end and his legs propped up at the other.

"'Lo, Iris." He looked better today, except for his knee swollen with wrappings and the crutches on the floor by the couch.

"Hey yourself. I brought you some stuff to eat." I made some room on the coffee table in front of Doug and set out the Chinese food that I had picked up.

"Thanks." Doug used the remote to turn off the television.

"How'd you get up the stairs?" I asked.

"Mike and Tom—put my arms over their shoulders and came up one step at a time."

"Nice guys."

"Yeah."

I went into the kitchen and tried not to look in the sink. If Doug had lived alone, I would have been tempted to clean the place. Instead I looked in the cabinets until I found two passably clean dishes and took them back to the living room to make a plate for Doug.

"Can you get around on those?" I pointed to the crutches.

"I can, but it still hurts."

I passed Doug his plate. We ate, mostly in silence broken by a few comments about the good food.

"I've been thinking," Doug said when he had finished and rested his plate on the debris layered on the coffee table, "about the accident and my career."

"You mean the operation?" I had assumed that he was planning to have the operation. After all, he had been on the Canadian all-star hockey team, not to mention his talent for dance.

"No. Or only sort of. I was thinking about dancing. How being hurt in an accident is like getting old all of a sudden. Because if you're hurt or you're old, you can't dance. What I started to think was kind of strange."

"What?" I asked. Doug was so big and strong, and moved with such an easy grace, that I often forgot his thoughtful side.

"That as a career, dance will never take me anywhere. If I did the best I could, I'd probably still be working at odd jobs to support myself. One day I'd be thirty or thirty-four or, by some miracle, maybe forty-one, and I'd wake up and know that my body couldn't do it anymore. Then I'd have to find a real career."

"Dancing is real," I protested, because dance was the dream for us both.

"It's not a career. It doesn't go anywhere. Maybe a few dancers become choreographers, but I'm not going to. Even if I did, what kind of living would I make? Maybe this is better." He gestured toward his knee. "It's a message."

"Who from?"

Doug shrugged. "The gods, the universe, the banks and card companies that I owe money to. The message is to move on. If I'm smart, I could start my second career now. Instead of losing ten or fifteen years to dancing, I'd be gaining ten or fifteen years of being a lawyer or an accountant or whatever I'd end up being."

At that moment I thought Doug was talking about both of us, saying that I was wasting my time wanting to be a dancer. But then I realized that it wasn't about me, and that his conflict about whether to dance or do something else had been bothering him before his injury.

"You're upset."

He opened a hand toward his bandaged knee. "I just feel so frustrated," he answered, spacing and emphasizing every word. "People get injured in sports even more than in dance. I never thought I would. No matter how much I was willing to sacrifice, it wasn't enough, because I'm not going to be a dancer."

"Give it a few days," I tried to comfort him. "You're down, but you can come back."

Doug looked around the living room.

"This place is a dump," he said. "I don't know how I've been able to live here."

If Doug had said that a month earlier, I would have been delighted. Frankly, I didn't know how he could stand to live there, either.

But today it made me sad. It felt like his whole view of the world had changed. He didn't seem to want me to soothe him. He was thinking about something else, almost as if he wasn't quite there. We talked some more, but I realized that he was too miserable and in too much pain for me to lift his spirits.

It's hard to be with someone when nothing you do can change their mood. I would have liked for Doug to see things differently. He had told me not to expect much from our relationship because we were both dancers. If he wasn't going to dance, he might have wanted a deeper relationship with me. But he didn't. That couldn't have been clearer. He wanted another life, one that would have nothing to do with art, shabby apartments, and a girlfriend who made a living as a receptionist and a waitress while she dreamed of dancing.

Nonetheless, I opened my purse and took out the envelope. I had decided on a thousand dollars, because it was a large amount but would still leave me two thousand dollars on the rest of my credit lines in case of an emergency. I had thought a lot about the treadmill, and I had felt terrific fear, but I had also considered the debts that can't be measured in money. The debt to our teachers, the debt to love others, the debt to our families, although I had never known my blood family. I imagined myself in Doug's position. There would be no one to help me if people like Doug, Tina, or Rachel wouldn't stand by me. Maybe he and I had failed at love, in fact I was pretty sure that we had, but I still cared for Doug. He was my friend. For me, without any family, what could be more important than friends? If I worked hard, I could earn back the thousand dollars, but this moment to stand up for Doug, to support him and show love for him, would never come again.

"This is for you," I said and handed him the envelope.

He opened the flap, blinked a few times, and I saw his eyes glisten with tears. Inside were ten rectangles of paper with a portrait of old Ben Franklin. Brand-new, crisp hundred-dollar bills. I knew that borrowing the thousand dollars would obligate me, but life is obligation. At least that's what I thought in that moment while Doug looked in the envelope. He looked at me with intensity, passion of a sort I had never seen in him but which I still knew had nothing to do with love.

"Thanks, Iris." His deep voice had become huskier. "I'll never forget it. You've truly helped me."

"I'll be going," I said, which might have seemed strange except that I had nothing further to say. This had been the purpose of my visit and, unless Doug had some surprise, I was ready to go. I bent over and kissed him good-bye, and a few minutes later I was standing at the bus stop down the street from his building. I realized that he hadn't said anything about paying me back. If it was a loan, we hadn't discussed whether it would have interest and, if so, at what rate. Gazing out at the city as the bus sped along its route, I felt complete. Maybe it had been a gift. Whatever it was, I had done what I had to. Giving and giving up. With the gift, or loan, I had given up my hopes about a relationship with Doug. It wasn't giving up in a bad way, but more accepting reality. If I felt sad, as I did, I also looked forward to something new, to the future with its mysteries and abundances.

That optimistic mood proved to be about as wrong as anything. As soon as I got to my apartment, I found my mail in a pile on my bed and I started going through it. Nothing personal, there never was anymore—just ads, sweepstakes, and credit card bills. Except for an envelope from the Internal Revenue Service. I was perplexed, because I had filed on time in April but I didn't have a refund coming. Unless there'd been a mistake and I was going to get a refund after all. When I opened the computer printout, I couldn't believe what I read.

The IRS advised me that my return had been selected at random to be audited. To save me the annoyance of coming to the IRS office or going through my records, the IRS did a computer audit using certain guidelines that had been ascertained from the examination of millions of returns. Because my occupation had been listed as waitress, they had included an analysis of my tip income based on the total income reported by The Golden Plate. This had showed that my tip earnings appeared to be underreported. Due to this underreporting for the prior year, they had then conducted a similar analysis for the two preceding years and concluded that I had failed to report tips received in the amount of fourteen thousand two hundred thirty-one dollars. Based on my tax rate, I now owed them three thousand two hundred fourteen dollars in additional taxes plus another nine hundred eighty-seven dollars in interest and penalties. More than four thousand dollars.

I kept looking at this IRS letter as if I couldn't see. How could this have happened? Could it be a joke? But this letter definitely looked like it had come from the IRS. I wished that I could think of someone who disliked me enough to play a truly cruel joke on me, because if it wasn't a joke then the IRS actually wanted forty-two hundred dollars that I didn't have. I shook my head and stared at the type to make it change, but the words clung to the page. All that hard work that I'd done to pay off my debt had actually gotten me nowhere. Thanks to the IRS, I had been going deeper into debt as they tallied up unpaid taxes and then topped it off with penalties. They just hadn't let me know.

I didn't see a way out. I sat on my bed like a lump, a statue of concrete, heavy with fear and depression. I couldn't add forty-two hundred dollars to my debt. I didn't have enough left on my credit line to pay even half of forty-two hundred dollars. And if I could borrow it at 19.6 percent, I would be paying it back for years. I thought of how many telephone calls I would have to answer at Castle Advertising and how many tables I would have to wait on at The Golden Plate to pay back what the IRS demanded. This letter, this piece of paper with its computer printout, was a jail sentence for me.

That wasn't all. At least I had believed that I knew how to get out of debt. I had believed that working two jobs would bring me my freedom one day. Suddenly I found myself doubting that I would ever be free of debt. If I could find a way to pay off this forty-two hundred dollars, I had a fatalistic feeling that I would get unexpected bad news from somewhere else. It would keep on like that, all my efforts to be free like the futile struggles of a fly gummed to a spider's web.

All at once I regretted the money that I had given to Doug. What a few hours earlier had struck me as generosity, now appeared to be madness. I couldn't afford such an outlay, whether as a gift or a loan. What was wrong with me? How had I imagined that, deep in debt as I was, I could still give away my money? The rationales that had struck me as persuasive lost substance, became shadows, and vanished. I was a fool, and not even a fool in love. I didn't know how to handle money. My misery gathered force as I berated myself. I had my arms pressed tight to my sides, my hands clenched in fists, a tightness through my whole body. Failure. I was a failure. I was a person who had failed.

And I couldn't turn to Saidah, not after borrowing on my credit card to give to Doug. It would be an insult to her. She had been gone for such a long time and I had wanted so badly for her to return. But I had failed her, too. I couldn't face her, no matter how much I wanted to see her. I would have to go it on my own. At least that's what I thought, as the shock let up enough for me to cry and the drops of my tears splashed on the letter from the IRS. Maybe bankruptcy *was* the only answer. At least for people like me, who have no courage, no foresight, no fight. I felt bankrupt; why not make it my legal status as well as my miserable mood?

I wished that it was time to go to sleep, but hours of the evening remained. Finally I stirred and reached under the bed. When I didn't contact the green garbage bag, I slid to my hands and knees on the floor and reached further until I touched the plastic and pulled the bag into the light. I dropped in the letter from the IRS, twisted closed the top of the bag, and shoved it back into my private storage area.

That done, I knew that I didn't want to see Tina and Rachel. I felt too raw and beaten down. Taking the blanket from my bed, I opened the window and crawled out on the roof. I watched the three-quarter moon loft itself in the dusky sky. As the light faded from the edge of the world, my thoughts expanded and contracted. By putting the IRS letter in the trash bag, I had determined that I would not deal with it. I would deny its existence. Let them come and find me.

Watching the moon rise and the stars come out, I thought of the bigness of everything. Distances vast beyond imagining, galaxies filled with millions of stars. From this big perspective, my problems seemed minute. What could a letter from the IRS matter compared to the inferno of our modest sun? What did the IRS weigh on such a scale? Or my own life?

In the end, the vastness of the universe always overcame my imagination. I couldn't fold it into my thought, and tonight I felt the same way about my handling of money. I didn't comprehend money any better than I understood the Milky Way. What had the letter from the IRS been but a black hole, a pulsation of energy that destroyed everything around it? Its immense gravity sucked my hope and my energy into its darkness.

Because I was numb, I didn't feel too bad about Doug when the repetitive cycles of my thoughts would bring him to mind. Doug's image sparkled like something I could put my hand through. As if the physicality of him wasn't the final truth. In this odd moment of my thoughts, he seemed to me to be more like a passage. He had been close enough to me to evoke the idea of family. Not the kindly Cassidy family that I had known, but the lost family of my birth. What if I had been the eldest, the first child of a woman too young and poor to raise and care for me? But after my adoption, she might have had more children. These would be my brothers and sisters. I might have a father, her husband. There might be cousins and grandparents of mine in Peru, Bali, or Bangladesh. In that foreign land, whichever one it might be, the letter from the IRS would be meaningless. My debts would be meaningless. All that would matter would be my family, the family that would recognize me and welcome me back into their fold. I would come as a stranger, a westerner speaking an alien tongue and unfamiliar with their customs, but they would know me by the way my face would mirror their own.

With thoughts such as these, and sorrow that I couldn't seek out Saidah so she could comfort and help me, I let the evening slip away. At last I saw Tina get into bed and turn out the light. Then I opened the window, came back in the bedroom, and settled in my own bed.

"How long were you out there?" Tina asked.

"A couple of hours."

"Oh." Tina yawned in the dark. "What were you doing?"

"Thinking."

"About what?"

"Nothing."

"OK." Tina rolled on her side so that her back was toward me in the dark. In a few minutes she was asleep.

For maybe the hundredth time I was calculating how long it would take to pay off my new debt, the thousand dollars to Doug and the forty-two hundred dollars to the IRS. Before today's fiasco my plan had been to pay off the credit cards in three years and the student loans in the two years after that. I didn't know how the IRS would handle me when they tracked me down. I certainly wasn't going to contact them, but I figured they'd want all their money. If I avoided them long enough, I might have cleared two thousand dollars more off a credit line. Then I could max out my last card and pay the IRS in full. If I could do that, it would take four years to pay off the credit cards and two years for the student loans. I had added a year to the time that I would be in debt. I felt sad about the time, but worse about failing. I would be a waitress at The Golden Plate forever. It was no longer a part-time job but an arrangement that would continue until I was nearly thirty.

Thirty! I couldn't believe it. Lying on my back, my tears pooled in the cups of my ears and slithered into my hair, and I felt swallowed up by the darkness of the night.

CHAPTER 15

The Etiquette of Tipping

That miserable night began a series of miserable days and nights. All day at Castle Advertising I worried about the IRS tracking me down, the credit cards that would take the rest of my youth to pay back (thirty! I might as well drop dead now), the fact that I didn't have a boyfriend, and, way down on the long list, that I wasn't dancing. At The Golden Plate I waitressed like my life depended on it, tearing at breakneck speed from the dining room to the kitchen, smiling too hard to please the customers, wondering whether I'd get a big tip or a little one. I felt tired and covered it up by acting energetic, but it was more like frenzy. I didn't think I could do this for six more years. I was running down. If I weighed the six years of work ahead of me against the pleasures I had received from borrowing, I would find myself unable to remember the pleasures. Six years, the term that an indentured servant might have had to work for his or her master back in colonial times. At least those servants had borrowed to seek new lives and opportunities in the New World.

Even the little kids in the Saturday morning dance class started fraying my nerves. I had been able to handle them easily at first, but the more tension I felt about the money the more I found myself being short with them. Watching them learning to dance, I would think about how I wasn't getting paid to be there. I would argue with myself, saying that money wasn't everything. But I need to be paid, I would answer back. Saidah's advice about the value of good deeds felt more and more remote to me. After all, I had been merely desperate when she gave me that advice, and helping the kids had made me feel better. But now I felt beyond desperate, the fear was worse, and my hopelessness made anything that didn't pay off debt seem beside the point. After the class I went to Chalma's little office where she had hung reproductions of Degas's paintings of ballerinas on the pale green walls.

"Hi, Iris."

"Hi. Do you have a minute to talk?"

Chalma opened her hand to offer me one of the chairs in front of her desk. Sitting down, I kept looking at the ballerinas, the graceful youth of the women costumed in their frilly white tutus, their bodies in so many poses that spoke to me of the life of the dance studio.

"What's up?" Chalma asked, following my eyes to the dancers in the paintings.

"Did you dance?" I asked.

"I studied," she said with a smile. "How is your dancing coming along?"

I shook my head. "I'm too busy working."

"But why?" Chalma looked concerned.

"I just have to." I didn't want to tell Chalma my problems and added flatly. "I have commitments."

"You should be dancing," she said. "Just watching you teach I know that."

Her words warmed my heart. I realized that no one had encouraged me to dance since I broke my arm. Doug could have, but he hadn't. Neither had Rachel or Tina. To my surprise, my eyes filled with tears that I tried to conceal by looking down. I had been crying so much lately that I had been considering not wearing eye makeup anymore. Chalma saw the moistness of my eyes before I could hide it.

"What's going on?"

"I need to earn more money."

"Don't we all," she smiled.

"I'm enjoying teaching the kids, but…"

"You need to be paid," Chalma finished the sentence for me.

"Yes," I agreed, relieved that she had said it.

"I felt that from the beginning, but I couldn't convince the powers that be."

"So I'm going to have to give it up," I went on doggedly, imagining that I would find paying work for Saturday and Sunday during the day, "because I have to increase my income."

"That would be a shame." Chalma looked at me in that way she had, with her blue eyes intent, like I had her full attention and nothing could possibly interrupt us. "But tell me, why aren't you dancing?"

I shook my head. "I don't have the time."

"How much do you work?"

I explained about Castle Advertising and The Golden Plate.

"Isn't the point of having jobs like that so you can dance?"

She was right. If I had been working at a job that I loved, that would have been something else. Not that I had any idea what that might be, but I had planned my life around dance, not paying off the balances on my credit cards.

"Yes, that's true."

"So?" she smiled as she elongated the word into a question, but she challenged me, too. It was like someone shaking me or dousing me with cold water. I remembered why I had come to the city, and I despaired to have lost my passion and determination to do what I loved.

"I'm not doing what I want to do. It's true." Looking at Chalma, I wondered what kind of dancing she had done and why she had stopped.

"Maybe hurting your arm discouraged you. It can be tough to come back from an injury."

"I never thought of that."

"I'm just guessing. And maybe you were a little discouraged even before the accident."

"I kept auditioning, but not getting to dance."

"A lot of things are a struggle until you get them going. This nursery school is a good example. You hit some bumps, but you keep going. If you go far enough, it gets a lot better."

I felt her compassion for me. Why hadn't anyone else been encouraging? All of a sudden, I wanted very badly to take dance classes again. I had been discouraged by the rejection at the auditions, but a few kind words from Chalma made me want to rush to an audition. Only I needed to get back in shape with classes, and auditioning wouldn't help with my debt.

"Thanks."

"Listen, let me go back to my partners and see if we can't work something out. I really want you to keep teaching the class. It's been getting bigger every week. The parents love it because the kids love it. We might be able to do something. Let me try and I'll give you a call."

I knew the nursery school didn't have any money to pay me, but I appreciated how much Chalma wanted me to continue teaching. I said I'd wait to hear from her, and headed home for a nap so I'd have some energy to waitress later at The Golden Plate. The restaurant did a big business. The food was good and, on most nights, reservations were necessary to get a table. Saturday nights were the busiest, which I welcomed because I made the best money. I had eight tables, enough to keep me running back and forth all night. This particular Saturday, even with the reservation list, there was a crowd of people waiting all night to be seated. This gave them time to have a drink or two at the bar and spend some money before getting seated. For some people, it also loosened whatever meager restraints sobriety normally imposed on their being crass and mean to waitresses.

It started with too many tables being seated at 8 P.M. I was moving like a track star, but some tables had to come first and others had to wait their turn. Pretty soon a guy started waving at me and wouldn't take no for an answer. He was the loudest one at a table of six, three couples in their forties, the guys looking like lawyers or bankers in suits.

"I'll be right there," I said as I speeded past the table trying to take care of the drink orders from the first three tables.

"That's not soon enough," he said.

I ignored him, but it went downhill from there.

"Did you finally notice that we're here?" was his reaction when I did come to take their order.

After their rounds of drinks, they ordered a bottle of wine to go with the entrees. When I brought it and poured him a sip, he swirled the wine in the glass, lifted it to his nose, inhaled, and frowned.

"It's corked."

"I'm very sorry," I said, taking the glass from him and hurrying back to the kitchen with the bottle. In the bustle of the Saturday night craziness I got Bertrand to taste the wine.

"There's nothing wrong with it."

"He's giving me a hard time."

Bertrand shrugged in that Gallic way that meant, What can you do with fools? "Give him another bottle."

I gave him the second bottle, which he accepted with a big show of tasting the wine. Later, when I had served their meals, he said, "You should be proud. Are you?"

Of course I had to ask, "Why?"

"Because I've been all around the world, and you get the award for the worst service ever."

I was having quite a night, but I contorted my face into a smile and said, "Thanks, I'll put that on my résumé." At least one of the women at the table was looking in her lap with embarrassment. The guy must have had four or five drinks, not to mention the wine. Great customers for the restaurant, but miserable for me as the waitress.

When the busboy was clearing the station, I saw that familiar hand waving me to come to the table. I went with dread, feeling the power this miserable little tyrant could wage over me just for the price of a dinner.

"I have a complaint."

"What else is new?" The words came out before I could stop myself.

"My meat was bad."

"Then why did you eat all of it?"

"The sauce hid the flavor of the meat, so that I couldn't tell until the last bite."

"Well, there's nothing I can do now."

"Yes, there is."

"I don't think so."

"Tell the manager that I'm not paying for this meal."

"You can't eat the whole meal and then not pay for it."

"Yes, I can. And if I get sick from eating that meat, I'm going to haul this restaurant into court. The Golden Plate—what a joke!"

"You'll have to speak to the manager."

"That would be a pleasure. I'm going to mention the lousy service to him, too."

Even then I kept my cool. I read somewhere that using the word "cool" to mean "calm" comes from Africa where it's always hot. So if you can be cool when it's very hot, you have dignity, stature, and charisma. In the midst of handling the other seven tables, I had to find Bertrand to deal with this problem guy.

He and Bertrand hassled it out, and Bertrand actually conceded the cost of the one entree just to avoid having a noisy scene in the dining room. But when I picked up the credit card receipt, I could hardly believe it. I know I should have expected the worst, but for a two-hundred-dollar tab, the guy had left no tip. Instead, inside the leather folder, he had put about twenty pennies and written on the edge of a small sugar package, "Your tip."

I lost it. I picked up the pennies and ran for the entrance. They had already gotten their coats and gone into the parking lot, but I went right out the door after them. I didn't care about my other tables, I didn't care about anything. I heard somebody screaming— it was me. They turned in surprise.

"Here's a tip for you!" I pelted him with the pennies, my words rushing out like demons. I called him names I didn't think I knew. At last, my lungs raw, I turned and trudged back to the entrance of The Golden Plate. That fraction of a minute had been timeless. I left the six customers frozen behind me in a tableau of disbelief. Ahead, where the huge neon golden knife and fork rose on either side of the doorway to support an equally outsized golden spoon that finished the framing of the door, I saw Bertrand waiting for me.

"Come."

I followed him into his office. We hadn't even reached the middle of the room when he turned to speak to me.

"Iris, I'm letting you go."

I felt betrayed. All the reasons why I had been right to do what I had done came bubbling up in my mind. I started to speak but he waved his hand.

"Don't tell me that the wine was good, that his food was good, that he insulted you, that he didn't leave you a tip. I'm running a business. My staff is professional. If a customer is out of line, you have to be all the more professional. You have to rise above it."

"But…"

Bertrand shook his head to silence me. "I don't know what's troubling you, but you can't bring it to work. I wish I could let you stay, but I can't."

I didn't answer. All my energy vanished. I slumped, felt barely able to walk, and started slowly toward the door.

"Iris," Bertrand stopped me. "Do you need some money?"

"No."

"You know Chantal and I like you. But you need a break or something. Please let us know how you're doing."

"OK."

I left the glowing golden knife, fork, and spoon behind me. In the dark streets, passing through the circle of light beneath each streetlight and into the darkness again, my thoughts stuck in a loop. I owed the IRS money because of the tips I received. This guy who didn't like the wine, the food, and the service had given me no tip. So, in a crazy way I couldn't explain, I felt that getting no tip should solve my problem with the IRS. I kept thinking it over and over again.

I must have walked halfway to my apartment before another thought finally broke this cycling. By losing my job at The Golden Plate, I was back to a monthly deficit. Fear reached its bony, chilling fingers into my guts. Yet I seemed to be two different people, because I didn't just feel fear. Replaying the scene in the parking lot, I felt triumph to fling the pennies back at that man. It wasn't just that he had demeaned me and I flung his behavior back in his face. It was bigger than that. Maybe it had been time to leave The Golden Plate. I had been burning out. But if leaving might be right, I still had no idea how to make the money I needed for the future. I could go back to playing the lottery, or search for a new second job, but I saw no way to escape years of overwork and frustration of not doing what I wanted.

At home I had a message on the answering machine to call Doug. I didn't much want to talk to him, because seeing him made me think over and over that I should never have loaned him the money. Talk about the blind leading the blind. I was in debt myself, but still foolish enough to lend money to somebody else in debt. Rachel and Tina had already gone to sleep, so I tried not to turn on any lights. I sat on my bed in the darkness and had the dull thought that most of my time was spent sitting or lying on this twin bed or working. Was this the good life? My body felt leaden. I couldn't even take off my clothes. I wanted to call Saidah, but I felt that I couldn't. I needed her advice, but I had failed in so many ways that I felt ashamed to face her. As much as her advice, I would have welcomed the warmth of her upbeat spirit. But I had gone against her when I chose to lend Doug the money. I had lost my job at The Golden Plate. I had gotten in trouble with the government about my taxes and who knew how that would end up? It would be bad. That struck me as a certainty.

I kept trying to add the pieces of my life together. Find a theme, a direction, a harmony that would offer hope. But it was like a column of numbers that couldn't be added in a total. I didn't see a big picture. There were a lot of miserable fragments. Maybe Chalma was right and not getting parts when I auditioned had made me falter in my pursuit of dance. My exhaustion glued me to the bed like the gravity of Jupiter. How many nights had I fallen asleep feeling miserable? In that hopeless moment, it felt like every night. At last, without undressing, I kicked off my shoes, made a supreme effort to raise my legs onto the bed, and simply fell on my side. As soon as my head touched the pillow, the darkness of the night changed to the darkness of sleep and an escape from my constant worries.

CHAPTER 16

Facing the Music

For someone who felt as rushed and run-down as I did, I didn't welcome having all of Sunday free to myself. Knowing that I wouldn't go to work that evening at The Golden Plate especially bothered me. If I stayed home, I'd probably drag out the trash bag from under my bed and work some more on my budgets. The thought of doing that filled me with futility and despair. It was like trying to fill a pot that had holes in its bottom. In fact, the holes in the bottom of the pot were larger than the opening at the top. More would always pour out than I could put in. Feeling that way, I wanted to crowd things to do into the day. That would avoid the hours of free time that opened like an abyss.

I started by calling Doug, who wanted to see me. I told him I'd come over to his place early in the afternoon. The day looked beautiful, as if a dam had burst and let sunlight come pouring over the world. I had taken a couple of lessons on my in-line skates, so I considered whether I could skate all the way to Doug's. When I thought of all the trucks and buses that I'd encounter on the streets, not to mention the potholes and the rough spots where the surface had been patched, I decided the best plan would be to go skating in the park after I saw Doug. That way most of the afternoon would be accounted for and I would only have to get through the evening with nothing scheduled. I didn't feel good to be thinking like this, filling time, killing time, but I was afraid to look at my money situation. Not only had the IRS put me a lot deeper in the hole, but losing my waitressing job meant that I was back in the red every month. I didn't feel like I could just bounce back and get another job. And I didn't want to have free time, because the best thing to do would have been to figure a new approach to my financial worries and I felt like I couldn't. Not right now, when my confidence had been shaken and I figured every plan of mine would end in failure.

As I rode the bus toward the city's outskirts, my in-line skates in a backpack on the seat beside me, I began thinking about the dance studio where I studied. It had been five or six months since I had been there, but there was a technique class late on Sunday afternoon and I doubted that their schedule had changed. Maybe what Chalma had said got me thinking about the class. When I thought about going, I felt I wouldn't be able to enter the studio. I realized that Chalma must have been right. Before I broke my arm, I had been going to calls for tryouts but never getting selected to dance. After being the pride of the dance department in college, I had expected to succeed in the city. It had been a lot of failure that I wasn't used to.

As I walked up Doug's steps, I thought knowing him hadn't helped either. Instead of finding a companion to commiserate with me as we went from tryout to tryout, Doug started landing parts. I didn't feel competitive exactly, but his success gave a greater intensity to my feelings. Only now he had injured himself, too.

"Come on in," Doug yelled in response to my knock.

I stepped through the door into a transformed apartment. I couldn't believe my eyes. The litter of the living room had been picked up. It had been a sediment of magazines, clothing, sports gear, old mail, and who knows what else that I had thought archeologists of the future would unearth in layer after layer and imagine that an earthquake had created the mess. But my heart sank when I saw the three large suitcases placed along the wall near the front door.

"What do you think?" Doug was on the couch with pillows propping up his back and his injured knee. He waved toward the empty cleanliness of the room, and for a moment I missed the debris that had been so familiar. It had made this apartment into Doug's nest, his home.

"I can't believe it."

"Everybody pitched in. I couldn't stand it anymore."

"But," I pointed to the suitcases, "are you going somewhere?"

"Yeah, I'm going home."

"Why?" I was still standing by the front door.

"Do you want anything to drink? Or eat? There's some stuff in the fridge."

I shook my head. "No."

"Sit down, at least."

I sat in the chair across the coffee table from Doug. It sounds strange, but all of a sudden I wanted my money back. I hadn't loaned him the money so he could go home. I had thought he was on his own, that he had no one to turn to but me, that I was like family to him. With an unpleasant rush of insight, I saw this as my own fantasy, my desire for a husband or a brother who would take away my aching. In my college philosophy course, I had been impressed with Plato's idea that each individual is only half of a whole, that we are separated before birth from the other person who would complete us, and our lives are spent yearning and searching for that healing other. I figured that I had been joined to someone on my left side, which was why sometimes I felt such pain there.

"Why?" I demanded.

Doug cleared his throat and looked down. "I've been accepted to law school," he said.

This didn't add up. "When did you apply?"

Doug raised his head, assessing me with concern. "About six months ago."

"But you were dancing."

"I've been feeling for a while that dance isn't doing it for me. I mean dancing would be great, but I can't deal with not making a living."

"What law school?"

"In Toronto."

"That's good?"

"One of the best."

"Why didn't you tell me?"

"I wasn't sure I'd get in." Doug shrugged. "I thought maybe you wouldn't like me as much if you knew. Hanging out with a future lawyer, instead of a dancer."

"You held out on me."

"I didn't think you needed to know."

"It would have been nice." I realized that Doug's easygoing manner hid a willfulness or selfishness that I hadn't seen before. Or maybe I had seen it in the way that he had been unavailable much of the time. Strange that I didn't care whether he would have been my boyfriend or my friend, either would have been fine, but leaving the city, in fact leaving the U. S. of A., wasn't OK.

"Well, you know now."

"Doug," I hesitated, then ploughed forward. "I'd like back the loan I gave you."

That startled him.

"But you just gave it to me."

"I need it back."

"Why?"

"Could be my student loans, my credit cards that are shot to hell, or maybe the big hit the IRS just put on me. They say I didn't pay taxes on all of my income from tips."

Doug whistled. "When did you find that out?"

"Right after I lent you the money. I wanted to help you out, but I wouldn't have done it if I'd known about the IRS thing. I shouldn't have done it anyway. You know I'm in as much debt as you are."

Maybe I shouldn't have said it that way, because I opened myself up to the answer that Doug gave me.

"If you know how much debt I'm in, then you know I can't pay it back. Not now, much as I'd like to."

"Doug, you shouldn't have asked me to lend you that money. You knew I didn't have it."

"So how did you get it?"

"Drew cash on my credit lines," I admitted miserably.

"You shouldn't have lent it to me, then."

"Why can't you give it back?"

"I don't have it. I had to pay for the hospital bills and clean up a lot of odds and ends before I could leave town."

"You're cleaning up everything but what you owe me."

"Iris, I will pay you back. I promise."

"When?"

"As soon as I can."

"When will that be? Aren't you going to borrow more to go to law school? Am I going to have to wait until you're Mr. Malpractice or Mr. Big Corporate Lawyer? I mean—that could be years. I need that money back now. I lost my job at The Golden Plate last night. My finances aren't in such great shape and I'm really tired of running around, working all the time, and worrying." I hadn't meant to expose myself to Doug in this way, but it did feel honest. I started crying, like the downpour of a sudden rainstorm. This burning in my eyes and wetness on my cheeks was becoming a familiar sensation.

"Iris."

Through the mist of my teary eyes, I saw that Doug had opened his arms to me. I walked around the coffee table and knelt by the couch to embrace him and be embraced. It was an awkward position, but his chest and arms around me made me feel better. For those moments he became my friend who suffered from debt as I did, not someone who owed me money and was leaving town.

When my tears stopped, I snuggled longer in Doug's arms. At last I stood, rubbed my palms over my face, and straightened my clothes.

"I'm going to pay you interest," Doug said.

I didn't even ask how much. I had the odd sense that I was leaving Doug, not that he was leaving me. I realized that he wanted to pay me back, just like I wanted to pay off all my own debts. He simply couldn't.

155

"Good luck in Toronto," I said, picking up my backpack.

"You don't have to go."

"Yeah, it's best if I do. I mean it, Doug—good luck at law school. I hope your leg heals OK."

I didn't feel much of anything for the whole bus ride back through the city. In the park, I sat on a bench and buckled my in-line skates, then fastened my knee, elbow, and wrist guards, before putting the fire-engine red helmet on my head. As soon as I was skating, I started to cry. All of a sudden I felt betrayed by Doug's leaving, by his borrowing money, by his not being able to repay me. I skated the easy paths, level, smooth blacktop that wound among the small lakes. Through my tears I could see the brightness of the day. I kept wiping my eyes so I could watch for pebbles and ruts in the walkways, but my heart was like a spring that constantly replenished my tears. I kept moving my limbs, hearing the whir of the wheels beneath my feet as my legs pumped and my arms swung side to side. I wanted the tears to vanish in this rhythmic move-ment of my body. I wanted to be as thoughtless as the afternoon, like a breeze or the swelling summer daylight. Yet I kept thinking about how Doug had applied to law school and not told me. That hurt me more than the fact that he couldn't pay back the loan. I knew he didn't have any money. But applying to law school meant that he had imagined a whole life other than the one he lived here, a life with law-school classmates for buddies and a well-paying job in his future. I wouldn't have objected to that if he had told me, if I had known that for him dance was a flirtation and not a lifelong love affair.

I must have skated an hour before I sat on a bench to rest and cool off. Beads of perspiration replaced my tears at last, and I took off my helmet and padding to enjoy the breezes moving nimbly through the trees and over the lawns. I glanced at my watch. If I wanted to go, I had time to get to dance class. Then, like something of great beauty— a mermaid, perhaps—that rises from the hidden depths of the sea to be visible for a few moments, I had a memory of my childhood. Dad and Mom had taken me to a ballet. I might have been eight or nine, and I had been dazzled by the beauty of the elegant ballerinas standing on pointes, leaping, turning. The ballet was *Swan Lake*, and I was enthralled. Afterwards I asked Dad if he thought I could be a dancer.

"You could be a wonderful dancer," he answered with a smile, bending to give me a hug.

Why had he believed in me? There was so much I didn't know. He had never danced. As far as I knew, he had very little exposure to any of the arts. He worked in a large plant about half an hour from our home. I don't know if he liked it or not, but he went every day. He was an executive, but in the middle levels, not a mover and shaker. Mom stayed home when I was little, then worked in a smaller company when I started going to school. Whatever the reasons, the next thing I knew they took me to a dance studio and often stayed to watch me while I took the classes.

Remembering all this, I felt how important their love had been to me. Death has such a strangeness, or maybe it's memory. I saw Mom and Dad in my mind but I could never touch or speak to them again. It occurred to me that separation is like a small death. As if Doug had died, in a way. Unless he wrote to me; then, for me, he would regain some of life's animation. And that my refusal to see Saidah was killing her for me. The more I thought about this, the more I thought that each person I knew changed me in some way. Saidah had become part of me. I had taken in her ideas about debt, her warmth, her loyalty to her teacher. I didn't want to let that new aspect of me die, any more than I wanted to lose my friendship with the woman whom I had met on a bench in this very same park. I had been candid with Doug, why couldn't I be candid with Saidah? Because I had shown how little I valued Saidah's advice when I gave Doug the loan. But, I argued with myself, if I let my embarrassment keep me from seeing Saidah again, then I would be showing that I placed very little value on her and on our friendship. I wanted to turn to her. I needed her help.

I let the time float by until I knew that the dance class had begun. It wasn't important that I go today. What was important was that I knew I wanted to go. Still, I felt that dealing with my debts was going to take all my energy. I wouldn't be able to dance until I had paid off the last penny. I put my padding on again and skated more slowly on the sloping curves of the walkways. The skating lessons had helped me a lot. The more I skated, the more at ease I felt and the less I worried that I would fall again and hurt myself. The park always seemed to me to be the center of the city. In fact, it was at the center, but I mean in that bigger sense. It was the place where I came to recharge—not the business district that bustled during the day, or the theater district where crowds moved from the small cafés and restaurants to the entertainment emporia. I loved the lakes and trees, the slopes and breezes, the calm of this great green circle that brought disorder to the grid of streets and established its unruly presence in spite of the encircling artifice of the city's buildings.

I stopped at the edge of the park and sat to take off my padding, helmet, and skates. In the skating, the movement, I had finally let go of thoughts of Doug. My energy had returned, and I wanted to study my numbers again and work on my spending plan. But more than that, I wanted to call Saidah. Was I such a big deal that I couldn't admit a mistake? Especially when I knew that not getting Saidah's help was a mistake in itself? I probably goofed by chasing my customers into the parking lot at The Golden Plate and tossing the pennies back at them. I certainly made a mistake to put on in-line skates when I didn't know what I was doing. It would be worse to tell Saidah I had ignored her advice about Doug, but I never told her I was perfect. It couldn't be more humiliating than the sadism of that customer at The Golden Plate, the way that Doug had let me down, or the prospect of six years of working at jobs I didn't love to pay back money that in large part I couldn't remember spending.

These thoughts, especially the prospect of seeing Saidah again, energized me. When I got to the apartment, I took a quick shower, dressed in clean clothes, and dragged the green trash bag out from under my bed. The trash bag had deflated a bit and slid out more easily than when I had first begun picking through its contents. That was because I had discarded a lot, but I didn't think I'd ever get to the bottom of it. I considered going back to my receipts from The

Golden Plate and adding up my tips again, but what good would that do? I had put that number on my tax return, but the IRS had its own way of calculating tip income. I'd have to accept that.

Instead of working the numbers directly, which I knew would lead to the conclusion that I needed a second job, I started by noting down some of my good deeds. What was the value of giving one thousand dollars to Doug to help him out? That seemed like a trick question, but I had been there for him. Even though I had given up money, I thought that helping him might have been worth five thousand dollars to me. I had told Chalma I wanted to quit, but I was still teaching the little kids for free at Little Folks Nursery. I figured that was worth at least two hundred dollars each Saturday. I had been too busy working two jobs to have a long list, but this short list bolstered my spirits.

My next step would have been to figure out what job could pay me the income that I needed to pay the IRS, the credit cards, and my student loans within a reasonable period of time. I don't know if six years is reasonable, but at least it wasn't forever. I could simply work in another restaurant. The moment I thought this, I could feel my happiness vanishing. I wouldn't make it through six years if I had to work as a receptionist and a waitress. Of course, I didn't see any alternatives, but I didn't want to feel miserable. I simply packed up the trash bag and slid everything back under the bed. Considering that my finances were out of balance, it's amazing how good it felt to push the trash bag into the darkness. Out of sight, out of mind. But that wasn't really it.

I picked up the phone and dialed.

"Hello?"

"Saidah, it's Iris."

"How was your weekend?" Saidah asked.

We chatted a little about this and that.

"Can I see you after work tomorrow?" I asked.

"Not tomorrow," she said. "I have to give a talk to the local chapter of AWED after work."

"What's that?"

"American Woman's Economic Development Corporation. It's a nonprofit organization that teaches women how to start and run their own businesses. It also helps women who are already in business with moving ahead."

"Oh."

"But Tuesday would be fine."

"Same time, same place?"

"Yes, I'll see you then."

"Thanks, Saidah."

I was going to get the help that I needed. No matter how bad my situation might seem, the idea that Saidah would help me put my mind at rest. And I hadn't been proud and refused her help just because it might be embarrassing to tell her about the loan to Doug. I hadn't thought that I was arrogant—flippant maybe, lively, beyond any doubt—but I realized that refusing to see the truth is a kind of arrogance. Denying my debts, forgetting my dreams. As if I could make my problems disappear by saying they didn't exist. Calling Saidah put an end to all that. I might not be dancing, but I would have to face the music.

CHAPTER 17

Work as Love, Work as Sharing

Home on Monday night, I spent much of the evening thinking about my career. Or my lack of a career. I had taken whatever work I could get so that I could dance, but now I wasn't dancing. I had never minded working hard, even doing work I didn't like, as long as I also got to do what I loved. It made me want to go back to the dance studio, but that wouldn't pay my debts. Why couldn't I be practical, like Doug? Go to law school, start a job that had a future? Only there was no school that I wanted to go to. I couldn't think of any job that would make me happy.

I knew that I couldn't keep on with what I had been doing. Working at Castle Advertising and The Golden Plate had burned me out. It wouldn't be hard to find another job as a waitress, but I didn't see how it could work in the long run. I'd get run down. There wouldn't be time to dance. I wouldn't see any way out, any way to have a better life. For a moment, the idea of getting an M.F.A. in dance flashed through my head. I could see myself as a teacher. Most dancers, after they get to their thirties and certainly by their forties, have to move on to another career. Since I wasn't a choreographer— and hardly anybody could make a living being a choreographer anyway, I thought that being a dance teacher might be fun. But that avenue was closed to me. The only way I could go to graduate school would be to plunge deeper into debt. Adding the years at graduate school to the years that would be needed to pay off the new debts for graduate school, I saw my life vanishing.

I couldn't find any solution. The heaviness of despair insinuated itself in my limbs and my gut. I could see how pressure could build and build until I would have to give up, take whatever jobs came my way, and struggle to at least pay my minimums every month. I tried to understand the bigger picture of which my miserable struggling was a tiny part. Who benefited from the debt that I carried? The interest that I paid? The fact that I would have to work two jobs until I was thirty if I wanted to be free? I didn't know, not in a concrete way. It was all plastic and paper, not people. There was no one to go to and say, "Let's talk about this. It isn't working. It's wrecking my life." I felt angry to crawl into bed with misery as my companion again, but what choice did I have?

Nor had my feelings changed much when I went to see Saidah after work on Tuesday. She sat on the bench, reading the newspaper the way she had been the day I first met her. I felt the muggy heat, but I welcomed being outdoors and out of the air conditioning. Saidah had worn another flowing and colorful garment, with fabric of black and gold that made me imagine lions basking in the sun and dark shadows of an African veldt.

"Hi, Saidah."

She looked up with her rich smile and I felt happy that I had decided to meet with her. After feeling that I had to avoid seeing her because of the loan to Doug, now I felt that I couldn't wait to confess. I might have been carrying a heavy stone in my backpack and wanted to unburden myself. As soon as she asked me how I was, I started.

"Not so great. For one thing, I made that loan to Doug that you told me not to. I know I shouldn't have, but I gave him a thousand dollars. Then, when I got home, there was a letter from the IRS saying that I owed them for back taxes." I was crying already and Saidah put her hand on my arm to comfort me. Speaking released the pressure I had been feeling and the words rushed out of me. "Doug's leaving for Toronto to go to law school. He's not going to dance anymore. I lost my job at The Golden Plate. Without my tips, I'm going further into debt every day."

Saidah shook her head when I had finally finished.

"Iris, I didn't say that you shouldn't lend money to Doug."

"You didn't?" I was shocked, because I was sure she said not to.

"I asked you if you could afford to. You had to make the decision."

"But," I didn't understand her, "you knew I couldn't."

"I had an opinion, but it's no use telling someone else what to do. If you're going to handle this debt issue, you have to take responsibility. You make the decisions, good ones and bad ones. After you make them, you have to stand behind them. Why do you think it was wrong to lend the money to Doug?"

"Because I'm already in debt."

"Then you know."

"Isn't that what you think, too?"

"It's what you think." Saidah smiled at me. "Stay with that. I want to hear about the IRS."

I explained to her about the letter, the underreported tip income, and how adding the penalties to the extra taxes brought the amount I owed the IRS to more than four thousand dollars.

"What have you done about that?"

I felt embarrassed to tell her, but I was seeing her because I wanted to be honest.

"Nothing."

Saidah looked perplexed. "You must have done something."

I shook my head. "I haven't got the money, but I was hoping maybe I could pay down a credit card enough so that I could pay off the IRS. Of course, I can't do that now that I'm not working two jobs."

"You didn't write back to the IRS?"

"No."

"But you kept the letter?"

"Yes." I started to say where, but then stopped.

"What?" Saidah encouraged me to go on.

"I put it in the plastic bag under my bed where I keep all my tax stuff, banking, credit card bills."

"The stuff you don't like to look at."

"But I have been."

"How did you figure the tip income that you reported?" she asked me.

"Every night I kept the tips separate and counted them when I got home. Then I wrote the amount on a piece of paper and stuffed it in a brown bag."

"And the brown bag went in the plastic bag under the bed?"

It sounded ridiculous, but I couldn't deny it. "Yes," I answered in a small voice.

"Did you pay estimated taxes?"

"Yes." I had done that every three months, because I knew I'd get in trouble if I didn't.

"How did you add up the amount of tips that you put on your tax return?"

"I got out the brown bag and added all the slips."

"And you had a slip for every night that you worked at the restaurant?"

"Right."

"With dates?"

"Yes."

"Iris, you've got to contact the IRS."

"But they figured it out a different way."

"They're guessing, estimating, but you actually have records. You know the exact amount."

"Don't I need a lawyer?" I knew I couldn't afford a lawyer. By the time the lawyer got done with me, I'd probably wish I'd paid the IRS.

"Maybe it would be best with a lawyer, but you don't have to. You write back to them and tell them you want a meeting. Take your slips and whatever you've got that shows how you tallied up the tips. That's what you've got to do."

"You are telling me what to do." I was kidding, but the chance that I didn't owe the IRS gave me the thrill of hope.

"You bet I am!" Saidah answered. "Now tell me about the restaurant."

I related the whole sad story, from feeling burned out and irritable to chasing Mr. Big Tipper into the parking lot and hurling his pennies back in his face.

"It's been said many times," Saidah responded when I had finished, "that if you love what you do, you'll earn a living."

"I don't love waitressing."

"What about the day job?"

I shook my head. "Do what you love and the money will follow. I've heard that, too, but I tried to dance and didn't make any money."

"I look at it a bit differently," Saidah said. "I believe that careers should be based on the Golden Rule."

"Do unto others as you would have them do unto you?"

"Yes." She nodded emphatically. "By that I mean that to work is to think of yourself in relationship to others. Work is a form of service, a way of serving others as they serve us. Work is an important way that we join in community and share. Money is simply a tool of this sharing, but to focus on the money is to lose the more important image of the sharing."

"But…" I certainly had never looked at work this way, and I couldn't quickly find words to express my doubts about Saidah's viewpoint.

"So I believe that every form of work is good and should be valued," Saidah went on, "from the least prestigious to the most exalted, from the temp to the CEO. If we understand that by giving our labor we are helping nourish each other and build the community, then we can feel that all work has value."

"What about being a receptionist or a waitress? Who loves to do that?"

"If you understand that you are part of the community when you do that work, that you are sharing your energies with the energies of others, why wouldn't you love your work? It's a form of relating and giving to others. Don't you love to give and share?"

Her idea flickered in my mind, but dimly.

"What about dancing?" I asked. "I love to dance."

"To share is an honor. It's not about the egotism that our consumer culture encourages. It's not about being the best dressed, owning the neatest car, or living in the biggest house. It's not about being a rock star or a rich entrepreneur. It's about seeing the value of everyone's contribution and respecting each person and what he or she gives. If it's hard to accept, because we've been taught to value money and individual fame, then it's all the more important lesson to learn. There is value in whatever you do. If you want to do something that takes years of training, then you'll have to learn patience. If you're in the arts, you'll have to accept that not everyone succeeds by performing. Some people succeed because they learn from failure and become wise. Others succeed because they learn to value what they do apart from whether it matches their dreams. There can't be only one way to share, but many ways."

"Should I try to get back my job at The Golden Plate?" I didn't understand what Saidah meant, although I would give it a lot of thought later.

"I don't mean that. You're telling me that you can't work that much. I'm not sure if that's true, but I do understand one thing."

"What's that?"

"You need to do what you love."

"But…"

"Maybe not as your job, not now, but you can't live if your deepest feelings go unexpressed. You can't live if your entire life is devoted to earning money to pay off debts. You have to embrace what gives you joy. A lot of people fear that, or don't know what would give them joy. Why aren't you going to your dance classes?"

I was about to answer, then didn't.

"If you don't make space and time in your life for what you love, then everything else will lose its luster and feel lifeless. We have to find joy in each day. To live for the time five or six years from now when all your debts are paid is like a living death. You have to balance the repayment of debt with the joy of life. It's the joy that gives you the energy to pay the debt, that makes it possible for you to see being a receptionist, a waitress, or a flight attendant as a form of service and a gift of love. All work has honor. Every person has the capacity for joy." Saidah was confirming her words with emphatic gestures of her hands, like a conductor swinging a baton. Then her mood shifted and she looked wistful.

"What is it?"

"I was thinking about Elizabeth." Saidah breathed deeply and let go a long exhalation. "Actually, I was thinking how Elizabeth was there for me. I feel like I was gone too long. I let you down."

"No, you didn't," I shook my head.

"I'm going to do something about it today," she said. "But before that, I wanted to tell you a story. Are you ready?"

"Sure." I wondered what she was planning to do today. She was being a little mysterious.

"Before I start, I wanted to say one other thing. If what you love requires that you spend money, then you have to include that as an expense in your spending plan. If everything you earn is simply going to pay off debt, it's no wonder you'd get burned out. In your case, I think you need to put dance classes as a spending category. You have to feel that you're taking care of yourself."

"But it will take longer to pay off my debt that way," I protested.

"So be it, but you'll be living with joy."

My thoughts kept returning to the possibility that I didn't owe money to the IRS. As soon as I got home, I intended to write them— or it, whatever you call the IRS—a letter.

"What's the story about?"

"Having people to rely on. It's a folk tale from Afghanistan. Once upon a time," Saidah lowered her voice to intone those magic words, "there were two brothers who lived in such poverty that they bare- ly had enough to eat. To better their lives, they decided that the older brother would seek work elsewhere and send his wages home to the younger brother. So the older brother left home and walked a long distance until he came to a prosperous farm where the owner offered him a job, but with certain unusual conditions. If the boy lost his temper, the boy would have to pay the farmer fifty pieces of gold. And if the farmer lost his temper, he would pay the boy one hundred pieces of gold."

I was listening intently as Saidah wove the fabric of this peculiar bargain.

"The boy protested that he didn't have fifty pieces of gold to pay if he lost his temper. 'In that event,' the farmer said, 'you will have to work for me for seven years without receiving any wages.' The boy agreed to this because he was so desperate for work. Then the farmer made him work as long as there was light, including not just sunlight but moonlight as well, so that at last the boy lost his temper and cursed the farmer for his inhumane treatment."

"Owing fifty pieces of gold or seven years of labor, the boy returned home and told his younger brother how he had been cheated by the farmer. The younger brother sought out the farmer and accepted the same proposal, except that if he could not pay he would work fourteen years for the farmer. But this brother, knowing the farmer's tricks, did everything very slowly until the farmer at last lost his temper and had to pay the brother one hundred pieces of gold. The brother then paid off the fifty pieces of gold for his older brother's freedom, and went home with fifty pieces of gold for his family and a joyous heart."

"What happened to the farmer?" I asked.

"When he realized how unsuccessful his trickery had been, he decided to offer better working conditions. His workers became much happier and got a lot more work done. Over time, he gained a reputation as a generous employer and always had a lot of people eager to work for him."

"But who would agree to a bargain like that? To work seven years if you lost your temper? Or fourteen years?"

"It's involuntary servitude, but you and I both agreed to work for years to pay off our debts. How many years do you have left?"

"Five or six," I said, uncertain about the IRS but uncomfortably aware of the parallel she made between the story and my own situation.

"I finished paying my debts off a long time ago, but it was hard and took years. What do you think made it easier for me?"

I said what came first to my mind. "Having Elizabeth as a friend."

"You're right." Saidah's eyes moistened. "That was a big part of it. For me, that is the point of the story. It isn't about someone who is in poverty and alone in the world. It's about two brothers. The older brother goes into the world to help the family. He intends to give what he earns to the younger brother. They have the support that comes from love, from shared concerns."

All I could think about as Saidah spoke was how little the story applied to me. I had no brother, because I had no family. In that instant I knew, if I ever had money, that I would seek out my birth mother. Wherever in the world she might be, I would pay for whatever help I might need to find her and any blood family I might have left. I would hire a private investigator and travel on whatever obscure journeys would be necessary to do this. We might meet as strangers, but love has the power to overcome every obstacle. As soon as I had money, I would do it.

"Yes," I replied to Saidah after a hesitation filled with the thought of meeting people whose golden skin and angular faces would resemble my own.

"Twice I've mentioned to you the group of debtors who meet to give each other support."

"I know."

"This is the third time I'm mentioning it."

I couldn't help but smile. "I hear you."

"Do you?" Saidah spoke gently, but she challenged me. "Then why haven't you gone?"

I shrugged. "I don't know."

But I did know. I hadn't gone because I felt ashamed to be in debt. It marked me as a failure. More than that, I didn't want to admit that I was in debt. To admit that to others would be to surrender the image that I had of myself as fun-loving, happy, and spontaneous. I would have to see myself as deficient. That deficit would swallow me up, like Jonah into the belly of the whale, and I would emerge pallid, sad, and introverted. It would be like the emperor admitting that he wore no clothes, embarrassing and unthinkable.

"I'm working on my debt by myself," I finally replied, "and I have your help. Why shouldn't that be enough?"

"I understand," she nodded and sighed. "I didn't want to go myself. I thought that it would make my life worse. I was living off my credit cards. That's how I experienced it. I didn't have money because I worked. I had money because I had some more left on credit lines where I could borrow. I figured if I went to a group like that and had to admit that I was abusing the cards—I mean that I was abusing myself by the way that I used the cards—that I would have to stop using them. But how could I stop using them and live? What would I use for money? Miserable as I was with the debt, I figured my life would be a lot worse if I didn't have the cards. I was scared, and I didn't know how much I owed or how much I was paying in interest. So I understand when you say you don't want to go. It's like a whole new life, up ahead, kind of scary and out of reach. You know how you make it work now, even if it really isn't working, but you don't have any idea how to make it work some other way."

"And why can't I do it by myself?" I repeated my question.

"Because you need the other people. I'm speaking from experience. You gain so much by hearing their stories. You realize a lot of people have gone through what you're going through. You aren't by yourself. Many of the people have stopped running up debts, some of them have even been out of debt for years."

"Why do they keep going to the meetings?"

Saidah paused to consider her reply. "Sometimes I think of debt like an object that could be reflected in a mirror. But what you see when you look in the mirror isn't debt, but wealth. Debt and wealth aren't true opposites, but more like sister and brother. At different times in our lives we may have more of one and less of the other, or we may have a lot or very little of both. But once you've found a spiritual path that lessens debt, you may want to continue on that path even after the debt is gone. That's why people, like me for example, keep going to those meetings. It keeps me clear in my purpose."

I frowned. It sounded good, but I had the feeling that I'd go to some meeting and get brainwashed and have to give up what I liked and live a grey life without any pleasures. Not that I was having a lot of fun anyway, but to have less struck me as unbearable.

Saidah saw my indecision.

"You remember the story about the hunter and the trickster god?

How everybody ate the lion and ended up with the debt that the elders feared and wanted to get rid of?"

"Yeah."

"Debt can isolate us or it can join us together. If we feel bad about ourselves because of the debt, then we're isolated and the debt becomes harder to overcome. But if we see that everybody has debt, even debts that don't involve money, then we feel the freedom to join with others to face our money debts. There is strength in numbers. I mean that in more ways than one. Fellowship is a key to making your life bearable while you're in debt and helping you move out of debt. That's what these meetings offer—fellowship."

I couldn't quite give in. I understood that she wanted the best for me. She was trying to help me, but part of me held back.

"Make me a promise." Saidah smiled at me. She could see she wasn't getting through and was trying another tack.

"To go to the meeting?"

"No, you have to want to go to the meeting. And I'm not going to mention it again. If you want to go, you let me know. I want you to rent a video and watch one of my favorite movies."

"Which one?"

"*It's a Wonderful Life.* Have you seen it?"

I shook my head. "But I've heard about it."

"Definitely a golden oldie. I especially love the scene in the bank when the people all come at once for their money. Think about fellowship and see that movie. Will you do that?"

"Sure." I felt relieved that I wouldn't have to go to that group.

"And write the IRS. It's important."

"I will. Thanks, Saidah."

We chatted a little more and I paid her ten dollars for the consultation. It felt a bit strange to pay her, because I liked her so much and she obviously wasn't doing it for the money. But it did make sense to pay for what I valued. I had a lot to think about. Saidah knew how to stir me up. As I started for home, I thought that I would stop by the video store on the way home. I liked Jimmy Stewart and I could certainly use some entertainment.

CHAPTER 18

Dear IRS

stopped at the video store, but *It's a Wonderful Life* had been checked out. To be truthful, I was relieved. Once I saw the movie, whatever I thought of it, I would have to make a decision about the group that Saidah kept talking up to me. I told the clerk that I'd come back the next day after work and to save it for me if it came in. First thing I did when I got home was to reach under my bed, pull out the green trash bag, and find the letter from the IRS.

One of the hard parts of the letter to the IRS was the salutation. What do you call the IRS? "Dear Sir" sounded sexist; "Dear Sir/Madam," hopelessly out of date; "Dear Sir/Ms.," like a comment on the ambiguity of the woman's marital status, etc. I finally settled on:

> Dear IRS:
>
> I am writing about your recent letter to me, Reference TE31248749. I have kept receipts of all of my tip income and would like to meet with you to show you my receipts. These receipts add up to what I claimed on my tax return. I don't know how you figured out the higher amount, but whatever revenues The Golden Plate may have, I know how much I actually received in tips. Also, my receipts are

my permanent, accurate, and complete records. I am ready to meet with you at your convenience. I look forward to hearing from you.

The part about "permanent, accurate, and complete records" I put in because Saidah told me to. It seemed like a bold way to describe my brown paper bag filled with scribbling on scraps of paper. I also thought the letter rambled a bit and repeated itself. It didn't feel incisive, but I figured I'd type it at the office the next day and send it out. I didn't think I could make it any better, by which, I guess, I meant more persuasive. Also, when I thought about actually going to the IRS offices, I felt clammy and had goose bumps all over, but it would be worth it if I could get out of that debt.

Next I covered my bed with the receipts. I had added them up, but I'd never put them in any order. I arranged them by date, then copied each amount until I had four pages showing my tips in chronological order. Then I added it up again and came out with almost the same amount that I had shown on my tax return. I decided to send copies of these pages along with my letter to the IRS, and added another sentence, "Please find enclosed my list of dates and amounts to confirm the tips that I reported on my income tax return."

My meeting with Saidah had given me a lot of thoughts. For example, the group that she wanted me to go to. If I knew that I resisted going from shame and a sense that I would be admitting failure, why couldn't I overcome these feelings? Saidah said I would meet people with all kinds of debt issues. Some would be where I was, others would have paid off their debts a long time ago. She had said that I had to do things that gave me pleasure. I couldn't devote all my time to working to pay off the debt. Why wasn't I going to dance class? My leotards and tights were neatly folded in the bureau drawer. All I had to do was take out a set and get myself over to the studio. Thinking this, I felt a pang of loneliness for my dancing friends. I was friendly with so many people at the studio. I had missed seeing them all these months.

The loneliness intensified as I thought of my decision to seek out my birth family. If only Jim and Mary had given me that information…I guess they must have been afraid, but of what? That I would replace my adoptive parents with the birth parents who had chosen not to raise me? Or that I would learn something that would make me unhappy? Who could know? But my determination to find out remained.

I wondered whether I had to wait until I had money to find my birth family. So many things seemed to require money, but when I looked more closely at them, what they really required was determination. With money, I thought, I could hire a private investigator. In some way that I couldn't describe, he—I assumed it would be a guy—could open the secrets surrounding my adoption. Maybe he would be able to find the agency that had handled the adoption or the court where the adoption had been finalized. Maybe my blood could be tested and my DNA would reveal the region in which people like myself lived. Then the researcher could speak to the consulate for that country and find out which agencies might have placed me. I imagined my journey to that exotic place, my fruitless searching until some chance encounter would bring me home. Then my family would have an enormous gathering, a feast with parents, brothers and sisters, aunts and uncles, nieces and nephews, and cousins whom I had never known.

I put my receipts in two neat stacks and wrapped a rubber band around each stack. Then I returned the receipts and the IRS letter to the brown paper bag and put that wrinkled bag into the plastic trash bag, which I slipped back under the bed like a file drawer. I kept the yellow notepad with my financial projections, the draft of my letter to the IRS, and my newly created ledger. And I had the thought that I should call my parents' lawyer the next day. He had handled their wills and might know something about the adoption. I noticed that curious way in which decisions took shape for me. Due to Saidah's talking about having joy each day, I'd go to a dance class soon. Again because of Saidah, I would keep going back to the video store until I rented *It's a Wonderful Life*. I had liked the books that she recommended to me, so I'd probably enjoy this movie, too. The letter to the IRS was also prompted by Saidah, so I could see the big influence she had on me. I wished everybody could have a friend like her. And I would call or write my parents' lawyer. It was hard to say where that idea came from, but it had something to do with cleaning up my debts. When I was out of debt, I would be able to pay for the search for my birth family and my true identity. Maybe I could find a way to begin sooner.

Before getting into bed, I studied the yellow notepad with my spending plan. Here I was, in the red, but I knew that I had to add dance classes for myself. Only if my plan included joy for me could it possibly work. I added twenty dollars per week for dance classes. That would be two classes each week, a bare minimum considering my desire and dream of dancing professionally. I made a funny—not funny, strange—mistake when I thought how much these classes would cost. Three thousand dollars came into my mind, but when I multiplied twenty dollars times fifty-two weeks the total was only one thousand and forty dollars.

Through this mistake I understood the enormous role that fear played in terms of money. More, the role fear played in relation to what I actually did. To spend three thousand dollars on dance lessons for myself frightened me when I had debts that would take years to pay off. Better to live without pleasure in the hope that I would be debt-free sooner. But that wasn't the reality, the cost for dance classes would be closer to one thousand dollars than three thousand. I couldn't wait to begin my dance career. I couldn't live a daily life that had no pleasures in it. I had to balance my need for joy against the fear that could overtake me so easily. The spending plan offered me a practical way. I could provide for myself, but not by out-of-control spending with my credit cards.

I carefully marked down the weekly, monthly, and yearly amount for my dance classes on the yellow sheet. It might slow down my getting out of debt, but maybe it wouldn't. So much seemed paradoxical to me. Owing the IRS so much money, I didn't think I should be adding any expenditures to my spending plan. But spending money on dance might give me more energy, more life. It might lead me on an unknown path that would help me pay my debts more quickly. When I finished writing the dance classes into my spending plan, I vanished in the soothing forgetfulness of sleep.

The next morning I took the first lull in phone calls to start the letter to the IRS. I was interrupted a few times, and a little worried that somebody might catch me doing personal chores on office time, but by the midmorning coffee break I was able to seal the cover letter and a photocopy of the supporting ledger into an envelope addressed to the IRS. One of the good things about being a receptionist is that you appear to have no privacy, but really you have a lot. Most of the time nobody's in the waiting room or, if anyone is, they're from some other company and don't know what you should or shouldn't be doing. Also, I was mainly supposed to answer the phones and give a pleasant greeting to visitors, and no one complained as long as I took care of this.

By the middle of the afternoon I finished a short letter to Caleb Cromwell, Attorney-at-Law. Caleb had been my parents' lawyer and I had gotten to know him a bit when he handled my Dad's estate. Caleb drove a Rolls-Royce and had that upper-crusty polished distant feeling that made me want to call him patrician, like a senator in ancient Rome. He had a big frame, big handsome features, silver hair, and the air of someone put upon by life's having details instead of great vistas and noble victories. What finally made me like him, though, was that he cared and wanted to do the right thing, so after my fear of him wore off I could see why my mom and dad had chosen him for their lawyer. I told him I had been thinking a lot about my birth family and asked if he knew anything that would help me find them. I didn't know if he had any information about my adoption or, if he did, whether he would share it with me. But because I'd gotten to know him a little bit, I trusted him to do the right thing. When I dropped the letter in the mailbox, I felt relieved that I had taken a step, even if I couldn't know what the result would be.

On the sidewalk, I found myself enjoying moving easily through the crowds coming home from work. One of my dance teachers called it a sixth sense—to know where all the dancers are, every moment, even if they're behind you. The more you dance the more—I think—you can enjoy the feeling of your body moving in space, moving among the bodies of other people who may be dancing or just be pedestrians rushing this way and that on the sidewalks. I found my feet wanting to move in little patterns and I restrained myself from sweeping forward and spinning as if the city were a set and I were dancing with somebody like Fred Astaire or John Travolta.

Next stop was the video store where the clerk had stashed *It's a Wonderful Life* under the counter.

"Thanks for holding it for me."

"You've never seen it?"

"No."

"It's a great movie," he said. "My wife and I always watch it at Christmas and cry."

"That's something to look forward to," I kidded.

"It's a treat. Enjoy."

I felt like dancing all the way home. To be happy like that—I had forgotten the feeling. It must have been taking action about the IRS and the adoption. I might be in debt all the time, and be miserable about it, but if I lived each moment to the fullest I could still experience joy. I came up the stairwell with a rush of energy and burst into the apartment.

"That's impossible." Tina was talking in a loud voice to Rachel.

"I swear it's true," Rachel replied.

"Hey," I greeted them as I came into the living room. "What are you talking about?"

"It couldn't be," Tina continued the conversation without cluing me in.

"This guy said he knew," Rachel parried again, "and why would he lie to me?"

"Why do all guys lie?" I asked cheerfully, pushing my way in even though I didn't know what they were talking about.

"Oh, give me a break." Rachel rolled her eyes. Dark-haired and petite, she made a sharp contrast to Tina who was blond and taller, about my height. "He said it happened to a friend of his."

"My dad would know about stuff like that. Banks don't do it."

"Do what?"

"Rachel says banks program ATMs to give people an extra twenty dollars every once in a while."

"It's how banks get people hooked on ATMs," Rachel said, "so they won't use tellers any more."

"This guy at the dance studio told her," Tina said dryly.

"The banks save a lot of money because they don't need as many tellers. That's why it's worth it."

"They don't need as many tellers because of the ATMs," Tina argued. "They don't have to make the ATMs into slot machines."

"I didn't say slot machines. I said every once in a while."

Rachel's eyes were shining and I could see the idea appealed to her a lot.

"If they're not doing it, maybe they should be," I said. "It would be cheap advertising for the banks."

Tina shook her head. "When they advertise, they advertise. They don't secretly give away money."

"They secretly take our money with all their fees. If they secretly gave some of it back, that would only be fair." To show my expertise in advertising based on my months as a receptionist at the agency, I continued, "And advertising isn't always sensible. What if they gave airline miles for using ATMs? They use airline miles for everything else—like credit cards—and that's a kind of advertising and nobody says that's impossible."

"So giving twenty-dollar bills is like giving airline miles?" Tina demanded.

Rachel and I nodded.

"You're impossible," Tina shook her head, but we were all in high spirits.

"Want to watch a movie later?" I asked.

"What did you get?" Rachel asked.

"*It's a Wonderful Life.*"

"I've seen it," Tina said. "It's on every Christmas."

"I wouldn't mind seeing it again," Rachel offered.

Tina shrugged. "Sure."

"OK, great."

"So did it happen to the guy at the dance studio?" Tina demanded.

"No, to a friend of his."

"Was he there?"

"No."

"So you believe him and he believes his friend. He doesn't know for a fact."

"It sounded plausible to me," Rachel responded.

I started the film and we settled in on Rachel's convertible couch.

To watch *It's a Wonderful Life* struck me as ironic. I expected it to be sentimental and unconcerned with the troubling realities of my life. I wished that happiness didn't depend so much on the events and people around me. If only each of us had something inside like a sun that gave off happiness like light. What could a movie say about credit cards, friendship, or love?

CHAPTER 19

It's a Wonderful Life

Right from the start, the movie engrossed me. Jimmy Stewart plays a bright young man named George Bailey who yearns to leave the small town where he grew up and make his mark on the world. George's father runs a Building and Loan Company that gives loans to ordinary people to better their lives and competes with the evil banker Potter, who is in a wheelchair and uses money to get people in his power. When George's father dies, Potter wants to close down the Building and Loan, but George persuades the directors to keep it going. The directors' only condition is that George run the business. He agrees in spite of his desire to leave Bedford Falls, because he wants to continue his father's good work for the townspeople.

George falls in love with a wonderful woman and plans to travel for his honeymoon, but Potter causes a run on the Building and Loan, and people rush to withdraw their money. George knows he has to keep the doors of the Building and Loan open until 6 P.M., but all the money he has is the few thousand dollars that he has saved for his honeymoon. When he pleads with the people crowded in the Building and Loan not to withdraw their money, to remember that the money each person deposited helped someone else in the community to borrow to build a home or start a small business, I had tears in my eyes. I saw what a good bank could do for a community, moving the excess from one person to help another who would pay back in time and so help more people. The people overcame their fear and withdrew what they needed instead of taking all of their deposits. At 6 P.M. George had only a few dollars left and knew he couldn't go on his honeymoon, but I felt as thrilled as he did that the Building and Loan had survived.

Later, the banker Potter steals eight thousand dollars from the Building and Loan, which creates a crisis in which the Building and Loan could be forced to close and George could be accused of being a thief and face criminal charges. George considers suicide, but an angel named Clarence is sent from Heaven to save him. Clarence shows George what would have happened if George had never lived and the Building and Loan had closed with his father's death. Bedford Falls is transformed into a nightmarish town called Pottersville. At last George decides not to kill himself and is overjoyed to return to his loving wife and family. The townspeople have heard of the missing eight thousand dollars and take up a collection that saves the Building and Loan. The movie has a happy ending, even though Potter is never punished for stealing the eight thousand dollars.

The movie touched me, but it had an even stronger impact on Tina. Maybe because her dad made lots of money in banking, like Potter, she kept uncharacteristically silent when the movie ended. Later Tina sat on the end of her bed and looked over at me.

"I realized something tonight," she said. "I'm living a fake life. Pretending to be a poverty-stricken dancer."

"Aren't you?"

"Look at my wardrobe. If I feel like buying something, I use my plastic. If I want to eat out, it's plastic to the rescue. My life is plastic."

"But if you're paying for it…"

"I'm not," she snapped. "How could I? My Dad's been picking up my credit card bills. The more he pays, the more I spend. It's like I want to be in debt."

"I didn't know he was paying."

"He wasn't at first. He kept offering and I kept saying no. But when it looked like my credit rating would be ruined, I finally gave in."

"What if you stopped using your cards?"

"I don't want to."

She said this sadly, not willfully.

"Can I help in any way?" I didn't have any solutions, and I couldn't think of anything better to say.

Tina shook her head. "I need to help myself."

I thought of introducing Tina to Saidah, and had the words on my lips when Tina continued.

"I could start by being honest with myself. This life isn't for me. I'm not made for scrimping and sacrificing. I was raised rich and taught to consume—great clothes, travel to the ends of the earth. It's amazing how the ends of the earth always have luxury hotels. The best schools—private schools, where you meet the right kind of people. Pretentious designer-name brands for everything. That's my life. That's who I am."

"Yeah, you're like everybody else," I said.

She smiled, but she wasn't the same Tina who had told her banker dad to take a long walk on a short pier. "Except that I'm used to having more. It's about excess. More dresses than you can wear. More trips than you can take. More parties than you can go to. More money than you can spend, but you spend it anyway. Bigger credit lines, bigger credit card bills. It spins around and around. You don't know where it started—you, meaning me. Then, it's like a vision, a flash, and suddenly you see the truth. That I'm nobody without money. And what's worse, it doesn't bother me. I don't think I should be somebody else, some saint who heals the sick and loves animals and wears rags and eats scraps from handouts. I want to have a closet full of clothes. In fact, I don't want to share a closet anymore. I want to go to fancy restaurants and charity fund-raisers for rich people wearing tuxes and evening gowns. I want to charter a yacht for vacations with my socialite friends and cruise the islands of the Caribbean or Mediterranean. I don't want to be ordinary. I don't want to be smothered by some job I hate so I can dance. I want better than that, and I want it easier."

As I listened to Tina, I realized that what she said was true for her. Maybe exaggerated, but it was how she felt. I wanted to protest, or suggest that she meet Saidah, but I would have been imposing my vision of who I wanted her to be on her own vision of herself.

"What are you going to do?" I asked.

"I'm going to business school in the fall. It's late, but my dad can pull some strings and get me in. When I come out, I'm going to make a career for myself where I earn a lot of money. That's what I want, so I can pay my own way. I want to pay my own way."

She was deserting me the way Doug had. In one way I couldn't believe it, but in another way it made a lot of sense. I couldn't understand how anybody would give up dance, but I could see that Tina understood her life and her needs a lot better than I did. In fact, I had given up dancing for no reason at all except maybe discouragement. At least Tina had a reason. But I felt she was starting up a slippery slope, like that guy who got punished by the gods and had to keep pushing a boulder up a hill but could never get to the top before the boulder rolled back down. Tina's view of things seemed wrong to me. Making a lot of money wouldn't be any help if she couldn't control her spending. At least she would be on her own, paying her own way, and not dependent on her Dad.

"I'm going to miss you Tina, if you go."

"I'll miss you, too," Tina said.

We talked a little more and turned out the lights, but I couldn't stop thinking. First Doug, now Tina. Each one going back to school to get ready for a lucrative career. Should I be like them? But I had no desire to go back to school. My life wasn't about being like or unlike them. I had to be me. It sounded trite, but there it was. Who could know what would make for happiness? A graduate degree? A big salary? My mind kept coming back to the movie. George Bailey hadn't gotten what he wanted—to be a big man in the world beyond Bedford Falls. In that way, it hadn't been a wonderful life. But what the angel made him realize was that George's expectations and dreams had missed the obvious. He had *made* a wonderful life, and not just for himself but for his family and the townspeople, too. He had done it with innumerable small acts, sticking in the town of Bedford Falls and day after day playing his role as a banker for the people and a good husband and father for his family. All at once I wondered whether small acts might be more important than great ones. I wouldn't be a banker or a lawyer, but if I did my utmost to be caring and loving, might I not change the world a little bit?

Sure, it was a sentimental movie, but isn't sentiment a big part of life? I kept seeing those salt-of-the-earth people in the Building and Loan, George pleading with them not to take all their money and destroy their own bank, and the fear and worry on their faces. The first man withdrew everything, but the next took less, and so on and so on. People caring for each other. Not like a line at an ATM owned by a bank that makes its money off cheap-shot fees and interest on credit cards. The Building and Loan had been about people who knew each other and felt a common loyalty to help each other and their town. Each of those people had to trust.

That word arrested my thoughts. When those people who had worked so hard for their money left it on deposit despite their fears, they trusted in George Bailey and in each other. When George Bailey chose life over death, he trusted in the goodness of his own life, his family, and his town. In that moment of trust, no one could know the future, the outcome, whether happiness lay ahead or disaster. If each person had taken his or her money, then Bedford Falls would have become Pottersville. Trust allowed something more, something much bigger to affect the outcome. An angel, like Clarence, might come down from Heaven, or the townspeople might take up a collection for George and save the Building and Loan. But no one could know for certain, that was the risk of trusting. If George committed suicide, he controlled his destiny; if he trusted in life, then he might face ruin or joy.

Had my thoughts only been about the movie, it would have been so much easier. But thinking about the movie I was really thinking about myself. I felt cut off, the way those people who withdrew all their money must have felt cut off from the shared risk and potential of the Building and Loan. I had been trying to go it alone, because it felt safer. I didn't want to show people the ways in which I felt myself a failure. Each time Saidah spoke to me about the group of people in debt, I thought of them as losers. Of course, that meant I was a loser, too. I didn't want to go, but I could feel how I needed what had been such a help and comfort to the townspeople in the movie. I needed other people. I needed to trust, because I couldn't see a way out by myself. I had already tried to solve my debt problem alone, and that effort had ended with my flinging the pennies in the parking lot of The Golden Plate. Something bigger than I am, maybe something like the angel Clarence, had to lift me up. I felt humbled and agitated to think of this group of strangers that I would face, but I was ready.

I didn't sleep too well, and the first thing I did at work the next morning was to call Saidah.

"I'm ready to go."

"Slow down, where are we going?"

"To that group."

I told her about watching *It's a Wonderful Life* and how a beautiful image of sharing shaped itself in my mind and made me see the value of community.

"Let me check the schedule." There was a pause, then Saidah came back on the line. "You're in luck. There's a meeting after work in the basement of St. Gregory's. Want to meet me there?"

I did and didn't want to meet her there, but I wasn't turning back now.

"Yes," I answered.

"Can you get there by six?"

"Sure."

"See you then."

The day moved slowly at Castle Advertising. I'm not sure why some days hardly anybody called or came by the office. It must have been chance, the happenstance of scheduling and who was traveling to see clients. My mind wandered from place to place, stopped for a moment on the meeting with Saidah and the group of debtors, and then moved on to Tina's leaving the apartment. What would Rachel and I do about the rent? Then for a while my head would be filled with numbers. What the groceries cost, the electricity, the gas, hair styling, clothes I couldn't live without, like new black slacks when the old ones wore out, how much it would add to my expenses to start dance classes again. The numbers made me feel like a juggler who is always dropping a ball or two. No matter how many numbers I could

186

keep up in the air, I couldn't wrap my head around all of them. I needed paper for that.

I wondered if I should be hunting for a second job. Maybe I'd waitress two nights a week instead of four, bring in some extra income, and hold onto my sanity. If I chose Friday and Saturday, I'd make good tip income. That brought my thoughts to the IRS. It was hard to imagine a person working for the IRS. That my letter would go to a person who would make some decision about what the IRS called my tax deficiency. I could understand being deficient in all sorts of things, but to be deficient in taxes would have seemed funny except that it wasn't. If only there were a face that I knew, my friendly IRS agent. But my friendly IRS agent had gone the way of my friendly banker, vanished into an ATM, a computer, or maybe the Internet. I'd probably get another computer-generated letter, and it was beyond me to imagine what it might say.

Toward the end of the afternoon, when I was feeling a bit queasy thinking about the debtors' meeting, my nebulous drifting was interrupted by a call from Chalma.

"I want you to know I'm talking to them," Chalma said.

"Thanks." It was nice that Chalma kept me in the loop, but I couldn't imagine that the school would come up with any money, much less enough to make a difference in my life.

"I should have an answer by Saturday, when you come to teach."

"Great." I sounded enthusiastic for Chalma. They would probably offer me ten or twenty dollars an hour, if anything. Since I only taught for one hour, that wouldn't help me very much, especially considering how long it took me to get there and back. I multiplied ten and twenty dollars by fifty-two weeks and realized how small amounts do add up over a year. Five hundred or a thousand dollars—not a huge amount, but certainly something, enough to let me keep teaching the little kids, which I definitely wanted to do. That had amazed me about all my numbers, how small amounts add up in the course of fifty-two weeks.

"Taken any dance classes?" Chalma asked.

"Not yet, but I'm planning to."

"Good."

We talked a bit more about dance, then Chalma promised again to have an answer on Saturday, and we hung up. The end-of-the-day flow of people leaving the office began. The little clock on my desk showed that five o'clock had come and gone, but I sat immobilized.

"Good night, Iris."

"Good night."

"Have a good evening."

"You, too."

I knew so many people at the agency. Even casual friends were friends, and I liked the familiar faces passing by and saying "Take it easy," or "See you tomorrow." It was so ordinary that it became reassuring. Unlike the meeting at St. Gregory's that I was heading for. Filled with people I didn't know, strangers, losers as unable to handle their debts as I was unable to handle my own. Would there be a few people or a crowd? What would happen? My workday had ended, but I felt glued to my chair. Wasn't the unknown supposed to be exciting? Did the great explorers fear the unfamiliar? The craving to know the globe, to circle it, to reach the poles. The body of a famous man frozen solid in his hut, his last noble words on a slip of paper, and his supplies only a few miles away. A small mistake in navigation cost him his life in that white world. How romantic, to live balancing on the edge of life and death! Only I wasn't talking about discovering the North or South Pole. I was talking about a room full of unfamiliar people. All that I knew I would have in common with them was debt. "Owe no debt to anyone, except the debt to love." Saints could see the big picture, and they didn't have credit cards when Jesus drove the money changers from the Temple and Paul preached in Asia Minor. At last the moving hands of the little clock forced me to ask myself: What have I got to lose? I didn't want to answer that question. I had promised to meet Saidah at the church, and I was going to meet her.

CHAPTER 20

The Meeting

met Saidah at St. Gregory's, the tall-steepled church on the far side of the park. Before I continue, however, I'd like to say that I almost feel I shouldn't tell what happened next. At this meeting of debtors we were told to keep what we heard there to ourselves and never disclose the identity of anyone. It reminded me of a story that I had heard in my college course on dance and theater in ancient Greece.

Each year in Athens there were enormous religious festivals in which everyone, including women and slaves, could participate. This procession snaked from Athens to the holy site of Eleusis, a sacred shrine dedicated to the mother-goddess named Demeter. At Eleusis, sacred dramas were performed and the worshipers learned the mysteries of eternal life. These mysteries were truly to be kept secret. The penalty for revealing what happened at Eleusis was death. When one of the famous Greek playwrights, Aeschylus, I think, dramatized in a play what appeared to be parts of the sacred ritual, he was chased through the streets of Athens by an enraged crowd ready to kill him. That he escaped, and later was forgiven on the grounds that he had not intended to reveal any secrets, didn't change the life-and-death nature of the religious mysteries of Eleusis. In fact, the secrecy was so effective that today we know almost nothing about these rituals.

I feel much the same way about the meetings that I began to attend at St. Gregory's and in the basements of other churches around the city. It's amazing how much a city can contain, and how we only become aware of it when we're ready. While this group is hardly secret, I do feel that a person comes to a meeting when he or she is ready, so my telling about it is almost beside the point. To encourage people to go before they're ready, before they've been through enough fear and desperation to want to reach out for help and hope, would be futile.

"How can you come here," I asked Saidah as we sat on the folding metals chairs in the large room, "if you're not in debt?"

"I'm a recovering debtor and under-earner," Saidah answered. "The fact that I've been solvent for years doesn't change the need for vigilance. Solvency means not entering into unsecured debt, one day at a time."

"Unsecured?"

"You can only borrow against property that you own. So a mortgage is all right, because you own the house, and you could give a guitar as security for a loan because you own the guitar. But you can't just buy stuff on credit or borrow money."

Debtors Anonymous proved to be a twelve-step program like the more famous Alcoholics Anonymous. Watching the room fill up with people, I couldn't see how their faces or physiques differed from the people I saw crowding the streets during rush hour. Both sexes, all races, handsome or beautiful to not so attractive, well dressed to slovenly, cheerful, and worried. As I watched, I realized that anyone could be in debt. I couldn't know by a person's appearance or demeanor whether he or she was rich or poor. If I had met one of these people in the office or on the street, I wouldn't have known to think of him or her as a loser.

Promptly at six o'clock, everyone stood, held hands, and recited together, "God grant me the serenity to accept the things I cannot change, courage to change the things I can, and wisdom to know the difference." I liked holding Saidah's hand and the hand of the man on the other side of me. One thing that struck me about the prayer, because I did experience it as a prayer, was the reference to God. I quickly learned that God was an important part of the process of getting out of debt, because a paper was handed from one person to another and each person read aloud one of the twelve steps. But before they read the step, they would introduce themselves by saying, "I'm Bob, a compulsive debtor," and everyone would call back, "Hi, Bob," or "I'm Sarah, an under-earner and abuser of credit cards," and everyone would chorus in response, "Hi, Sarah."

When the first step was read, it made an impact on me: "We admitted we were powerless over debt—that our lives had become unmanageable." That was a hard thing to admit. Was I living an unmanageable life? I didn't want to think so, but in terms of debt it certainly seemed to be true. I didn't have time to finish this thought before the second step had been read: "Came to believe that a Power greater than ourselves could restore us to sanity." I had never thought of myself as lacking sanity, but debt had its own craziness. The idea that help might come from a greater Power, like the angel in *It's a Wonderful Life*, gave me a feeling of hope.

The third step made the source of this help even more explicit: "Made a decision to turn our will and our lives over to God *as we understood Him*." I thought that "Him or Her" would have been a better way to say it, but I appreciated the openness of the program to many faiths and many beliefs. It soon became apparent that this was no cult. I always think of a cult as a bunch of brainwashed people, but those of us in the basement of St. Gregory's had only been brainwashed in terms of our willingness to enter into debt. I don't know exactly how that happened. Could it have been advertising? Or just the way everybody around us acted? In any event, I had tried to handle my debt problem alone so far, but even with Saidah's help something more was needed.

Alan, who said he was a debtor and an under-earner, read the fourth step: "Made a searching and fearless moral inventory of ourselves." Inventory was a strange word to choose, but I understood that it meant to look deeply and clearly at myself.

The piece of paper continued around the room, but I was already on overload. I was powerless over debt, but God would help me get out of it. I had to take a hard look at myself so I could start the process that would get me moving in the right direction. I had been looking at numbers, but here I had to look at what I believed. I couldn't focus my thoughts on the other steps that were being read aloud, but kept thinking about what I had already heard. I'm sure each person reacts differently to his or her first meeting, and reading about it can't be anything like being there. Saidah had pushed me to go, but being with other people facing the same issues made me feel a sense of relief and safety. Slowly I had been realizing that I carried a heavy burden. Here I found a place to set it down.

Tariqa, whose skin was darker than mine and who professed to be a compulsive debtor, read the twelfth step in clipped, foreign-accented English: "Having had a spiritual awakening as the result of these steps, we tried to carry this message to debtors, and to practice these principles in all our affairs." I was astonished by the words "spiritual awakening." After all, we were in the basement of the church, not sitting upstairs in a pew with our heads bowed in prayer. But when people started telling their stories, I quickly came to understand the use of these words. The first story was by a "qualifier," someone who had agreed to speak on the evening's topic— tonight, it was about using the telephone.

I thought that was a pretty odd topic and the qualifier—a skinny, white-haired man in his sixties whose name was Jonas and who described himself as a debtor—didn't get right to the telephone in his story about his experiences as a debtor. He explained that at times he earned a good income as a graphic designer. He had been solvent for nearly two years until he found a new way to become insolvent—the monthly charges from the bank that had created new debt of which he had been unaware. That seemed like a small thing to me, but he took it very seriously. Almost as a joke, at least he laughed when he spoke and many of the people joined in, he told how a bank that was pursuing him for thousands of dollars offered him a new credit card with a credit line of two thousand dollars and how tempted he was to take it.

He said, and I found it hard to believe, looking at this neatly dressed, mature man, that he had sixty cents in his pocket and no other money and that he had been desperate to find work. He took his Apple computer to a friend and left it as security for a loan that helped him pay the rent. He looked for work, any kind of work, and found an assistant's job with an interior designer where his computer skills and design background made him useful enough to earn a low hourly wage. With those wages he had been able to pay back his friend and retrieve his computer. Now he had some prospects for graphic design work that would be much better paying, and he was doing his best, one day at a time, to live within his means.

What stunned and thrilled me about his story wasn't the way he used the telephone to call his "pressure person," someone from the group who helped him look at money issues or to reach out to others in his search for work of any kind. It was how debt for him truly was a spiritual as well as a practical issue. He had been tempted by the offer of the credit card, but he had been strong enough to say no. He had braved the fear of having nothing and, step by step, had improved his situation. Even if he had no money—or only sixty cents, I learned to be very precise about amounts of money—he didn't go off the path of solvency.

Soon I realized that every story was similar in this way. Each person in the room was struggling to better his or her life, and the only way to achieve this was to face fear, depression, and failure and rely on the twelve-step principles to change entrenched and self-defeating behavior about money. It was a slippery slope, and people talked of their failures as well as their successes with an honesty that touched me. Once Jonas finished his story as the qualifier, people raised their hands and he selected those who would be allowed to speak for two minutes, which were carefully timed by a volunteer.

The first speaker was a beautiful woman named Mariana who looked a little older than I was. She introduced herself as a compulsive spender who was striving to succeed as an actress. Like me, she had a day job that earned her one hundred and forty dollars per week, but she was spending twenty-three dollars per day. I quickly computed the numbers and realized that she must be going further into debt every day, a lot like my own situation since I lost the job at The Golden Plate. She said that her divorce settlement had left her with enough money to live for a few years, but that she had simply spent her way through the money. Now she had nothing, which had been the case at other times in her life when she had been extremely poor, and she was afraid. She had what she called the consuming sickness: She shopped whenever she felt low. She had used the phone to call and get the schedule for the DA meetings (DA being the way most people referred to Debtors Anonymous). I thought that use of the telephone played a pretty tenuous role in her story, but I soon learned that nobody judged what anyone else said at these meetings. It made these basement rooms a safe place to speak about the many ways debt restricted people's lives and the courageous and sometimes desperate steps people took on their journeys to overcome their debts.

Next, John, a burly businessman who might have been forty and wore an elegant suit, told how he earned one thousand dollars per day. When he said that, I envied him and couldn't imagine what his problem might be. Then he described how he saw a dirty, smelly bum in the street with three dollars and realized that bum had more money than he did. He said that when he stopped coming to DA meetings he would simply blow his money. I wondered how anyone could spend so much, but he didn't give any details about that. He said his life was always much better during the times he went to DA meetings, but that whenever he stopped going, he would relapse into his old spending habits.

Part of John's problem, as he described it, was that his parents had been willing to give him money. I couldn't see how this was a problem, but he explained that it made him feel his supply of money was limitless. It encouraged him to spend without placing any boundaries on his spending. He also felt that the money he earned could never match the money that his parents gave him, which made him feel bad about his work and dependent on his parents. Listening to him, I realized how each person in the room had been forced to look deeply at his or her life in order to confront debt. Now he hadn't taken money from his family for several years, but he still had debt issues. He also hadn't had money to pay the rent when it came due and called his pressure person. She asked if he could sell something. He managed to sell some of his furniture and had just enough money for the rent. It was a disturbing story, as many of these stories were, but I saw him struggling to change his life.

Claire, who introduced herself as a student with no control over her credit card spending, said that she was fifty-five thousand dollars in debt. After a moment, she corrected herself and said that her debt was fifty-five hundred dollars. I realized that her slip of the tongue had been significant and reflected how large the debt seemed to her. She said that an eight-thousand-dollar student loan was coming in the mail, but she was afraid to accept it because she didn't want to go further into debt. Yet she needed the money to live and pay tuition if she was to continue her schooling. I had always thought student loans were a good idea, because the loans prepared a person for a good job. But a lot of my classmates hadn't gotten those good jobs and, like me, still had the loans to pay back.

There were more stories that night, and many more stories on the other nights when I attended DA meetings at St. Gregory's and other places around the city. What made a deep impression on me wasn't only that these people were striving to better their lives. It was the sense of community, the warmth and supportive feelings that filled those basement rooms. When someone would give a piece of good news, how he or she had held back from repeating self-destructive behavior or taken an important career step, often everyone would applaud with the spontaneous good will that pervaded this community to which Saidah introduced me. I had never been with people striving to understand themselves more deeply and change their behavior. Many people spoke of this effort to change as a spiritual struggle that made them grow. Frankly, I had never thought of growth as the process of facing destructive patterns in our lives, but I began to think differently. I saw how the meetings allowed people to be tremendously honest about their failures and shortcomings, and gain the support of a community in their striving to escape the grip of these old patterns. I admired their courage to face themselves, and realized that only if I had strength similar to theirs would I be able to overcome my own issues with debt.

Once the people had finished sharing their stories, and there were a lot of people who didn't get called on and would have to wait to share until some other meeting, everybody stood and held hands again. The serenity prayer from the beginning of the meeting was repeated and then, quickly and with a lot of smiling, the words: "It works if you work it, so keep on working, it's worth it." Promptly at seven o'clock the meeting ended. A lot of people rushed for the exit, but others broke into small clusters to visit, and still others crowded around a table in the back to look at the DA pamphlets for sale and get schedules for the meetings.

I followed Saidah up the stairs in a kind of daze. It was like a door had opened. I was stepping through that open door into a large room that contained many marvelous and frightening new things. It wasn't any particular story or part of the hour-long meeting that made me feel stirred and overwhelmed, but the cumulative impact of all of it. It promised not only freedom from debt but also a new way of looking at myself and the world. That new way required taking a lot of responsibility. One day at a time—that phrase had been repeated over and over again.

When we emerged from the church, the summer sun quivered with a sullen scarlet hue that spread itself ever more thinly over the high-flung ridges of clouds in the western quadrant of the sky. Saidah and I walked along the edge of the park, the humid air cooling with evening and the scent of lawns, leaves, and heated earth rising to waken my senses. I had been underground, cut off from the world. It was like those stories, when someone goes to another world, like the story of how the earth opened and the fertility goddess was seized by the god of death and taken to the underworld. Or, maybe, Alice in Wonderland, Dorothy in Oz, or Pinocchio in the belly of the whale. I had seen a strange landscape, a new vista, and I didn't feel quite myself.

"What did you think?" Saidah finally asked.

"It was good. I mean the people were so honest about everything, and supportive."

We walked some more in silence. I appreciated that Saidah gave me space. I needed to draw my thoughts together.

"One thing I wondered," I finally said, "is what the woman meant who said, 'Debt was my solution to underearning, and underearning was my solution to debt.'"

Saidah thought about this for a few more steps. We were nearing the spot where she would cross the street to catch her bus home.

"I think I understand," she said, turning to face me. "First, because she didn't earn enough, she would go into debt to get the extra money that she needed."

"That's what I thought. What about the rest?"

"Then, by not earning as much as she could, she limited her ability to borrow."

"Oh."

"Because you can get in a lot more debt if you earn a lot of money than if you earn a little."

I nodded my agreement. "Like the man who said his salary had doubled again, but it wasn't doing him any good because he kept overspending."

"Exactly. He ended up in more debt than if his salary had never increased."

I sighed. "It's like the world is upside down."

"For people in debt, it can be upside down."

"And inside out," I added with a smile.

"You'll be all right?" Saidah was ready to head off in her own direction.

"Sure, I'm fine. Thanks, Saidah."

Impulsively I gave her a big hug and we separated. I walked into the center of the park, the twilight shadowing the little dips in the lawns and leaving pools of darkness beneath the skyward-stretching trees. I felt happy to be walking. I felt happy. That meeting had been scary, and I couldn't imagine myself getting up and saying, "I'm Iris, a compulsive debtor and under-earner," and then going on with my own story, but I had seen how that community gave strength to everyone who joined in it. It seemed so curious to me, because I had always thought of a community as a little town, like Bedford Falls in *It's a Wonderful Life* where everybody knows everybody else. Here, in a big city, in a meeting where everyone was anonymous and no last names were ever spoken, I had found a community. I didn't have to be on the PTA or have a kid in Little League, because I was joined to this community by the challenge of debt.

And what was debt? I asked myself that, as I watched the red sun liquify to a molten stream that spread itself on the margins of the sky behind the skyscrapers. Wasn't it one way in which people connected to one another? It came down to responsibility. Money might be scraps of paper, but earning money was a way of sharing talents and resources with other people through our work. Debt simply meant that for a period of time I had taken more than I had given. Surely that oversimplified it. I could think of a hundred exceptions—thieves, whose work hurt others; people in debt because they had guaranteed other people's loans; gambling debts that didn't seem to be taking anything from anyone since the gambler had lost. But I wanted to take responsibility for myself. I wanted to carry my own weight. I wanted to give equally to others. If I was afraid, and I could feel that same old fear that debt always made me feel, I also felt the hope and the challenge of confronting my problems. And now I had allies. Not only Saidah who had been immensely helpful, but DA and so many people like me who were seeking solvency one day at a time.

The sunlight vanished as I reached the edge of the park. The streetlights had come on to guide me through the familiar sequence of streets. The words of St. Paul played in my mind: "Owe no debt to anyone, except the debt to love." That had been what I felt in the basement of St. Gregory's. I had felt love. Not love directed at me, but a love of humanity. A love that accepted failures and shortcomings while encouraging people to grow and seek a fulfilled and joyous life. Strange, I thought at first, that those who have so little are capable of giving so much. That those who may be unable to pay their debts of money are able to pay this debt to love. I realized the generosity, the human richness that had been present in that room. I had so many things to do—fight the IRS, find the right second job, search for my birth family—but the spirit of the meeting lifted me up, and I believed for at least a little while that with prayer, hope, and hard work all things might be possible.

CHAPTER 21

The Ceaseless Waves

On Friday evening, I went to another DA meeting by myself, and soon I was going to two or three meetings a week, but that weekend a lot of other stuff was on my agenda. At my Saturday morning class I felt happy to be with my little kids. I had them do an airplane dance and an eagle dance and asked how the dances felt different to them. That discussion didn't last too long, then I started them around the perimeter of the room in a tortoise-and-hare dance with some of the kids going very fast and some hardly moving at all. I didn't think Chalma would be able to come up with much money, but as the kids whizzed by me I kept wondering if I couldn't do it for free if I found the right second job. I didn't want to give it up.

As the end of the class neared, I saw Chalma watching through the window in the door to the studio. She waved and I waved back. When class ended and the kids streamed into the arms of their waiting parents, she hurried over to me.

"Let's talk in my office." She looked pleased with herself, which gave me a reason to hope that her news might be good. In a few moments I was sitting across the desk from Chalma and glancing at the prints of ballerinas in fluffy white tutus that adorned her walls.

"I spoke with everyone. They agreed that if the parents would pay an additional amount for the class, then I could share that payment with you."

"Oh." I wasn't sure what this exactly meant.

"So I called all of the parents and asked if they would pay ten dollars per class. I want you to know that the parents love your teaching. When they heard that you might be leaving, they absolutely wanted you to stay. Only one or two families said they couldn't afford to pay for the class. We're going to create a partial scholarship for their children. So we can offer you six dollars for each student who comes to class. In fact, we're starting this morning."

"OK." I nodded calmly, but numbers were flashing through my mind. I had four boys and seven girls in class this morning. Eleven students times six dollars was sixty-six dollars, which was more than I had ever earned in one hour. Sixty-six times fifty-two—well, I couldn't do that in my head, but I tried sixty times fifty. It would be more than three thousand dollars a year. That much money would actually affect my financial situation.

"You're sure?" Chalma asked.

Suddenly I wanted to get home and pull the trash bag out from under my bed. I needed to add this income to the numbers on the yellow notepad and see what it would mean.

"Yes."

"I'm sorry that it has to be based on the number of students, because you won't be able to count on it. But the school's on a tight budget, and it seemed a way to make the classes possible. I guess if the attendance falls, you may have to reevaluate teaching."

"It's fine. I mean it's terrific." I could feel myself smiling from ear to ear. "Thanks so much, Chalma."

"You're the one giving the great classes," she answered.

I left the nursery school with that same big smile. My mind couldn't hold a thought, words floated away like vapor. Chalma had gone to bat for me. And the parents liked me, too. I wanted to teach and I was going to be able to. It was too much good news to keep inside my head. I found myself walking jauntily with the joy of what had happened. I had done something from love, and that love had been returned to me by Chalma and the parents of my students. I might be paid in money, but that money was being given to me from love. I felt stirred to the depths of myself, touched that my teaching meant this much to others.

I was feeling more than thinking, and my feet found their way through the city without much direction from me. When I stopped, I found that my exuberant wandering had brought me to The Golden Plate. I stood before the doorway framed by the spoon, fork, and knife. I knew why I had come here, although I felt reluctant to enter the restaurant. At the DA meeting the night before, I had begun thinking about the eighth and ninth steps, which involved creating a list of people I had harmed and making amends whenever possible. I felt that I had harmed Bertrand. There had been no excuse for me to chase his customers into the parking lot and toss that insulting tip back at them. I didn't want to go inside, because I felt too proud to apologize. On the other hand, I wanted to let go of that pride. I knew it would be important for me to let it go. My feet started toward the door, even as I thought I should just skip it. That guy had insulted me that night with the pennies, and I had been right to go after him. As my feet carried me through the door, I had a worse thought. If I met that boorish customer, should I make amends to him? I was thinking how much I didn't want to as I knocked on the door to Bertrand's office.

"Come in."

Reluctantly I stepped into his office and saw his expression change to surprise.

"Hi, Bertrand."

"The waitress who throws the pennies. What do you want, I wonder?" Bertrand had that French accent that I think he kept on purpose. He wasn't being friendly and didn't offer me a seat, so I stood in front of his desk. Taking a big breath, I started to speak but it was hard to get the words out.

"I wanted to say that I'm sorry about what happened."

"Now you're sorry. It doesn't help me that I never saw that gentleman again. It was childish, Iris. You aren't a child."

"I'm sorry about it."

"He was a regular customer, and a drinker besides. Maybe I lost one hundred dollars a week in business because he never came back."

He was blaming me like it was still that night, and I could feel myself heating up. Instead of forgiving me because I had come to make amends, he was still irritated with me for what had happened.

"I'm sorry about that," I said.

"You're sorry, but I'm no richer."

At that moment I had an insight that I thought was surely the truth. Standing there in front of Bertrand and wondering whether to keep apologizing or get angry and tell him off for being so unforgiving, I realized that what was happening had very little to do with me. It had a great deal to do with Bertrand and I couldn't change him. I had heard a lot in the meetings about turning things over—that meant trusting in a higher power. I had to turn this over. I didn't know why Bertrand was being tough on me, but I had to accept it and go on. I had done what I thought was right; I couldn't control what anyone's response would be.

"Well, that's what I came to say. Since I've said it, I'll be going now."

With that, I turned, walked out of the office, and back into the warmth of the July day. Bertrand didn't try to stop me, and I figured my visit had been a failure from the point of view of having him forgive me. Only that hadn't been why I came to see him. I had come to apologize and I had done exactly that. From that point of view, it had been a success.

Back at my apartment, something didn't feel right. Tina's bed had been stripped and our room looked barren. I looked in the bureau that we shared and her drawers were empty. Feeling a kind of panic, I pulled open the closet door. My meager, worn wardrobe hung on its half dozen hangers, but all of Tina's clothing was gone.

"Dear Iris," the note from Tina read, "I'm going home so I can work as an intern until school starts. I'll miss you and Rachel, but this is best for me. Love, Tina."

Sitting on my bed, I stared at the barren, empty expanse of Tina's bed. She wouldn't be there to talk to anymore about our shared dreams of dancing and everything else. Who could say what was more foolish, to dance and juggle second jobs, or to give up our dreams and become solid, well-paid professionals like Tina and Doug intended to be?

I didn't think people could be replaced. Maybe it was because of my missing birth family, but I didn't think that new friends would replace Doug or Tina. Otherwise people would be like money, with any dollar bill the same as the next. Yet life couldn't be without change—was that what I wanted? That Doug would never have injured himself, gone on dancing forever, never thought about a profession? Or that Tina would have kept spending on her credit cards and letting her father take up the slack?

I reached into the darkness for the trash bag. For the first time I thought that maybe I should get a filing cabinet and sort all these papers into files. What did it mean, to keep financial records in a bag meant for trash? I wasn't sure, but I had other things on my mind, too. For example, what would Rachel and I do about the rent without Tina contributing her third every month? I pulled out my yellow notepad and the small calculator. Quickly I multiplied six dollars times eleven students times fifty-two weeks. It came to three thousand four hundred thirty-two dollars per year. I shook my head. Watching my financial picture was like watching the constant rising and falling of waves. One moment I was worried because of a five thousand dollar annual shortfall, then I signed on to work at The Golden Plate and imagined that I would have an extra seven thousand dollars a year to pay off my debts, then I lost that job as a waitress, loaned money to Doug, and got my deficiency notice from the IRS. The mountain of debt looked like the Himalayas at that point, then suddenly I got a break with Chalma paying me to teach dance that covered a lot of that five-thousand-dollar shortfall. How could it ebb and flow so much?

After I wrestled with this question for a while, I was struck by the idea that life is always in flux. Even if all my experiences, from my broken arm to meeting Saidah to going to DA, said life was change, something in me resisted with passion. I don't know why I so strongly wanted to see my life as stable, but I imagined that the loss of my birth family and my adoptive parents had an impact on me. I was like a bottle bobbing on the ocean and wishing that I could anchor myself to the ceaselessly moving waves. It would never work. If my financial life flowed up and down, and my emotional life, too, then I would have to find another place to seek calmness and certainty. It would be a place like prayer. Whatever the outer circumstances might be, I would feel the way that I felt when I prayed.

I wrote some numbers on the yellow sheet. My shortfall was now fifteen hundred dollars per year. Suddenly I had an idea. What if I went to another school and offered to teach dance classes for ten dollars, or even nine dollars, per student? In fact, what if I rented a rehearsal studio and offered to teach little kids? Then I could keep all of the money and simply pay the rent for the studio. I knew that a studio rental wouldn't cost more than twenty or twenty-five dollars an hour. I could make a profit.

If a bolt of lightning had struck me, I couldn't have been more shocked. I had never had an idea like this before. I sat on the bed in a daze. At that moment, it didn't matter to me whether I would actually do what I had imagined. What mattered was that I had been able to imagine it at all. Where had the thought come from? I didn't know, but I imagined that the pressure of my debt, my meetings with Saidah, and DA had all moved me to a new place. I had always thought of myself as an employee, willing to do any work as long as it left me free to dance. Now I glimpsed myself as an entrepreneur, finding students to teach and making my success depend on my own efforts. It was like a mirage, elusive, shimmering, far away. But if I could picture it, couldn't I also make it come true?

I think this surprising influx of new ideas made me do what I did next. Right on top of the sediment in the trash bag were my credit cards, wrapped in a big rubber band. I took the small deck of plastic cards, unwrapped them, and lay them out on the bedspread. Thirteen cards. Once I had seen a tarot reading, with the elaborately illustrated cards placed in rows, one after another. On Tina's bed I made three rows of the cards, two rows of four credit cards each and a third row of the five department-store cards. Even if these cards weren't as colorful and picturesque as tarot cards, I thought I could read my future in them. Then, and I almost couldn't believe that I was doing it, I went to the closet where I kept my sewing machine, and got out my largest pair of scissors. I opened the scissors like the crossbones under a skull and placed it on top of the rows of cards.

What did I mean by this? The proximity of the sharp edges of the blades to this plastic that could be so easily cut? When one of the speakers at DA had spoken of cutting up his credit cards, I had felt a chill go down my spine. How would he, or I, survive without credit cards? But a lot of people in the room had nodded. Then the man said how he stopped paying any debts until he worked out a payment plan that would settle all that he owed. Stopping his payments on his credit cards destroyed his credit rating, but he didn't care. He didn't want credit. He wanted to live without debt. It was an upside-down way of thinking, but I knew that having these cards had gotten me into a lot of trouble. I didn't do anything, but left the scissors and cards arranged like a thought suspended in midair.

Toward the end of the afternoon Rachel came in from a rehearsal, calling my name.

"Iris? Iris, are you there?"

"Yes," I came out in surprise. "You know Tina's gone?"

"She left when we weren't here. She didn't want to say good-bye."

We talked a little about Tina and how much we'd miss her, about her dad and the credit cards, about the hard-to-accept idea of her becoming a banker. I was going to bring up the rent problem when Rachel changed the subject.

"You know the piece I'm choreographing? I need someone to design the costumes. Would you do it for me?"

I wanted to. I have a great imagination for designs, I love to do patterns, and my sewing is really good. Also, I liked Rachel and her choreography and I missed being involved with dance and dancers. That was my first reaction, but my second was that I wouldn't be paid. And in that moment before I replied, I saw the perfectness of it. If I would be paid to teach my kids at the Little Folks Nursery, then I needed another outlet where I would simply give of myself without money being an issue.

"I'd love to."

"Great."

Rachel spent the next hour or so showing me the dance and explaining its story about a young woman who falls in love with fire, but by the depth of her love transforms the fire to a man. It had a lot of beautiful duets, but I would have to make six costumes for five dancers (with an extra costume for the dancer playing fire and the man). I felt like starting right away, and by the early evening had rough sketches for three of the costumes, when the phone rang.

"It's for you, Iris," Rachel called.

I went into the living room and took the receiver from her.

"Hello."

"Iris?"

I was surprised to hear a deep voice with that impasto of French accent.

"Bertrand?"

"Yes. Listen, I need your help."

I was completely surprised. After the way he had acted when I stopped by the restaurant, I had felt sure I'd never hear from him again. "For what?"

"Marcia quit on no notice today. She's in love," he said it in a mean way, "and she and her boyfriend are heading for the coast. To make a new start. Only I need a waitress. Can you come tonight? Right now?"

I could think of some good reasons to say no, such as the way Bertrand had treated me. But I had gone there to make amends for having wronged him. I saw that this overture from him might allow me to move ahead in the process. I could have squeezed him for some commitment about giving me Marcia's job. The arithmetic was certainly appealing, because if I had her five nights I could add fifteen thousand dollars a year to my after-tax income. But four nights had driven me crazy, and making amends wasn't about making money.

"Yes, I'll come right over."

There was a pause. Maybe Bertrand expected me to say no and was surprised. "OK, as soon as you can. Take a taxi. I'll pay for it."

"And Bertrand, thanks for calling me." I really meant it.

That night I danced at The Golden Plate. If anyone had choreographed a ballet about eating, then I would have been the leading ballerina, turning, twisting, bending, nearly leaping from one table to another only to imagine myself on pointes as I rushed back to the kitchen and into the dining room again. My energy was effulgence, a light that had to pour out of me. I felt joyous, and it wasn't about making the money for that evening. It wasn't about money. It was about what I had begun, the process of making amends. The process of looking within myself in a searching way, admitting what was worst and best about me, and trying to bring the best into my life.

As I moved with a quick grace from customer to customer, seeing each of them as a mystery worthy of my curiosity and respect, I thought the hardest part of any journey must be the decision to begin. Not to know the route, to be indecisive about starting, or to fear the journey and refuse it—that could cause much anxiety and frustration. But once the first step is taken and the road lies open to the future, then how easily step follows step! I hadn't gone to Bertrand with an expectation about what he would do. I only went because I had to do what I believed to be right. But I could feel that I was on a road, in a process that would carry me away from the old life that I knew and on to something different. I could even see that the way I was thinking had started to change. One day, someone— Saidah—had touched my heart and I had begun to transform. But I must have been ready before that. I must have been waiting or yearning for the crisis that would bring a person like Saidah into my life.

These were the kind of thoughts that filled me as I danced that night at The Golden Plate. When the evening had ended, Bertrand called me into his office. I went a bit unwillingly, because of my memories of my last two encounters with him there. But this was a different Bertrand, all Gallic charm and smiles.

"I want to say thanks, Iris."

"Thank you for giving me another chance."

Bertrand surveyed me. If he hadn't been happily married, I might have wondered about the way he was looking at me.

"You've changed," he said finally.

I smiled and shrugged.

"Maybe you just needed a rest," he went on. "I was hasty. Yes. Would you come back and work here again?"

I thought of the ocean waves, how they fall and rise quite apart from human wants and desires. I felt calm inside, happy with Bertrand's offer but aware that I had been overwhelmed when I tried to waitress four nights a week and hold down my full-time job at the ad agency.

"I'll have to think about it," I answered, visualizing getting out my yellow notepad and working over the numbers to see what this might mean.

"When you're ready," Bertrand was smiling, like he had seen me in a new way, "we'll talk about it."

Leaving his office I felt like I had been receiving the applause of a curtain call, a fitting finish to my dance among the tables at The Golden Plate. My feet swept me homeward through the dark streets. In the bedroom I contemplated Tina's empty bed with my thirteen credit cards neatly arranged beneath the open-bladed scissors. As I turned out the light, it seemed I had so much on my mind that it would take me hours to fall asleep. But the moment my head touched the softness of the pillow, I slept without another thought.

CHAPTER 22

A Woman Who Knows She's Right

On Sunday I attended a 6 P.M. DA meeting. When one of the guys at the meeting had asked me out for coffee afterwards, I realized I had a judgmental feeling about him. His name was Tom, a tall and slender fellow with a mop of dark hair and sensitive features, especially his brown eyes. He told me his story: how he inherited almost a million dollars, started a film production company in his mid-twenties, and by the age of thirty, had gone bankrupt and owed almost half a million dollars on loans that he had personally guaranteed. Now he had been solvent more than a year, although it would take him several lifetimes to pay back what he owed at his present rate of repayment. However, he had no intention of going bankrupt. I respected him for that, but I still judged him for having less than nothing.

Once I got home I kept thinking about this attitude in myself. After a while, I knew I could let go of it. I really respected and cared for the debtors who spoke at the meetings. The group was different from one person. The group had a way of celebrating the movements, whether little or big, that a person made in understanding his or her issues with money. That process had a spiritual feeling to it, the way a person had to trust in something greater to transform and discover an inner treasury of resources. What really mattered wasn't the past but the place to which a person had come now. At the meetings I heard about people who squandered money in every conceivable way—credit cards for compulsive shopping, business ventures that failed, loans that were never repaid, gifts that couldn't be afforded, even spending a little too much to live modestly month after month. But the important point was to be fairer with myself. I wasn't bad because I was in debt. I wasn't worthless. I hadn't failed. I had only begun—that was the truth. I had to trust myself, not measure myself and others in terms of money and debt.

During the next month a lot of things crowded in on me. I had taken back my job at The Golden Plate, but only for Friday and Saturday when I made the most in tips. I was pretty sure I could manage this without burning out, especially since I hoped to move on to something better. Suddenly I was paying off my debts again. I also contacted a nursery school on the other side of the city. They were interested in having me teach dance there, especially since I was a success at Little Folks, but they only wanted to pay me twenty-five dollars a class. I knew that I wanted a deal like the one Chalma had given me, so I turned them down. I couldn't remember turning something down because it wasn't good enough for me, and it made me feel strong. It had to do with that equation I often heard at the meetings that "time is money." If I only had a limited amount of time, then I had to put each moment to the best use. I also thought that the saying could have been changed to "time is opportunity." If I spent all my time working at safe and familiar jobs, I wouldn't be available for something that might be new, different, and perhaps better.

On a sweltering day near the end of August, I came home from the office perspiring just from the walk through the park. Looking through the usual collection of bills and advertisements in my mail, my heart skipped several beats when I saw that the IRS had finally written back to me.

I tore open the envelope; the scene in my mind was like one of those bad gladiator movies. Would the emperor point his thumb up or down? I could hardly believe what I read:

Dear Taxpayer:
    Thank you for your recent communication with our office regarding the above referenced matter. To ensure that you

have the opportunity to present in full all relevant information with respect to this matter, we have scheduled an
appointment for September 19th at 3 P.M. with auditor M.
Stevens. Kindly bring with you all records and other data in
support of the information contained in your return…

The letter went on, but I was going to have to face an auditor by
myself. The IRS to me had always been like a big computer, completely impersonal, existing far away from real people living ordinary lives.
I called Saidah to tell her.

"You gather up all those receipts and that daily ledger you made and
take them with you," Saidah said. "Look at it this way. Before, you figured you were going to have to pay. Now, the worst thing that can happen is that you'll have to pay."

"But the best thing…"

"Is that you won't have to pay," she finished. "You know you're right,
so don't accept anything less than a complete wiping out of the tax bill
and penalties. If the auditor asks you to pay in full or even to compromise
and pay part of it, remember that you reported your income correctly.
You can always ask to appeal to a higher level in the IRS. If you don't get
any satisfaction there, you can appeal to the tax court."

"OK," I said, but I must have sounded dubious.

"Iris, I know you can do it."

"But shouldn't I have a lawyer? Or an accountant?"

"That might be nice, but I don't think there's anything more powerful in this whole world than a woman who knows she's right. If you
don't succeed, you can always get a lawyer later. But this isn't a case
before the Supreme Court. They're saying you earned money you
know you didn't earn. You've just got to stand up and be heard."

After I hung up with Saidah, I thought how easy it sounded. I simply had to tell them the truth. It was only when I imagined the vast,
faceless bureaucracy of the IRS that doubt would slip in around the
edges of my resolve. But I knew I would do it. For better or worse I
would go down to the government office building on September 19th
and meet with auditor M. Stevens.

The same day, a letter finally came from Caleb Cromwell, my parents' attorney. His stationery was stiff as parchment, with his name and address engraved in an antique script of curves and curlicues.

Dear Iris,

In response to your inquiry, I have searched my files and found very little information that will assist you. Your parents used the Lockwood Agency in Baltimore to handle the adoption. Unfortunately, your adoption was closed, which means that no information about either the birth family or the adoptive family was ever to be shared through the agency. Such closed adoptions were the rule at that time. While there have been changes in the laws regarding disclosure of information to people who are adopted, I also discovered that the Lockwood Agency closed its doors nearly a decade ago when its founder passed away. I wish that I had better news. If I can be of assistance in any other way, please don't hesitate to contact me.

Yours truly,
Caleb Cromwell

I put the letter aside, feeling at a loss. How would I ever heal my sad feelings of incompleteness? I experienced them in so many ways. For example, I had no plans to marry or have children, but I did keep wondering if my children might have some hidden genetic defect, a medical condition that I should know about and could only find out from the medical histories of my birth parents. Any slight or odd connection made me feel the necessity to search for them. Only for now, I didn't know what other steps to take.

That night I had a light dinner and worked some more on the costumes for Rachel. My mom had taught me how to sew when I was nine. I had practiced on my own and become skillful. I took a lot of pleasure in designing these costumes, selecting the fabrics, carefully cutting them to my patterns, and sewing them with the machine that had once belonged to my mother. Sheets and scraps of fabric piled up on Tina's bed—the bed that had been Tina's, I should say—along with spools of thread, my pin cushion, thimbles, the list of the dancers' measurements, drawings of the costumes, and so on.

Rachel and I figured that our rent was low enough that we could each contribute a little bit more, and I added the increase into my spending plan. It was a pleasure to have extra space and be messy if I wanted to. Under these piles on Tina's bed, the credit cards remained beneath the large pair of scissors. True, I used those scissors frequently, but always replaced them on top of the credit cards. At the least, the scissors served as a warning, and I hadn't used my credit cards at all. But I kept considering the long run, the years and decades of the rest of my life, and wondering whether these credit cards would continue to torment me. The cards seemed to sing to me like sirens: Think of all the pleasures that we gave you, all the gifts, the wonderful meals, the things that you would never have been able to afford without us. Then the seduction would change from the past to the future, and the cards would whisper: We can give you all that again, all that and more. Only we can provide for you, only we can be trusted to be caring and loving for you.

The sewing helped a lot to silence the voices of the cards, because I felt so calm and at peace with myself as I created these costumes. When I felt troubled, I would pull out my yellow notepad and study the figures of my spending plan. What pleasures did my spending plan promise to compete with the chant of the credit cards for more, more, more? My plan offered the minimum, the certainty of rent, food, transportation, modest additions to my wardrobe, the payment of my estimated taxes, the whittling away at my debts. For pleasure there were only the two dance classes each week, classes that for whatever reason I had not yet begun to take. But I had to correct myself, because to say that my plan offered the minimum was certainly wrong. It wasn't a minimum, to live within my means, to pay my own way, to dig myself out of the grave of too much debt, and escape from the fantasies that more and more things would bring me happiness. When I thought like this, I wanted to pick up the scissors and cut the credit cards into little pieces.

That would end the enchanting spell of these plastic magicians. Yet the long Labor Day weekend came and went, the costumes were finished and my sewing supplies and fabrics put away, and still the credit cards remained intact and whispered promises like lovers who fear the dawning of a new day.

CHAPTER 23

A Secret Sacrifice

My name is Iris. I'm a compulsive debtor, credit card addict, and underearner."

"Hi, Iris," came the chorus of voices from thirty or so men and women assembled in the basement of the church for the DA meeting.

My face flushed, standing to speak for the first time. I felt shamed by the words I had just spoken, although I had heard so many other people admit the same. I looked at the expectant faces of the people sitting on the folding metal chairs around me. I had two minutes to have my say, whatever I wanted. I hadn't written a speech. I hadn't even planned to thrust my hand in the air. I felt brimming over, like I had to speak.

"I feel lucky there's a noon meeting today, because I really need support. I've taken a personal day off from work to go to the IRS. I've never been to the IRS and, honestly, I'm scared. They claim that I owe more than four thousand dollars in taxes and penalties. I don't know how to talk to them. I'm bringing along my records. But if they don't accept what I say, I'm going to be in worse debt than I was before."

I could see that the faces remained friendly, some heads nodding with recognition of having faced situations similar to my own. I took a deep breath and continued.

"I owe thirty-seven thousand dollars for student loans and credit cards. Before I did my spending plan, I didn't realize that I was losing ground every month, that I was in the red. It hurts me to owe so much money that I'm not sure if I'll ever be able to pay it back. I want to be a dancer, but just to live and pay back a little bit I have to work two jobs. I'm a receptionist, a waitress, and I teach dance to little kids on Saturday mornings." I smiled to mention my class for the children.

"Being in debt has been the most terrible thing in my life," I said, "so terrible that I couldn't admit to myself how bad it was. It's made me feel worthless, depressed, and fearful. When I went to have my debts consolidated, they told me that I should go bankrupt. But I'm not going bankrupt.

"Being in debt has been the most wonderful thing in my life, too. Not wonderful in a pleasant way, but because it's made me look into my own heart. What I've seen there," I hesitated with a painful constriction in my throat and tears started rolling down my cheeks, "is how I've confused money and love. How I spent to make me feel better, more complete, instead of seeking that in myself or with others. I know I can't do that anymore. I finally looked at my numbers, what I earn and spend. I'd never done it before. And I've got that in balance. In fact, right now I'm lowering my debt every month.

"And I'm so thankful for you, for all of you. Because if I didn't have a place to come and hear what you say, and talk myself—today is my first time—I don't know what I'd do."

Applause broke out. All around me I could see clapping hands and faces smiling encouragement.

"Thanks," I said, wiping my cheeks. I didn't know if I had spoken my full two minutes, but I was finished. "Thank you."

My excitement kept my blood throbbing after I sat back down, but I felt such relief. Finally, unequivocally, I had stood up and told the truth about myself. I actually felt exhilarated, despite my debt and my fear of the IRS.

After the meeting, a number of people came over to encourage me.

"You'll find they're just human beings doing their job," an older man with a grizzled, outdoor look and a shock of white hair told me. "I made some bad mistakes and owed them a lot of money, but in the end they made a compromise."

"Don't be intimidated," a studious woman with eyeglasses said.

"Turn it over to a higher power," said another well-wisher.

Oddly enough, I felt calm walking to the IRS skyscraper and riding up in the elevator. It was only when I stepped onto the floor and faced the receptionist that the butterflies started fluttering their golden wings inside my stomach. The receptionist called M. Stevens and asked me to sit in the row of chairs next to the elevator. I looked around for magazines, but all that I saw were tax pamphlets and forms in a rack next to the receptionist's desk. I rummaged in my satchel, pushing my leotard and tights for dancing to one side, and pulled out my ledger and receipts so I could review them one more time. I had been studying them about five minutes when a deep voice interrupted me.

"Ms. Cassidy?"

I looked up and saw a man nearing fifty whose upright posture, fitness, and crew-cut hair made me certain he must be an ex-marine.

"I'm Maxwell Stevens," he went on, "the auditor in charge of your case. Would you please come with me?"

Everything that he said was polite, but I felt a sudden dread to be following him through a maze of aisles, past dozens of desks where I imagined the IRS agents were hard at work tracking down tax frauds, and into a small, windowless conference room that had a long table and grey plastic chairs.

"Please have a seat," he gestured to a chair and then sat across the table from me. He had been carrying several brown folders and opened one to study its contents. I could see my letter as he flicked through the sheets of paper.

"On your return, you put your profession as dancer."

"Yes."

"But I don't see a Schedule C here. Did you have any income or expenses from dancing?"

"Not last year."

He looked up at me. "It's unusual not to have any income or expenses from your profession. I see you have a W-2 here."

"Yes, I work at an advertising agency."

"But I have your returns for the last three years." He studied the documents in the folder. "I don't see a Schedule C for dance in any year. You understand that if you had income or expenses from dancing, they would go on Schedule C? That shows income or loss from your business or profession."

"Yes." Frankly, I didn't know why he was starting here or what he hoped to get at.

"So did you have any income from dancing in the three years at issue?"

"No."

"Any expenses?"

I thought carefully about this. "I paid for dance classes and dance outfits. Actually, this year I will have some income from teaching dancing. And I'll be taking lessons again soon. I broke my arm earlier this year."

"Ah." He had sharp grey eyes that flickered up to meet mine and then returned to his papers.

"But, prior to this year, your income did not come from dancing."

"No. It mainly came from waitressing."

"You understand that the deficiency assessed against you is based on studies of employees working in restaurants. An analysis of overall revenues and actual tip income allowed the creation of a statistical model to correlate tips against revenues. We lose a lot of money each year because people who get cash income underreport. That's why tip income concerns us. It's so easy not to write down everything that you received."

"But I didn't do that."

"Your letter says that you didn't do that. Did you bring the receipts that you mention in the letter?"

"Yes." I handed everything across the desk to him. "You already have the ledger that goes with them."

As he turned over the scraps of paper, he worked the muscles in his jaw. I didn't know if that was good or bad, but my anxiety had vanished. Here I was, in the belly of this great beast of the IRS, and I felt calm. I didn't quite know what Maxwell Stevens had been getting at with some of his questions, but he seemed like a decent, straight-arrow kind of man.

"Was the ledger kept contemporaneously with the making of the receipts?" he asked.

"You mean, at the same time?"

"Yes."

"No, I wrote the receipts every night when I came home, but I didn't create the ledger until I got the IRS notice about a deficiency."

"It would have been better if it were contemporaneous." He straightened in his seat and nodded his head. "But I can see that you systematically made records of your actual earnings. Record keeping is so important, but many people don't bother with it. If an issue comes up about their return, they have no way to prove the truth of the information that they provided. Let me see."

He had an adding machine and started entering the numbers from my scribbled slips.

"It's off by about ten dollars," I supplied.

"Thanks, but I want to check it myself."

While he busied himself with the numbers, I thought about what was happening with Rachel's dance performance. After I finished the costumes, which I enjoyed creating very much, one of the dancers had dropped out and Rachel asked me to stand in. That was why I had packed my dance clothes in my satchel today. I was finally going to take my first dance class since breaking my arm. Whatever the result with the IRS, I had made up my mind to go to the dance studio for the class that started right after the end of the workday.

Maxwell Stevens finally concluded his addition of the numbers. He checked his total against the return and then against the ledger that I had given him.

"Yes, the return shows too much income."

"It's only about ten dollars," I said again.

He raised an eyebrow. "When you're dealing with tax returns, you have to be precise. A little bit here and there can add up to something that's not small in the least. In this case, you've overpaid your taxes."

I wanted to protest and say that if the extra tax on ten dollars was three dollars, I didn't really care, but I had a feeling that would draw another reprimand. Also, if I understood what he was saying, I had overpaid. But if I overpaid, then I didn't owe the IRS the extra taxes and penalties.

"In fact," he went on, "I think you may have overpaid substantially. If you're serious about your dance career, you have the right to file a Schedule C and deduct your losses as a dancer against other income, such as that from being a waitress. Your dance classes, dance clothing, transportation to dance-related events—all the ordinary and necessary expenses of being a dancer—would be tax-deductible. I'm sure that you must have had such expenses and simply not recorded them."

I nodded, waiting for something bad to happen.

"Of course, I see many people in the arts who go for years with losses on Schedule C. That can raise tax problems for them. If the IRS determines the art activity is a hobby, any losses will be disallowed. If you don't show net income on Schedule C for three years out of every five years, you may be challenged as a hobbyist. So perhaps you're wise to wait until your dancing is helping to support you."

He closed the file.

"Do I owe anything?" I asked.

"You have records that prove your actual income. In the view of the IRS, that disposes of the matter." He stood and looked at me with a pleasant smile. "I want to thank you for being so cooperative. You'll receive official notification in the mail."

"That takes care of the penalties, too?" I asked.

"Yes. There can't be penalties if you didn't underpay in the first place."

"Thank you," I said. I wanted to tell him that I appreciated his treating me decently, but I couldn't quite think how to say it. "Thank you," I said again.

All the way down in the elevator and on the street as I walked to the dance studio, I kept repeating to myself: I don't owe anything to the IRS! It seemed to me like a David and Goliath story, except the IRS was a lot bigger than Goliath. I had marched right into their skyscraper and looked them in the eyes. And I had walked out a winner, because I had written down what I earned from tips.

I stopped at the first pay telephone and dialed Saidah.

"I don't have to pay," I said to her. "The agent said the IRS would drop it."

"Iris, that's wonderful."

We chatted a little bit about my meeting with Maxwell Stevens, then Saidah changed the subject.

"Two weeks from Sunday we're having some friends over for a cookout. You're invited, if you'd like to come."

"I'd love to."

"I want you to meet Cedric and the boys."

"Terrific."

When I reached the dance studio, I paid for the class and quickly changed in the dressing room. My leotard and tights had been worn and washed so many times that they felt good on my body like a comforting second skin. I stood in the doorway to the studio and watched the master class ending. Everything about the studio made me feel that I had come to the right place. The smooth grain of the wood under my stocking feet, the dancers moving gracefully across the floor under the watchful eyes of the teacher, the rhythm of the footfalls, the sense of movement and connection through space. I wanted my class to go well, especially because I wanted to dance in Rachel's piece. But to be here touched me, to be in this place of my dreams and strivings. Whatever happened, if I danced well or poorly, I felt gratitude to be alive, free of the IRS, and able to dance.

That night, when I reached the apartment, Rachel was waiting for me.

"Did you go to dance class?" she asked.

I nodded. "Um. Yeah."

"How did it go?" She wanted to know, because I had told her my decision whether to dance in her piece depended on how I danced in the class.

"It was great."

She smiled radiantly to hear me. "Then you want to dance?"

"Yes," I said with all my heart, "I want to dance."

"We can catch you up with some extra rehearsals."

We talked about how the rehearsals had been going, the skills and weaknesses of the other dancers, even the publicity for the performances, and how to draw everything together in the next month. All Rachel wanted to do was show audiences her choreography, but she had to become an entrepreneur—a producer—to do it. Of course, dancing for Rachel wasn't like being accepted into one of the city's dance companies, but it excited me. I couldn't wait to get in shape by taking more dance classes and to start the rehearsals so I could learn the intricacies of my role.

I had told Rachel about my troubles with the IRS, but I hadn't told her about my appointment.

"I went to the IRS today," I said.

"You did?" Rachel opened her dark eyes wide to show her surprise and concern.

"Yes. I showed them my receipts for my tip income. The agent, he was a really nice man, decided that I don't owe anything. No extra taxes, no interest, no penalties. In fact, I think he was kind of encouraging me to treat my dancing as a business. Deduct my dance classes, transportation, and stuff as an expense—maybe from the income I get for teaching dance."

Rachel nodded. "That's great, but I have the same problem. If these performances make any money, I have to show it on my tax return. If I lose money, I guess I can subtract that from my income as a temp."

"He talked about the risk of being a hobbyist, how it's best to have business profits in three years out of five."

"Well, we're certainly not hobbyists. But, in a strange way, we do seem to be in business. Not that I ever wanted to be in business, but you just can't help it. I have to pay for the space to perform, the material for the costumes, the fliers for publicity. I want to pay the dancers, even if it's only a little."

"You don't have to," I volunteered.

"You won't get rich," she countered, "but I want to. It's important to show respect for people who work so hard. I have to worry about whether enough people will come to cover the cost of everything.

Maybe I should have gone to school for business instead of performing arts."

"Me, too," I said and told her about Chalma's deal at the Little Folks Nursery and how I had turned down the other school that wouldn't pay as much.

"If we were selling something other than dance, we might become rich," Rachel observed.

"You never know…" I said, my thoughts turning to one more action I wanted to take before this remarkable day ended. Strange how months can pass with small steps forward and sometimes backward, then all at once I felt myself taking some big steps. I had spoken at the DA meeting. I had been vindicated by the IRS. I had finally gone to dance class and would actually perform in Rachel's piece.

Alone in my room, I studied the thirteen credit cards arranged on the bed. They were like old lovers. Once they had been my constant companions, but now I had left them behind and nearly forgotten them. I lit and placed three candles on the windowsill, then turned out the lights in the room. In the semidarkness of the flickering candles, I imagined myself to be a priestess of some ancient cult that demanded sacrifice. Not the sacrifice of life, but of old habits, old dependencies. I took the large scissors in my right hand and the first of the credit cards in my left hand. I lifted up my hands to the candles, the window, and the night sky brooding darkly beyond. In my mind I heard the plastic card cry out to me:

"But I clothed and fed you when no one else would have. I gave you flowers and took you to operas and concerts. No matter how much you owed, I never abandoned you. I gave myself completely to you and served you only. If we've had some misunderstanding and you want to spend less, I'm perfectly happy with that. If you want to have me to rely on for emergencies, that would be fine with me. I offer you safety and power in the world. Don't sacrifice me for some illusion of freedom."

I placed the card between the jaws of the scissors. Inexorably, mercilessly, I cut the plastic in half. A dozen more times I raised up a card and closed the blades of the scissors until all of the credit cards had been destroyed. When I had finished, I looked at the cut rectangles of plastic glistening in the amber glow of the candlelight. For a moment I felt fear: How would I survive without this extra help? How would I be able to make it on my own? Was my dream of freedom really an illusion? But I knew how far I had already come—the meetings with Saidah, the struggle to master my numbers, my efforts to lessen my expenses and increase my income, the DA meetings where I had finally spoken. Fear was the illusion against which I had to struggle. The fear that I didn't have enough to share with others, or that others lacked enough to share with me. If fear might overcome me at one moment or another, I believed now that I would be able to slip out of fear's grasp. I was coming to trust in a higher power and in my own riches of talent and determination.

Gently I blew out the three candles and settled to sleep on my bed, thinking that in the morning I would put these scraps of plastic into thirteen envelopes and return them to the companies that had hoped to profit endlessly from them.

CHAPTER 24

Saidah's Gift

"Iris, I'm so glad you could come."

"Me, too," I answered, surprised to find that Saidah lived in suburbia in a well-kept, two-story Victorian house with bay windows, a big porch, and lacy white trim. The large lawn stretched around to the back of the house where I could hear the murmur of lots of voices. I shouldn't have been surprised, I mean Saidah had to live somewhere, but to me she had been like a wise nymph who magically appeared at that bench in the park. I had never imagined her settled in a life that included a house, a lawn, a barbecue, and the legion of friends that I saw when she led me into the back yard.

Saidah wore a light, flowing robe striated with purple and gold. "Cedric," she said. "Honey, I want you to meet Iris. This is my husband, Cedric."

The man at the grill looked like an athlete, a little over six feet and lean in a way that made me think he would be quick and well-coordinated. He turned with a smile, the spatula in his left hand, and reached out to engulf my hand with his right.

"Great to meet you." He was lighter-skinned than Saidah, more my color, and looked as if he might have some Spanish ancestry. "Saidah tells me you're a dancer."

"Yes…" I was going to say something like "I hadn't danced in a long time," or "I hadn't performed much," but he didn't give me a chance.

"I love dancing. Saidah will tell you that. I studied dance, too—in college."

"What kind of dance?"

"Ballet. The coach made everybody on the football team take ballet classes." He shook his head with a big smile and flipped one of the patties on the grill, "Was that ever hilarious—those hefty linemen up on tiptoes in their dance outfits. But it made a big difference in my sense of balance. That's why we were doing it. I gained a lot of admiration for dance."

I had been in awe of Cedric before I met him because he had played major league baseball, but he couldn't have been friendlier, and I soon felt at ease. We chatted while he kept the food cooking on the grill suspended over the glowing charcoal. People would come by and exchange a few words, and Cedric would introduce me and then put a hamburger, a turkey burger, or a frank into a roll and add it to the fresh corn on the cob and piles of baked beans, garden salad, and cole slaw already on their paper plates.

"I've been teaching on Saturday mornings at a nursery school," I said, "and now I'm going to be teaching Saturday afternoons, too." The class had grown so large that Chalma asked me if I would teach two sections, one in the morning and one in the afternoon. This helped me a lot, because two dozen toddlers in one dance class is way too many. I didn't mention the financial aspect to Cedric, but my earnings had increased because of the popularity of my class. It wasn't just popular with the children, but with their parents as well. I was also making good tips on Fridays and Saturdays when The Golden Plate overflowed with people.

"Iris, come with me," Saidah came back for me and led me through the crowd. Their friends included every kind of person, old and young, skin colors from black to white and every hue between, people who looked like artists and others who looked like business types although I couldn't be sure. There must have been fifty or sixty people standing on the back lawn under the shade of old maples and a beautiful white birch.

"This is my son, Jesse," Saidah said, beaming with her pride in the young man who balanced his silverware and a paper plate in one hand while offering me the other. I took it, thinking how unmistakably he resembled his father.

226

"Are you a ball player?" I asked when Saidah went back to the other guests.

"Baseball?" he asked.

"Uh-huh."

"No, not me. That's my dad's sport. Right now I'm playing soccer."

"That's a great sport," I said enthusiastically.

"Then basketball, and tennis."

I liked the way Jesse's eyes held a liquid light. He was such a handsome young man. He was only a few years younger than I, and as we talked I kept thinking of Saidah. This was her precious son. Jesse asked me about my dancing, then told me a bit about his college. His junior year had just begun and he had a difficult curriculum of premed courses. This weekend he had come home for the party.

Saidah returned with a younger, plumper boy in tow.

"This is Alton, my little one."

Alton screwed up his face to be called her "little one," but Saidah took no notice. He was littler than either his brother or father, that is, shorter, although he made up for it with a roly-poly middle and chubby cheeks.

"Hi, Alton."

"Hello."

Saidah took Jesse aside. Despite having so many guests, she had made sure right away that I got to know Cedric, Jesse, and Alton. I had the odd sense that she was including me in her family. It made me feel good, and I fantasized about how the family could use another woman. I learned from Alton that he wasn't an athlete like his father and brother, but that he knew more about computers, the Internet, and chess than anybody I'd ever known.

"I play first board on the school chess team," Alton was proudly telling me, his eyes looking huge behind the gogglelike lenses of his eyeglasses. "We've won six matches in a row."

His private school played matches with many of the other schools in the area. In quick succession I learned about his involvement with the school poetry magazine, the drama society, and the debating club. He had a jaunty enthusiasm and an infectious smile that lingered on my lips after he had wandered off to refill his empty plate.

Alone for a moment, I felt divided. Saidah had honored me by her invitation to this party in her home and her attention to me as a guest. Certainly she was inviting me to know her in a new way that included her family, but the degree of my pleasure in being included also emphasized to me my sense of loss of a family of my own. I had pursued that through the attorney and come to a dead end. I found myself frozen, staring out at this gathering of Saidah's friends but thinking of myself as separate and far away from them.

"Penny for your thoughts," Saidah said as she came back to me again.

"You'd be paying too much," I kidded in return, reluctant to share what I had been thinking.

"Come on, Iris, why are you standing over here looking like a mystery?"

Since she was asking, and I liked her a lot, I decided that I would tell her.

"Everyone seems so happy, and your family is so nice," I said, "that I started thinking about how I don't know if I have any family. I mean I don't have any relatives that would come to a party like this." I didn't say that I had been wishing I could be part of her family.

Saidah nodded and considered what I had said. I liked the way she didn't respond right away but let her thoughts deepen before speaking.

"Someday, when you're married..."

"Oh, no," I laughed and shook my head in protest.

"Someday," Saidah repeated firmly, "when you have a family of your own, you may remember this feeling of loss very differently. When you have a family, you may appreciate them all the more because for a time you were alone in the world. You may have more love, understanding, and patience to give to them. They may make you feel complete and fulfilled in ways that you can't imagine today. A wise person once said, 'Compare and despair.' It isn't good to compare our lives to others'. We simply have to live to the fullest. You keep looking to the past for a family that you feel you lost, but in the future, maybe not so far from today, another family is waiting. That family doesn't exist yet, but your love can bring it into being."

"Thanks, Saidah." Her words touched me, and my eyes moistened.

"I have a little present for you," she said.

This surprised me.

"What is it?" I asked her with candid interest.

"Come into the house and I'll get it."

I followed Saidah up the back porch, through the large kitchen, and into a study off the front entranceway. While Saidah moved the papers neatly piled inside her rolltop desk, I looked at the wallpaper and mahogany wainscoting. Whoever had restored the house had done a beautiful job.

Saidah pulled a sheet free and gestured toward an antique couch with a curved back, maroon fabric, and knobby legs. "Have a seat."

We sat side by side.

"When you told me about speaking at the DA meeting," Saidah said, "I felt proud of you. Actually, I felt proud of myself, too. That I had played at least a little role in helping you with your finances. It made me want to give you something. After thinking about it a lot, I thought I would write down some of the things that we've discussed. These ideas seem like common sense to me, but I know as a financial planner that these are secrets to many people. They don't know how to handle debt. You're going to the DA meetings, so you know what I mean."

"Yes. I appreciate everything you've done for me." I meant it, too.

"While I was writing, I realized that this wasn't just a gift from me to you. That it was a gift I had received, too. From my teacher, Elizabeth, and maybe she had received it from other teachers before her. I don't know how far back it goes. But if it helps you, think of it as ancient wisdom. That's why I wrote it on such heavy paper."

"It's like parchment," I said, looking at the paper in her hand. "Like a scroll."

"The scroll of Saidah," she said with a smile. "Very ancient wisdom handed down through the generations, at least as old as the pyramids. Secrets that are now yours to transmit to others."

Though she was joking as she handed me the paper filled with her neat handwriting, I understood that our relationship as teacher and student was coming to an end. She was ending it, giving me a summation of her teaching. More than that, she was telling me that I could become a transmitter of what I learned, that I could be a teacher. Slowly, I read what she had written.

Saidah's Money Maxims

1. Debt makes money your master, while you must make money your servant.
2. Know your numbers, your income and expenses, your assets and debts.
3. Prepare a spending plan that will not only let you live solvently but also bring you joy.
4. Banks and credit card companies only seek profits, so be vigilant and protect yourself against unfair charges and practices.
5. Never mistake credit cards for money, and remember there is no such thing as free money.
6. Even more important than being debt-free is the process of living solvent day by day.
7. Never make decisions when you're under pressure to please others, but take the time you need to feel confident about what is right for you.
8. In debt or prosperity, seek the support and sharing of community.
9. Esteem your teachers, but find solutions in your own potentials and truths.
10. Never forget the debt to love.

Reading her insights, I realized how far I had come since I first met her. That first day on the park bench I wouldn't have understood her gift, but now I knew the truth of her money maxims. Only I didn't feel ready to let her go.

"Thanks so much," I said, aware of the time and thoughtfulness that she had put into creating this gift. "But aren't you going to be my teacher anymore?"

Saidah smiled and shook her head. "I'm happy to be your teacher, but you don't really need me."

"Yes, I do."

"You remember, I said, 'When the student is ready, the teacher will come'?"

"Yes."

"There should be another saying like that, maybe 'When the student is ready, the teacher will go.'"

"But I'm not out of debt yet."

Saidah shook her head again. "You're walking on the road. Once you begin, there may be detours, but you're heading in the right direction. You're doing it yourself. Why wouldn't you want me to find a student who does need me, someone I could really help? Not you. You're almost ready to teach."

"What about my debt?" I repeated.

"You've changed since I met you," Saidah told me. "You've learned to observe yourself. If you just accept that change, you'll be ready to move on. Once I could observe myself, I could also learn from my mistakes. It made me able to give you some help with your money issues. You'll be able to help others. Teaching is like letting good will flow from one person to another, from Elizabeth to me, from me to you, from you on to others. It helps pay the debt of love that we owe. You're already doing it by speaking at the meetings."

I wanted to protest, but my real fear wasn't to lose Saidah as a teacher. She had convinced me of that. And, while there's no certainty about the future, I knew that if I stayed on my spending plan, sooner or later I would be free of debt.

"I don't want to lose you as a friend," I admitted.

"I feel the same," she said, solemnly offering me her hand. "Let's shake on it."

I took her hand, and the glint of humor in her eye transformed to a large smile as she leaned forward and wrapped her arms around me. I hugged her in return.

"By the way," she said, when our hug ended, "Cedric and I are definitely coming to the premiere to see you dance."

"Great."

"Now I'd better get back to my other guests. There are some nice young men here, and I'm going to introduce you to all of them." She took my hand to pull me back to the barbecue.

"Please," I protested, but secretly I was happy to follow her.

True to her word, Saidah introduced me to five or six men whom she thought I might like, and I spent a pleasant afternoon chatting with them and then talking some more with Cedric and Jesse.

When I had a moment to myself, I thought of how my life had changed. Saidah hadn't given me her money maxims because I was her student. She had given them to me because she thought I might become a teacher. And her friend. Who can know the future? I certainly didn't, but I felt willing to offer myself to others as she had offered herself to me. I didn't know if I would have enough to give. After all, Saidah had two graduate degrees, yet I had learned from her and my own experiences. I knew that it would take time to pay off my debts, but I had patience now and a vision of the future. Just teaching the twenty-four toddlers in the two classes on Saturday earned me nearly seven thousand five hundred dollars per year. I had begun to think of a different day job and how I might cover my health insurance. I had a plan and the willingness to work to achieve my dreams. And I would be dancing.

Most important of all, I believe, was that I had come to trust. Call it trust in a higher power or life itself, but I felt that I could make a good life for myself and for others. Who did I mean? Certainly I meant a family of my own, a husband and children to love and cherish. I could even imagine that someday I might be a teacher. But there was more. I recalled something Saidah had told me. How when she was a little girl, her grandmother had warned her about people who are always waiting for their ships to come in. "If you want a ship to come in," her grandmother told her, "you have to send out a ship. That's the only way."

I felt ready to send out my ships. I had a lot inside me and I wanted to share it. I glanced down at the thick paper in my hand. Of all of Saidah's maxims, I thought she had saved the most important for the last. I owed a debt to her. Maybe I could never repay her, but I could give to others. "Never forget the debt to love," she had written. And I promised myself that I never would.

Epilogue

Almost three years have passed since Saidah gave me the scroll with her insights about money and debt. My life has changed in a lot of ways. I no longer work at Castle Advertising. Because of the costumes that I created for Rachel's dance, I began to get requests from other choreographers and even theater companies to design for them. It's a small business, but it pays well and I enjoy it. One or two of my designs were even picked up by fashion companies to be manufactured, and I made some money from that. I also temp two days a week, using the same agency as Rachel, and still waitress on Fridays and Saturdays at The Golden Plate. In terms of my finances, the most important thing may be that I was able to find another school where I could teach dance and be paid by the number of students. Without going into the details of the numbers that filled a lot of yellow notepads during the last three years, my finances worked out better than I had hoped. If you had asked me that day at Saidah's party, I would have told you that I faced seven or eight years of paying off my debts. As things have worked out, I expect to be out of debt within another eighteen months.

Maybe you feel that I should have continued my story through the time that I became debt-free. But I've told you about the crucial time when I changed my understanding of money and debt. It was the six months between when I met Saidah and when she gave me her money maxims. Once my understanding changed and I became more able to observe myself and seek support from others, the steps that followed merely reflected those changes. I sought to earn more as an employee and to take opportunities to create businesses of my own, such as teaching dance or designing costumes. But the change within me made everything else possible. If I had stayed at Castle Advertising, I would still have paid back my debt. Maybe not as quickly, but with the same determination to one day be free of money worries.

Of course, my story is a story, and some events had to be left out. I didn't go into details about Doug, for example, but I should say one thing—no, several things—about him. He's going to graduate from law school in a few more months. His dream is to have a practice where he represents artists and athletes. To think of him having dancers and dance companies as clients makes me happy. Most important, in terms of what I feel about him, is that after he worked for a law firm in Toronto last summer he paid me back the thousand dollars plus six percent interest. For him to be honest with me that way made me feel the world is a kind place and that he will always be my friend, even if Toronto is far away.

Rachel's performance was a success for her and for me. I'm taking as many dance classes as I can and performing with the company Rachel created. She's always worried about budgets, bookings, and rehearsals, but she's made a go of it. We still share the apartment. I don't know when that will change, but neither of us plays the lottery. Every once in a while we hear from Tina, who has finished her master's degree and gotten an entry-level position in investment banking. Her starting salary is more than Rachel and I earn together, but that does-n't bother me at all. I've made the choices that I had to make and, as Saidah says, "Compare and despair."

Saidah and Cedric are wonderful friends to me. When Jesse grad-uated from college, he headed for L.A. to spend a year waiting on tables and writing screenplays before applying to medical school. Alton finished private school and started college several hours from home. So Saidah and Cedric have kind of adopted me. I love them and feel a lot of love from them. Every once in a while I ask Saidah for some advice, but it's more like talking to a friend than a teacher.

She's been right about my becoming a teacher. At the DA meetings you can be a mentor to those who need help. After I had been solvent long enough, some people asked me to be their sponsor or one of their pressure people (who help look at their spending plans) and, after some hesitation, I agreed. Now I feel myself to be a student and teacher both. I'm always learning more, but I do have some information, understanding, and hope to offer to others.

Close as I feel to Saidah and Cedric, my desire to find my birth family remains. I made them a part of this story because that absence seemed to be about some larger sense of not having enough. I still feel that from time to time, but I also feel a deep gratitude for what has been given to me—my life, my talents, my friendships. I keep thinking about hiring a private detective, but I'm not sure if that would do any good. If the records are sealed by the court, and the agency doesn't exist anymore, I'm not sure what a detective could find out.

I've been dating quite a bit, but I'm still waiting to find the love of my life. I've given a lot of thought to the adage, "Time is money." What it's really about is limitation. I'm only human and I can only do so much in an hour, a day, a week. If that's true, it's important not to spend a lot of time dating people that I know aren't right for me. The more time I spend dating somebody like that, the longer it's going to take me to meet the person with whom I might share my deepest love.

My story hasn't been told because it's unique, but because it's a story shared by so many people who face debt every day. While the story leaves out some details, I feel that it is an accurate recounting of how I felt and thought during that crucial six-month period when I confronted my money issues and learned how to deal with debt. I certainly don't feel that I've told the full story of my life. I'm far too young to imagine attempting that. In fact, I hope that my life will have enough excitement to fill a few more books (whether or not those books are actually written down). But if my story helps one person lessen his or her burden of debt, then everything will have been worthwhile.

The Money Exercises

These exercises are intended to help you gain clarity and purpose with respect to your financial life. They cannot replace consulting professional advisers and expanding your own financial knowledge through research, reading, classes, and self-help groups. However, the exercises are useful tools that you should consider as you develop your financial plan and learn more about your attitudes and education with respect to money. One important effect of these exercises is to dispel any vagueness about such matters as how much you own, how much you owe, how much you earn, and how much you spend. If you are married, your spouse should be an active participant in using these exercises to create goals that work for the family.

YOUR FINANCIAL ATTITUDES

The following questions are designed to help you explore your financial attitudes.

▶ Do you make short-term and long-term plans with respect to money matters?

▶ Are you stingy or generous?

▶ Do you spend wisely or too much?

▶ Do you save enough and, if you do save, how do you diversify and protect your savings?

▶ Do you feel that any of your spending is addictive or wasteful?

▶ Based on your parents and other people with whom you are close, whose attitude toward financial matters seems to be the model for the way that you behave?

▶ If you can find a person who served as a model for your own financial attitudes, such as your mother or father, is there anything about that person's financial behavior that you would criticize or like to change?

▶ As you look at your own financial behavior, are you pleased or do you feel that there's room for improvement? In what way? What steps could you take to improve your financial attitudes?

▶ Do you believe that only positive thinking about money is needed to achieve your financial goals, or is a plan of action also necessary?

▶ Does charitable giving or service play a role in your financial life?

▶ Do your financial attitudes and goals dovetail with your personal goals in terms of family, friends, community, fulfillment in your work, recreation, and other nonmonetary activities?

YOUR MONEY PRIORITIES

▶ Is it more important to save or spend money? How can you bring saving and spending into balance?

▶ Would you rather use money for yourself (either to spend or save) or for others, such as your family, friends, community activities, or charity? Again, what would allow you to balance these desires?

▶ Do you find that money is often in dispute with your spouse, significant other, friends, or coworkers? If so, is there any consistent theme to these disputes?

❱ What is the proper balance for you between money and time? Would you like to work more or less? Do you want to spend your time differently than you do now?

❱ What things cannot be valued by money and yet are worth more to you than money?

❱ Are there any aspects of your financial life or what you own that you might like to let go of in an effort to simplify your lifestyle and lessen the amounts of money that you currently need to earn?

YOUR FINANCIAL EDUCATION

❱ Did your parents or any family member ever sit down with you and teach you how to handle money?

❱ Did you ever learn anything about handling money at school?

❱ If you did learn about handling money from family, friends, or at school, how would you describe the lessons that you were taught?

❱ If you feel your financial education has been inadequate, what steps would you take to strengthen your knowledge and ability to handle your finances? Reading books? Attending classes? Devoting more time to your finances?

❱ How would you like your financial education to help you in making an appropriate action plan to achieve your financial goals?

YOUR FINANCIAL IQ

❱ Do you always have precise knowledge of your net worth?

❱ Do you always know whether you are earning more than you are spending?

❱ If you use credit cards, do you know for each card how much you pay for an annual fee, what the interest rate is on the card, and whether there is a charge for late payments?

▶ If you pay the minimum monthly balance on your credit card debt of two thousand dollars (at nearly 20 percent interest), how long will it take to pay off the two thousand dollars, and how much will you pay in interest?

▶ If you save ten thousand dollars by the time you are twenty-five, and it earns compound interest of 5 percent, how much will you have at age sixty-five?

▶ How do debit cards differ from credit cards?

▶ How much do you pay each month in bank fees?

▶ What are the benefits of retirement plans such as 401(k), IRA, and Keogh?

▶ What is the benefit of having a will or a living trust?

▶ When necessary, do you use professional advisers such as accountants, attorneys, and financial planners?

From these examples you can see that the financial intelligence quotient is about education. If you feel that you would benefit from learning more, refer to "Further Reading about Money" for some helpful suggestions.

YOUR SPIRITUAL ASSETS

	Value
Your Spiritual Practices	_____
Your Relationships	_____
Your Good Deeds	_____
Your Contributions	_____
Other	_____

If you feel uncomfortable giving a dollar value to those invaluable activities, simply use +s to mark their importance to you (five +s mean very valuable, one + means slightly valuable). The point is to gain a larger view of economics and circulation than money alone can offer us.

WHAT YOU OWN   Date _____

	Amount
Cash and Deposit Accounts	_____
Value of Your Share of Any Businesses That You Own	_____
Marketable Securities	_____
Government Bonds	_____
Mutual Funds	_____
Primary Residence	_____
Real Estate Investments	_____
Loans Owed to You	_____
401(k), IRA, Keogh, and Other Retirement Plans	_____
Automobiles/Boats	_____
Collectibles	_____
Other Assets	_____
Total of What You Own	_____

WHAT YOU OWE

	Amount
Credit Card Debt	_____
Auto Loans/Other Consumer Loans	_____
Mortgage on Primary Residence	_____
Other Mortgages	_____
Margin Loans Secured by Investments	_____
Loans Payable to Your Business	_____
Loans Payable to Individuals	_____
Other Debts	_____
Total of What You Owe	_____

To determine net worth, subtract what you owe from what you own. The balance is your net worth.

WHAT YOU EARN Year _____

	Annual Amount
Salary/Wages (gross amounts)	_____
Bonus/Commission	_____
Interest	_____
Dividends	_____
Business Profit or Loss	_____
Capital Gains or Loss	_____
Profit or Loss from Real Estate	_____
Profit or Loss from Partnerships and S Corporations	_____
Retirement Plan Distributions	_____
Alimony/Child Support	_____
Other Income	_____
Total Income	_____

WHAT YOU SPEND Year _____

	Annual Amount
All Federal, State, and Local Income Taxes (including Social Security, Self-Employment, and other taxes usually withheld from payroll)	_____
Primary Residence—Rent or Mortgage and Real Estate Tax Payments	_____
Other Real Estate Payments	_____
Auto Loan/Consumer Loans	_____
Credit Card Payments	_____
Alimony/Child-Support Payments	_____
Life Insurance	_____
Disability Insurance	_____
Excess Personal Liability Insurance	_____
Homeowner's Insurance	_____
Auto Insurance	_____
Health Insurance	_____

Meals in Restaurants   _____

Prescriptions, Vitamins, Toiletries   _____

Household Items and Repairs   _____

Groceries   _____

Local Transportation   _____

Clothing/Wardrobe   _____

Vacations   _____

Entertainment   _____

Dependent Care   _____

Gifts   _____

Charitable/Spiritual Donations   _____

Savings/Investments   _____

Debt Repayment (Principal)   _____

Interest Payments   _____

Other   _____

Annual Total   _____

Keep track of all amounts spent, however small, by writing the amount down in a notebook as soon as you spend it. Create additional categories to fit your spending patterns. At the end of twelve months, your yearly-spending total will be easy to compare with your earnings. If you don't have figures for twelve months yet, make an estimate by multiplying the number of months you do have to see what an entire year would total (and make appropriate adjustments for large items that may come at particular times of the year).

YOUR MONEY LEDGER

This allows you to keep track of even the smallest amounts that you may spend. Whenever you spend money, write it down in a small notebook that you carry at all times. To make your work easier, you should use the categories from What You Spend to describe each transaction.

Date	Item	Payment Method	Amount
Jan.1	Rent	Check	$550
Jan.2	Groceries	Cash	$23.45
Jan.4	Clothing (shoes)	Credit card	$64.87
Jan.6	Health Insurance Premium	Check	$88

If you have a lot of transactions, you might want to transfer these amounts immediately to a spreadsheet, whether by hand or computer. The spreadsheet might continue to the right of the "Amount" column by including columns for each category and ending with "Miscellaneous." By entering what you spend twice, once under "Amount" and once under the particular category of the expense, you can easily total up the amounts of each type of expense, then add all the expenses together and check that total against the total in the "Amount" column to make certain they are the same and the addition is correct.

YOUR SPENDING PLAN

An effective spending plan must take your needs into account. It can't simply be devoted to paying off debt or, in all likelihood, you won't be able to live with it. The Spending Plan is really a reworking of What You Spend, so that you are planning what you intend to do in the future. You can start with an ideal Spending Plan, which would look at the categories in which you spend too much and those in which you deprive yourself. This ideal plan might be met by increasing your income, but until you can do that, the second step is to create a realistic Spending Plan. Before this Spending Plan includes amounts for debt repayment, it must have amounts for saving/investment, entertainment, and spiritual activities. As you work and rework your Spending Plan, you have the opportunity to make choices as to how you choose to spend on different categories. Large expenditures can be planned and saved for, rather than cause you to go into debt. Your spending becomes part of your conscious decision-making processes, rather than being based on impulse or addictive behavior, and new and more healthy spending patterns can emerge to help you.

Year _____	Monthly Amount	Annual Amount
All Federal, State, and Local Income Taxes (including Social Security, Self-Employment, and other taxes usually withheld from payroll)	_____	_____
Primary Residence—Rent or Mortgage and Real Estate Tax Payments	_____	_____
Other Real Estate Payments	_____	_____
Auto Loan/Consumer loans	_____	_____
Credit Card Payments	_____	_____
Alimony/Child-Support Payments	_____	_____
Life Insurance	_____	_____
Disability Insurance	_____	_____
Excess Personal Liability Insurance	_____	_____
Homeowner's Insurance	_____	_____
Auto insurance	_____	_____
Health Insurance	_____	_____
Meals in Restaurants	_____	_____
Prescriptions, Vitamins, Toiletries	_____	_____
Household Items and Repairs	_____	_____
Groceries	_____	_____
Local Transportation	_____	_____
Clothing/Wardrobe	_____	_____

Vacations	_____	_____
Entertainment	_____	_____
Dependent Care	_____	_____
Gifts	_____	_____
Charitable Donations/Spiritual Activities	_____	_____
Savings/Investments	_____	_____
Debt Repayment (Principal)	_____	_____
Interest Payments	_____	_____
Other	_____	_____
Totals	_____	_____

YOUR DEBTS AND INTEREST PAYMENTS

This will allow you to see quickly the debts that are most expensive to carry so you can pay them off first. If you owe anything to the Internal Revenue Service or other tax authorities, that should be paid first if there is any likelihood of your declaring bankruptcy. Credit cards and loans with the highest interest rate should be paid as soon as possible. Other charges on the credit cards, such as annual fees and late fees, should also be taken into account in deciding which cards to pay off first.

List all your debts:

	Amount	Interest Rate	Monthly Payment* Interest/ Principal	Annual Fee	Late Charges
Taxes	_____	_____	_____	_____	_____
Credit cards					
1.	_____	_____	_____	_____	_____
2.	_____	_____	_____	_____	_____
3.	_____	_____	_____	_____	_____
4.	_____	_____	_____	_____	_____
5.	_____	_____	_____	_____	_____
6.	_____	_____	_____	_____	_____

7. Other	_____	_____	_____	_____	_____
Auto Loans	_____	_____	_____	_____	_____
Mortgages/ Home Equity Loans	_____	_____	_____	_____	_____
Personal Loans	_____	_____	_____	_____	_____
Business Loans	_____	_____	_____	_____	_____
Other Debts	_____	_____	_____	_____	_____
Total Debts	_____	_____	_____	_____	_____

* Take note that the monthly payment does not simply pay off the loan, but is likely to be divided into a payment toward principal (paying off the loan) and a payment toward interest.

YOUR PLAN FOR CREDITORS

If you must default on timely payment with creditors, it is important that you have a plan to pay all of them on a regular basis, usually monthly, even if the amounts paid are small. However, your Spending Plan should provide enough money for you to take care of yourself and your family. Only after that do you begin to pay your creditors.

List of Creditors	Agreement	Balance Owed	Interest Rate	Monthly Payment* Interest/ Principal
1.	_____	_____	_____	_____
2.	_____	_____	_____	_____
3.	_____	_____	_____	_____
4.	_____	_____	_____	_____
5.	_____	_____	_____	_____
6.	_____	_____	_____	_____
7.	_____	_____	_____	_____
Totals	_____	_____		_____

YOUR FINANCIAL FUTURE

▶ How many years until you plan to retire?

▶ Have you planned for the major preretirement expenses you see ahead, such as college tuition for any children?

▶ Do you plan to continue working during retirement? If so, how much do you expect to earn?

▶ How much money would you like to have saved, including in retirement accounts such 401(k)s and IRAs, by the time you retire?

▶ How much will your savings give you in annual income during retirement?

▶ What amounts will you receive as a pension from your employer and as Social Security?

▶ To what extent will your retirement income from all sources replace your current income?

▶ Will your retirement lifestyle be satisfactory to you compared to your present lifestyle?

▶ Do you have adequate insurance, including health insurance, disability insurance, life insurance and, perhaps, long-term care insurance?

▶ Have you made an estate plan that will dispose of your property as you want and will protect you and your loved ones?

▶ Have you consulted with professional advisers such as accountants, attorneys, and financial planners with respect to your financial future?

YOUR IMPORTANT PAPERS

Do you, your spouse, and your trustee or executor know where all of your important documents and records are located? This can be important in the event of an emergency. Personal information about you, your spouse, and children can also be very useful to have.

Item	Location
Names and Addresses of Business Advisers	_____
Names and Addresses of Friends	_____
Names and Addresses of Relatives	_____
Living Trust	_____
Other Trusts	_____
Will	_____
Will Codicils	_____
Powers of Attorney	_____
Health Care Proxies	_____
List of Life Insurance Policies	_____
List of Disability Insurance Policies	_____
List of All Death Benefits	_____
Retirement Plan Statements	_____
Bank Savings Accounts	_____
Bank Checking Accounts	_____
Certificates of Deposit	_____
Mutual Fund Statements	_____
Stock Certificates	_____
List of Annuities with Statements	_____
Real Estate Deeds and Title	_____
Leases for Rental Property	_____
Car Ownership	_____
List of Personal Property	_____
List of Home Furnishings	_____
List of Collectibles (with Appraisals, if any)	_____
Property Loaned or in Storage	_____
Money Owed	_____

Credit Cards   _____

Insurance Policies   _____

   Health Insurance   _____

   Homeowner's Insurance   _____

   Car Insurance   _____

   Liability Insurance   _____

   Excess Personal Liability Insurance   _____

Tax Returns   _____

Birth Certificate   _____

Passport   _____

Marriage Certificate   _____

Adoption Papers   _____

Citizenship Papers   _____

Divorce or Separation Decrees   _____

Contracts/Business Agreements   _____

List of Copyrights   _____

List of Licensing Income   _____

Other papers _____   _____

Important Information   _____

Full Name   _____

Date and Place of Birth   _____

Social Security Number   _____

Residence Address   _____

Business Address   _____

Name and Location of Bank and Number

   for Safety Deposit Box   _____

Location of Safety Deposit–Box Key   _____

Safe Combination   _____

Location(s) of Safe   _____

Obtain the same information for your spouse, children and, perhaps, your parents if you are involved in their well-being and estate planning.

Supportive Organizations and Web Sites

There are many organizations dedicated to educating people about financial and consumer issues, including how to deal with debt issues. A selection of these organizations follows, along with their web site addresses. Many of the web sites include links to other helpful resources available on the Internet.

Consumer Action (CA), 717 Market Street, Suite 310, San Francisco, CA 94103; (415) 777-9635; www.consumer-action.org/

CA serves consumers nationwide by advancing consumer rights, a free hotline to direct consumers to complaint-handling agencies, educational materials, consumer advocacy, and price comparisons for credit cards, bank accounts, and long-distance services.

Consumer Counseling Centers of America, Inc. (CCCA), 601 Pennsylvania Avenue NW, South Building, Suite 900, Washington, DC 20004; (202) 637-4851; www.consumercounseling.org/

For people who are falling behind in their payments, CCCA offers counseling and programs to consolidate and manage debt.

Consumer Federation of America (CFA), 1424 16th Street NW, Suite 604, Washington, DC 20036; (202) 387-6121; www.consumerfed.org

CFA is a proconsumer advocacy organization as well as an educational resource on many consumer-related issues. It offers conferences, reports, books, brochures, news releases, and a newsletter.

Consumer.gov; www.consumer.gov/

A governmental site that focuses on consumer issues and allows the location of on-line information by category (such as "money") and subcategory. (See also First.gov below.)

Consumers Union, 101 Truman Avenue, Yonkers, NY 10703-1057; (914) 378-2000; www.consumersunion.org

Consumers Union, the publisher of *Consumer Reports*, is a non-profit organization serving consumers by providing objective advice about many consumer concerns, including personal finance.

Debtors Anonymous (DA), P.O. Box 920888, Needham, MA 02492-0009; (781) 453-2743; www.debtorsanonymous.org /index.html

This organizational web site offers information on how to obtain publications (such as the monthly newsletter, *Ways and Means*), how to contact DA, and background information on DA and the Twelve Steps.

Debtors Anonymous Information, www.solvency.org/

This Web site, while not affiliated with DA, offers helpful information about local and on-line DA meetings, personal recovery stories, information on steps needed to get out of debt, and more.

Experian, toll-free (888) 397-3742; www.experian.com/customer/

Formerly TRW, Experian is a credit-reporting agency. Consumers can find out how to apply for their personal credit report and review other information about credit standing and credit repair. Experian emphasizes that consumers can repair their own credit and warns against paying fees to credit-repair clinics.

Family Money, 125 Park Avenue, New York, NY 10017; (212) 557 6600; www.familymoney.com

This magazine and its Web site offer practical, entertaining advice about how to make a better financial life. The Web site has a calculator so you can create examples and see the impact of compound interest on savings and debts over time.

Federal Consumer Information Center (FCIC), Pueblo, CO 81009; toll-free (800) 878-3256; www.pueblo.gsa.gov/
   An arm of the U.S. General Services Administration, FCIC offers numerous publications in such areas as consumer help, money, and scams/frauds.
FirstGov, c/o General Services Administration, 1800 F Street NW, Room 5240, Washington, D.C. 20405-0002; www.FirstGov.gov/
A government Web site that gives the public easy, one-stop access to search all on-line resources of the federal government.

National Foundation for Credit Counseling (NFCC), 8611 Second Avenue, Suite 100, Silver Spring, MD 20910; toll-free (800) 388-2227; www.nfcc.org/
   A national network of 1,450 nonprofit Neighborhood Financial Care Centers offering money management education, budgeting, credit and debt counseling, and debt repayment plans.

National Institute for Consumer Education (NICE), Eastern Michigan University, 559 Gary M. Owen Building, 300 W. Michigan Avenue, Ypsilanti, MI 48197; (734) 487-2292; www.emich .edu/public/coe/nice/index1/html
   NICE is a professional development center that promotes personal finance education in schools, workplaces, and communities as well as serving as a clearinghouse for personal financial education.

U.S. Public Interest Research Group (U.S. PIRG), 218 D Street SE, Washington, DC 20003; (202) 546-9707; www.pirg.org/
   Created by the state PIRGs as a watchdog for the public interest in the nation's capital, U.S. PIRG uses investigative research, media exposes, advocacy, litigation, and education to defend and protect consumers from abuses such as rising bank fees or the theft of financial identity.

Further Reading about Money

The Secret Life of Money by Tad Crawford (Allworth Press)

Credit Card & Debt Management by Scott Bilker (Press One Pub, Barnegat, NJ)

Credit Card Debt by Alexander Daskaloff (Avon Personal Finance)

A Currency of Hope (Debtors Anonymous)

Debt-Free Living by Larry Burkett (Moody Press)

Debt No More by Carolyn J. White (Clifton House)

Downsize Your Debt by Andrew Feinberg (Penguin USA)

The Financial Expert by R. K. Narayan (University of Chicago)

The House of Mirth Edith Wharton

How to Get Out of Debt, Stay Out of Debt & Live Prosperously by Jerrold Mundis (Bantam)

Life after Debt by Bob Hammond (Career Press)

Life without Debt by Bob Hammond (Career Press)

Little Dorrit by Charles Dickens

Money and Morals in America by Patricia O'Toole (Clarkson Potter)

Money and the Meaning of Life by Jacob Needleman (Doubleday)

The Money Mirror: How Money Reflects Women's Dreams, Fears and Desires by Annette Lieberman and Vicki Linder (Allworth Press)

The 9 Steps to Financial Freedom by Suze Orman (Crown)

The Oxford Book of Money, edited by Kevin Jackson (Oxford)

The Richest Man in Babylon by George S. Clason (Signet)

The Way to Wealth by Benjamin Franklin

The Wealthy Barber by David Chilton (Prima)

Your Money or Your Life: Transforming Your Relationship with Money and Achieving Financial Independence by Joe Dominguez and Vicki Robin (Penguin)

Index

About the Author

Photograph by Bill Beckley

Tad Crawford, President and Publisher for Allworth Press in New York City, studied economics at Tufts University, graduated from Columbia Law School, clerked on New York State's highest court, and represented many artists and arts organizations when he actively practiced as an attorney. He is the author of *The Secret Life of Money: How Money Can Be Food for the Soul*, which received the *Body, Mind, Spirit Magazine* Award of Excellence as well as the Athena Award–Publisher's Choice from *Mentor and Protege* for "work that Exemplifies the Spirit of Mentoring." In addition, he has authored or coauthored twelve books on business and the creative professions. The Business/Legal Affairs editor for *Communication Arts Magazine*, he has written articles for magazines such as *Art in America, Glamour, Harper's Bazaar, Lapis, The Nation, New Age Journal*, and *Self.* A member of the Jung Institute and the Analytical Psychology Club of New York City, he lectured on mythology at the Jung and the Humanities conference keynoted by Joseph Campbell and has spoken on money at such venues as the Open Center in New York City, Interface in Boston, Wainwright House in Rye, New York, and the New York City offices of Merrill Lynch. He has also appeared as a guest on television programs such as *Fox on Money; The O'Reilly Report; Good Day, Wake Up*; and *It's Only Money*, as well as numerous radio shows including *New York & Company*.

Books from Allworth Press

The Secret Life of Money: How Money Can Be Food for the Soul
by Tad Crawford (softcover, 5½ × 8½, 304 pages, $14.95)

Business and Legal Guide for Authors and Self-Publishers, Revised Edition
by Tad Crawford (softcover, 8½ × 11, 192 pages, includes CD-ROM, $22.95)

Business and Legal Forms for Fine Artists, Revised Edition
by Tad Crawford (softcover, 8½ × 11, 144 pages, includes CD-ROM, $19.95)

Business and Legal Forms for Illustrators, Revised Edition
by Tad Crawford (softcover, 8½ × 11, 192 pages, includes CD-ROM, $24.95)

Business and Legal Forms for Graphic Designers, Revised Edition
by Tad Crawford and Eva Doman Bruck (softcover, 8½ × 11, 240 pages, includes CD-ROM, $24.95)

Business and Legal Forms for Photographers, Revised Edition
by Tad Crawford (softcover, 8½ × 11, 224 pages, includes CD-ROM, $24.95)

Business and Legal Forms for Crafts
by Tad Crawford (softcover, 8½ × 11, 176 pages, includes CD-ROM, $19.95)

Legal Guide for the Visual Artist, Fourth Edition
by Tad Crawford (softcover, 8½ × 11, 272 pages, $19.95)

The Artist-Gallery Partnership: A Practical Guide to Consigning Art, Revised Edition
by Tad Crawford and Susan Mellon (softcover, 8½ × 11, 144 pages, $19.95)

The Writer's Legal Guide, Second Edition
by Tad Crawford and Tony Lyons (softcover, 6 × 9, 320 pages, $19.95)

AIGA Professional Practices in Graphic Design
Edited by Tad Crawford (softcover, 6½ × 10, 320 pages, $24.95)

Please write to request our free catalog. To order by credit card, call 1-800-491-2808 or send a check or money order to Allworth Press, 10 East 23rd Street, Suite 510, New York, NY 10010. Include $5 for shipping and handling for the first book ordered and $1 for each additional book. Ten dollars plus $1 for each additional book if ordering from Canada. New York State residents must add sales tax.

To see our complete catalog on the World Wide Web, or to order online, you can find us at *www.allworth.com*.